TRANSPORT AND REGIONAL DEVELOPMENT

About the Author

Dr. Sukla Bhaduri (*b. 1949*) is M.A. (Presidency College) Calcutta University, recipients of two medals: Sudhira Ray Memorial Gold Medal and Ranjit Lahiri Memorial Silver Medal. She was also awarded Ph.D. from Calcutta University as a Ph.D. Research Scholar (1975).

She taught in the Lareto College Calcutta and was Senior Research Fellow in the Calcutta University. She was also attached to the Centre for Urban Economic Studies of this University as Research Associate.

At present she is associated with the Department of Geography, Burdwan University as a Teacher. She has published, several papers in reputed journals.

TRANSPORT
AND
REGIONAL DEVELOPMENT

A Case Study of Road Transport of
West Bengal

SUKLA BHADURI

CONCEPT PUBLISHING COMPANY PVT. LTD.
NEW DELHI-110059

The Indian Council of Social Science Research gave the financial support towards the publication of this work. However, the responsibility for the contents of the book — facts, opinions, conclusions, etc. — is entirely that of the author and not of the ICSSR.

ICSSR Consultant: R.P. Misra

ISBN: 978-81-7022-342-9

First Published 1992

Published and Printed by

Concept Since 1974

Concept Publishing Company Pvt. Ltd.
A/15-16, Commercial Block, Mohan Garden,
New Delhi-110059 (India)
T: 91-11-41101460
E: publishing@conceptpub.com, *W*: www.conceptpub.com

FOREWORD

Development of an economy is dependent, among others, on the growth of its system of transport. The ease and rapidity with which goods and people can flow between two areas also determine the volume of trade and migration, as also the degree of interdependence between regions. Of various modes of transport, the present study by Dr. Sukla Bhaduri concentrates on road transport, the oldest and still now the most widely used mode. The study is specific to West Bengal, but many of the observations made here would apply to other areas of India. The book has been written from the point of view of a professional geographer, but, nevertheless, it provides useful material and observations which would be of value to economists, sociologists, regional planners and other schools of social science.

The study, begins, logically, with a historical perspective. When British colonial rulers took over the administration of Bengal, they were primarily interested in trade and economic penetration, and in skimm-off surplus in order to promote development in their own country. For them it was captive market, a source of raw material and labour power for use in other parts of the empire and also a springboard for aggression and take over of other areas in the subcontinent. The last thing they were concerned with was the wellbeing of the people they ruled, and, as a consequence, the famine of 1770 occurred which took a heavy toll of 20 per cent of the population of Bengal. The colonial system was characterised by many such famines, while the region was virtually free from this calamity until then, the last and one of the most devastating ones took place on the eve of the departure of the British, in 1943, at the time of the Second World War. However, it is not without significance that transport facilities was one of the reasons why both of the two famines took place, though, most probably, the nature of causation was different between 1770 and 1943. In 1770, some development of road transport under the British, for military purposes, helped to take away food surpluses from the villages in the good years for feeding the urban population and the army, which left nothing to fall back upon when the disaster struck in the form of drought. The self-sufficiency of the pre-British village economy was destroyed by the colonial penetration, while no measure was taken to provide food insurance in deficit years. In contrast, the 1943 disaster was due to the destruction of country boat in order to contain the advancing Japanese army, which disrupted the flow of rice to various regions. It is not without significance that the droughts in recent years have led to fewer deaths, largely because of the development of transport, which helps the victims to get away and find jobs and relief, if for a temporary period, in surplus area or towns, and also to make the movement of food possible, by way of imports or from surplus to deficit areas.

There can be no doubt that the core of the transport system we observe in West Bengal today was established by the colonial rulers – the railways, the Calcutta port, the long distance roads etc. But the development carried the footprint of their own colonial needs. They were mainly interested in imports and exports via Calcutta port, and not in the development of transport *per se* between various nodes, which explains the concentration of roads and railways around Calcutta, or from Calcutta to mining and plantation areas. This particular feature of the colonial road system has been amply demonstrated by various measures worked out by Dr. Bhaduri in this study.

In one sense the development of road transport should have been easier in West Bengal, as the terrain is flat with very few hills, mountains, lakes etc. However, through this flat plain also flows innumerable rivers and channels, and the soil is not hard enough for maintaining good road conditions. Maintenance is a serious headache, as the required road building material is in short supply, and both heavy rain and soft soil cause heavy damage after every monsoon. The partition of Bengal has also created political difficulties in accessing many areas in North Bengal, which were not so inaccessible during the pre-1947 days. In terms of length of roads, per capita, the position of West Bengal is quite low among the states, while, per square kilometer geographical area the position of the districts in the northern and western areas is quite bad Dr. Bhaduri has marshalled a great deal of data to make those points in Chapter 2.

Chapters 3 and 4 provide various statistical measures of accessibility of major urban areas in West Bengal, such as alpha, beta and gamma indices of relationship between vertices and edges, correlation matrices, principal component analysis as well as a simple application of network analysis in terms of flows between a pair of nodes. Almost all these measures virtually point to the same features – regional concentration of transport around Calcutta, and, to some extent also around Durgapore-Asansol, the other major urban complex, and the utter neglect of the northern and western districts. Chapter 6 also provides a measure of transport efficiency, linking the route connections with population served in various towns from the point of view of a particular node.

Both in Chapters 2 and 5 we find a historical background regarding the growth of road and automobiles during the plan period. It shows that while a certain amount of progress has been achieved since the independence of the country, we are still a long way to go. Still now a high proportion of villages are inaccessible from the main roads. At the same time, there appears to be a growing decline in the priority given to roads from the First Plan onwards, when the need for road construction is so urgent for national development, particularly for the growth of the backward areas.

Dr. Sukla Bhaduri's study on roads in West Bengal would fill an important void in the literature. The study contains a very large number of useful tables and maps and provides a comprehensive picture of the situation will regard to roads in this state.

29 May, 1991 PROF. BIPLAB DASGUPTA
Calcutta

PREFACE

This book aims at assessing the total road transport development in West Bengal under P.W.D., Local Bodies and Municipality from the turn of the century to the early period of Independence 1900–1974. The discussion follows with quantitative description of the road transport problem in the different districts of West Bengal and its future plan for mass transportational facilities. Thereafter, the problems of growth, organisational set up, finance, functional criteria of the road transportation media have been studied since their inception.

Transport system happens to be a pace setter of a growing economy. It, therefore, forms the base study of growth potential. Transportation links communities, provides for the movement of men and facilitates the flow of goods and services between zones which are socially and economically interdependent.

Therefore, transportation is a measure of relation between areas. Today, transport is regarded as a geographical phenomenon rather than economic one, reflecting the pattern of resource utilisation and demanding objective analysis of spatial structural formation.

Transport and power are the two most important planks of the infrastructure for economic growth. The flow of inputs to production centres and that of finished goods to consumers would be impossible without an adequate transportation network. Therefore, transportation network constitutes one of the most important element of cultural landscape.

With the progress in the stage of development, mode of transport also changed from bullock carts to supersonic jets. Speed has become the most important factor of transportation in the modern neo-technic world. Notwithstanding these changes the economic importance of transport has remained constant all the while. Since the dawn of civilisation it has been playing a vital role in production, exchange and distribution.

Transportation is intimately linked with spatial development. The importance of transport as a measure of resource utilisation indeed varies from place to place over the surface of the earth. Various factors determining the need for developed transportation are also numerous all ultimately linked with the local economic set-up.

Economic progress in any place very largely depends on the development of cheap, fast and efficient methods of transport.

A study of road transport in West Bengal gives insight into the detailed transportational phenomenon provided by the integrated transportation network which linked the state with whole of eastern region which in turn is centered on Calcutta industrial complex. Relevant to this study among theoretical work, the research paper of K.J. Kansky deserves first mention. Analysing some of the transportational characteristics, e.g., the accessibility, circuity traffic, etc., he has magnified the structure of transportation network of a region with a view to correlate the structure of transportation with that of economy. This is an empirical study wherein theoretic measures have been successfully used by way of graphical methods. The use of graph theory as a method of transport network analysis has received considerable attention. It was introduced by Garrison (1960) and was elaborated by Kansky (1963), later by Haggett and Chorley (1969).

The recent study by E.J. Taafe in association with R.L. Morrill and P.R. Gould entitled *Transport Expansion in Underdeveloped Countries: A Comparative Analysis* (1963), has presented an ideal typical sequence of transportation development in few under-developed countries like Ghana and Nigeria and suggests that it is realistic to think of the entire sequence as a process rather than in a series of discreet historical stages. B.J.L. Berry worked on "Recent Studies Concerning the Role of Transportation in the Space Economy" (1959). In Germany, the transportation studies are more concerned with the role of transportation in the economy with a little bent towards formulating an articulated transport network.

Recently in India work on transportation geography has received considerable importance of which very few relevant to this study may be mentioned, such as *Transport Geography of South Bihar* by Jagdish Singh (1964), *Transport Geography of Uttar Pradesh* by R.B. Singh (1966), *Transportation and Urban Attribute in the Coimbatore Region: A Case Study of an Interacting System* by H. Ramachandran (1977), *Urban Transport – Calcutta: Case Study* by D.K. Haldar (1977),

Accessibility of Roads in Mysore State by S.J. Hullur (1971), *Geography of Transportation in Eastern India under the British Raj* by Sunil Kumar Munshi (1980).

West Bengal is often rightly referred to as the problem state of India. With about 3 per cent of the land area of India this state supports about 8 per cent of the total population of the country.

Extreme regional polarisation of industrial activities in the state has created uneven development of transportation system. Accelerated pace of industrial development in the state and its spatial diffusion demanded a balanced development of the transportation network. The overwhelming majority of the people (70 per cent of the total population of the state) still live in rural areas (97 per cent of the total area of West Bengal being rural) and depend mainly on agriculture. Rapid agricultural development demands a system of transport network which will facilitate the distribution of fertilisers, better seeds and improved agricultural implements to the remotest of farm lands as well as the collection of surplus farm products to be marketed at distant urban centres. It is generally recognised that the capacity and connectivity of a road network is a very important factor in regional and national development; one of the foremost priorities of transport policy is, therefore, the improvement of rural road systems. While transport development at this level may assist agricultural activity and the promotion of rural industries at an intermediate technological level, improved transport links between rural areas and urban industrial growth centres may tend to increase the polarisation and exacerbate the problems of the towns.

The study is designed to make a comprehensive survey of road transportation and road mix of the districts and the problems and constraints thereof with a view to getting at the root of the problems, scanning them for the purposes of suggesting measures for improvement and ensuring inhibited growth of the region. The chain action and reaction of any adverse factor relating to road transportation development and its effect on the regional economy has been kept in view in this study.

The study has attempted to analyse the road transportation efficiency in relation to overall view of the economic conditions of the districts, their population and the industrial potential, by taking into account the local factors and intra-regional factors of mobility and the inter-regional factor mobilisation for an integrated development of the state of West Bengal.

In total road length, the state ranks next to Uttar Pradesh. The existing facilities are under severe strain and have to be expanded in order to handle the increasing volume of traffic in the around West Bengal. The products of the vast hinterland of Calcutta, the State itself, eastern Uttar Pradesh, Bihar, Orissa and Assam, move to Calcutta for export through West Bengal. Foodgrains, tea, various oilseeds, hides and skin, iron and steel and many other export items as well as various import items including machinery, drugs, chemicals, clothes, etc., move to and from the hinterland of Calcutta through West Bengal. West Bengal, therefore, has a remarkable geographical entity and it is worth studying how transport has responded to these contrasts.

Moreover, transport also influences the economic organisation of an area. That is, the response is reciprocal. Indeed, this is the central problem of this research, the response of transport to geo-economic factors and the response to transport of geo-economic factors.

The roadways are responsible for carriage of about a third of total goods and half of the passenger traffic in West Bengal.

The Second World War brought into special prominence the necessary for the integrated road system. Lack of well developed through routes and bridges at important crossings and the fact that there was a limit to what the railways could carry. Importance of roads in West Bengal before independence were not so important as like inland waterways and railways. But importance of realignment of transport lines after Independence is a very unique case for West Bengal. Next to railways, Road transport plays a key role in the country's transport system.

This study is mainly concerned to establish a proper picture of road transport in West Bengal after independence so as to find out the insight into the declining importance of inland waterways and increasing importance of roadways in West Bengal during the early post Independence period, the study is restricted to the period 1900–1974.

After partition, lot of changes took place and West Bengal became the focus of those changes, West Bengal of today has passed through many changes of its boundaries. West Bengal of today is a name derived after the partition of the Province in August, 1947, when it emerged as a state in the Indian Union. The last substantial changes in the area of West Bengal took place in 1956 when the Islampur sub-division of Purnea district and a major part of

Manbhum district formerly parts of Bihar, were joined to West Bengal and its area became 87,617 sq. km. in 1961 (Sunil Munshi, 1975).

Mid-nineteenth century witnessed the introduction of steam boats as well as railways in Eastern India. But railways quickly replaced inland navigation in all areas except the delta proper, railways spread like light ways from Calcutta linking distant region directly with this metropolis.

Immediately after the Second World War there was a rapid expansion of Goods vehicles (trucks) in the country and their number was 40,107. The entire transport system in the country was subjected to a heavy strain during the War and a number of new roads were constructed. Particularly in the eastern border region, for military purposes. It provides the only means of mechanised transport in hilly, rural and backward areas which are not connected by rails.

The Department of War Transport of the India, Government set-up in 1943 a technical sub-committee on transport to consider the future of India convened a conference at Nagpur by the Chief Engineers of the Province and States to devise a plan for a co-ordinated system of road. The conference was expected to anticipate the transport needs of the country for a period extending up to 20 years after the end of the war. This study begins from this point to what achievement was made from Nagpur Plan to 1974. After a brief historical background of West Bengal, this research mainly aims in finding the roots of the cause of such development of roads, disparities, problems and constraints thereof and to suggest the proper measures to fill up the gap which are the outcome of the study. Importance of Calcutta, the Capital of British rule till 1911 was also focussed immensely along with all others growing transport node.

The aim of the Nagpur Plan (1943–1963) to build 1,96,800 of surfaced roads and 3,32,800 kms. of unsurface road within this period with the objective that no village in well developed agricultural areas should be more than 3.2 km. from a road, 8 km. from a main road, the corresponding distances for non-agricultural area being 8 kms. and 32 kms. respectively. Classification of roads into National Highway, State Highway, major district roads, other district roads and village road come into being. It was decided to have balanced development of all above classes of road.

The present study is an attempt to provide an integrated picture of transportation geography of West Bengal with special emphasis on roads.

The study is mainly limited upto 1974 for the purpose of mapping, because of unavailability of systematised data. But data of more recent years have been used in discussion wherever possible.

The study is divided into seven chapters. The first chapter comprises the physiographical background of West Bengal to which the patterns of road transportational features are closely interlinked. It, however, includes the historical development of roads during the early twentieth century (1900–1947). It gives a clue to the various historical forces that have moulded the existing transport network.

Chapter 2 surveys the development of roads in post-war period, a systematic and analytical survey of the transport arteries and examines their distributional pattern, characteristics and density in different regions. The spatial distribution of roads have been analysed.

Chapter 3 presents the nature of accessibility and the effectiveness of the existing transportation cover. Physical accessibility has been considered as the most significant element for this purpose.

Chapter 4 deals with the structure of transportation network. This chapter is sub-divided into two sections, the first section described only the general properties of the topology as found in West Bengal. The second section analyses the ranking of accessibility of nodes selected on size criteria.

Chapter 5 described the nature of road transport in pre- and post-independence periods. Unavailability of data, however, led to restriction of the work only to motor and bus transport. Commodity and passenger flows are not covered since accurate data are not available. However, passenger transport so far as but (STC) is concerned, has been analysed in detail and graphs have been drawn to establish the evidence.

Chapter 6 presents transportation efficiency of different nodes of West Bengal. Based on the space potential model an attempt has been made to delineate some efficient and inefficient transport regions in West Bengal.

Finally, Chapter 7 sums up the transport problems at inter-regional, intra-regional, urban and rural levels, some suggestions have been mentioned to cope with these problems and to establish a smooth operation of transport in the future.

Methodology

The study cover mainly two aspects:

1. Growth of roads and road transport;
2. Growth potential of roads based on accessibility and transportation efficiency.

In order to understand the actual position of road transport as obtaining today a thorough study of published and unpublished data have been made.

In the non-analytical historical part (i) physiographical background, (ii) development of roads under the British Raj during 1900–1947, (iii) development of roads during the plan periods have been dealt with through quantitative analysis.

The analytical part of the study includes analysis of (i) accessibility, (ii) transport structure, (iii) transport efficiency, (iv) problem of intra- and inter-regional mobility, rural-urban mobility with the help of graph theory, space potential model and other cartographic techniques.

I would like to take this opportunity to express my humble gratitude to those who have helped me in my effort to write this thesis.

The persons and institutions who rendered me help are numerous and it is difficult to acknowledge them individually. It is a pleasure for me to acknowledge the co-operation received from various organisations.

I owe a deep sense of gratitude to my supervisor, Prof. Kanan Gopal Bagchi, Professor and Head of the Department of Geography, Calcutta University, under whose inspiring guidance this work was carried out and accomplished. His affectionate guidance and thought provoking suggestions provided me with constant inspiration. His paternal affection was all along a source of inspiration for me.

I thank the authorities of Calcutta University most respectfully for the offer of a scholarship which sustained me in carrying out this work.

I am thankful to the Road Development of Public Works Department, Government of West Bengal, for the figures and facts which are up-to-date.

I specially acknowledge gratefully Mr. Barin Ghosh, Superintending Engineer, P.W.D. (Roads) for providing me with P.W.D. Road Map and Mr. N.C. Dey, Superintending Engineer, P.W.D. (Highways) for his kind assistance.

I am also grateful to Prof. Sunil Kumar Munshi, Professor, Centre for Studies in Social Sciences for his kind assistance and help.

I owe a debt of gratitude to Mr. Santosh Bagchi, Assistant Editor, Business Standard, for providing me with certain photographs.

The authorities of National Library (Annex), Commercial Library, Bureau of Applied Economics and Statistics, Writers' Buildings, British Council, Calcutta Metropolitan Planning Organisation, Calcutta University, have been kind enough to permit reference studies for which I am really grateful.

I offer my heartful thanks to Dr. Prithvish Nag, Deputy Director, NATMO for going through the initial writings and for making valuable suggestions. I would like to acknowledge the financial aid sanctioned by the Indian Council of Social Science Research, New Delhi for this publication. Last of all I extend my gratitude to Mr. Naurang Rai and Mr. Ashok Kumar of the Concept Publishing Company undertaking this publication.

Finally, I must acknowledge my indebtedness to my mother, brothers and my friends who have put up with considerable inconvenience and accepted various demands cheerfully so that the project could be successfully completed.

Centre for Urban Economic Studies
Department of Economics
Calcutta University
Calcutta

SUKLA BHADURI

CONTENTS

LIST OF TABLES

LIST OF FIGURES

1

HISTORICAL DEVELOPMENT OF ROADS IN BENGAL (1900–1947)

Any transport network is a reflection of the contemporary organisation of economy, social condition and political set-up. It carries a bold impression of the past and evolves gradually through the human history experiencing many stages.

Our task in this chapter is to set out the basic historical background to the state of roadways in West Bengal as it exists now (Fig. 1.1).

The relevant historical background is given by the development of roadways in Bengal under the British Raj which we may limit to the first half of the century or 1900 — 1947 to be precise. The geographical unit for this purpose cannot but be the basic administrative — political unit of 'Bengal' as it existed during the period mentioned. This is because all roads and source of information for road development in general for this period — which are mainly government reports pertain to this unit which is of course much larger than the present state of West Bengal. Let us first set out the geographical unit and its basic topography which has an obvious relevance for the study.

The road communication of a particular area cannot be fully understood except in the background of the basic terrain characteristics.

1.1 Geographical Units

Bengal during the British time (as it is more precisely designated as Lower Bengal) comprised the lower valleys and deltas of the Ganges and Brahmaputra and lay between 19°28′ and 28°8′ N latitude and between 81°37′ and 92°44′ E longitude.

Excluding Assam which was created into a separate administration in February, 1874, Bengal then included the four great provinces of Bengal proper, Bihar, Orissa and Chotanagpur. Bengal then was bounded on the north by Bhutan, Tibet and Nepal, on the east by Assam and lower Burma, on the south by Bay of Bengal and on the west by United Provinces of Agra and Oudh and the Central Indian Agency. The total area was 195,146 sq. miles.*

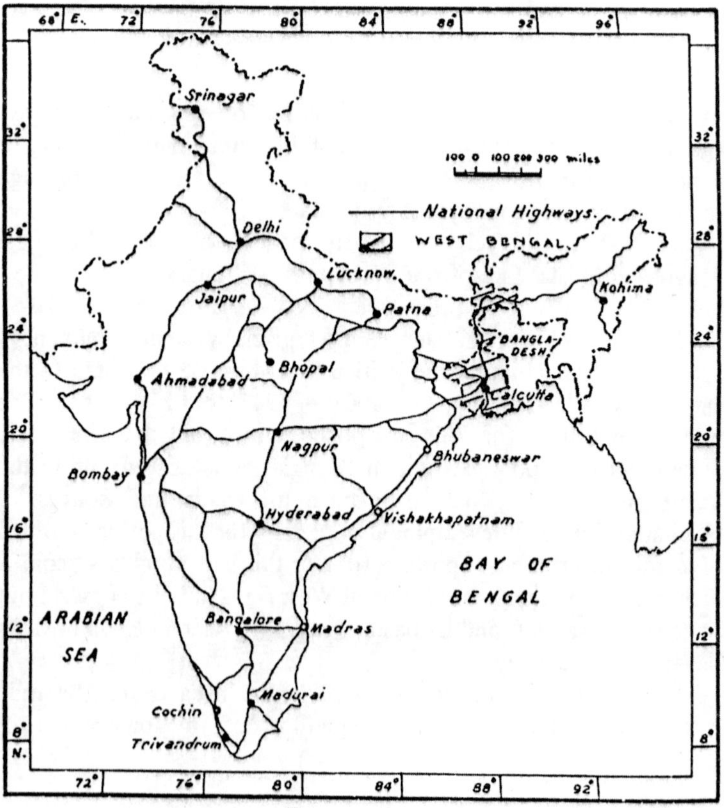

FIG. 1.1: Position and Extent of West Bengal.

* At present, West Bengal as the name implies, is the part of a larger regional entity named Bengal, lies between latitude 21°38′ to 27°10′ N and longitudinal extent 85°50′ to 89°50′ E comprising an area of 87,853 sq. km., i.e. 3 per cent of India's land area and supports 8 per cent of the total population.

1.2 Physical Set-up

In Bengal as elsewhere the natural landscape has considerably influenced the density of the road net. It is definitely longer in West Bengal than in East Bengal as shown on the map. The western part of the West Bengal has a moderate relief providing favourable conditions for road development. The Grand Trunk Road is by far the most important highway connecting Calcutta with the productive hinterland since the greater part of East Bengal is in extreme physiographic youth, the drainage is imperfect, and during the rainy season much of the country goes under water and become impassable except by boat. That is why rural East Bengal lacks good hard surfaced roads. In the eastern border of the province, however, the country is undulating and is served by good highways like the Dacca — Chittagong Trunk Road. Several hard-surfaced roads were built during the war years for strategic reasons (Fig. 1.2).

At the beginning of the British period the Bengal was a region where core was formed by the physical area called the Bengal delta of geologically recent origin. The essential geographic feature of Bengal is the highest mountain in the north, the Himalayas with its majestic peak Mt. Everest and Kanchenjunga and extremely dissected plateaus and hills rising abruptly from the plains in the north-east and east. It is only in the west that the topographic break is least pronounced, the plains merging almost imperceptibly into a slowly rising plateau. The plains can be broadly divided into three classes, the older deltaic and flood plains lying north of the Ganges – Padma axis, the younger deltaic and flood plains lying south of the axis, the erosional and flood plains lying west of the Bhagirathi – Hooghly river. The most conspicuous hills are found in the south-west of Bankura district and north-west of Midnapur district which rise to a height of over 1000 feet and have been considerably dissected.

There is another type of plain lying at the foot of the Himalaya. This is the typical piedmont plain of the Terai and western Duars.

Behind the Terai plain rise several ranges of the Himalaya to the stupendous heights of over 10,000 feet in Darjeeling district.

The hills in the Tripura and Chittagong Hill tracts run from north to south, intervened by valleys with an average width of 10 miles. They increase in height towards the east.

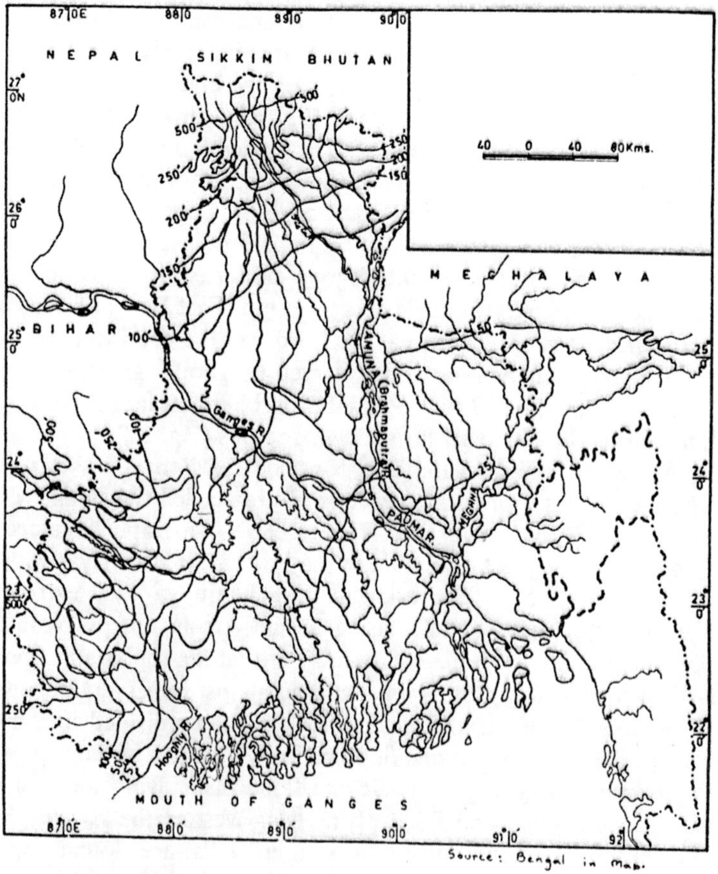

FIG. 1.2: Physical Set-up.

The most distinctive feature of the province is its network of rivers – the Ganges and the Brahmaputra, with their affluents and distributaries.

The three largest system of rivers of India, the Ganges, the Brahmaputra and the Meghna merge together in the plains of Bengal before entering the sea. South and north of Ganges locally known as Padma. The Bhagirathi is its western most and was at one time its principal channel, the lower reaches of which is named as Hooghly.

This river is of vital importance not only to the present Province of West Bengal but also to the whole of northern India as on its bank stands Calcutta, the largest port of India. Having its source at no great distance from that of the Ganges, but on the other side of the Himalayas, the Brahmaputra flows eastwards through Tibet where it is known as Tsanpo until it reaches a point due north of the western extremity of Assam, where it takes a southerly course and after forming its way through the eastern Himalaya, emerges in the plains of Assam. It then turns westwards and after traversing the Assam valley enters Bengal from the north-east.

Thus, it may be said that these are small groups of trunk streams flowing into Bengal Delta. These are Ganga, Padma, the Brahmaputra, Yamuna and the Meghna.

These physical regions around the Bengal Basin and the rivers flowing through them into the Basin imparted to it, the characteristics of a natural nodal regions of transportation routes.

1.3 Road Development in British Period

Due to the deltaic nature of parts of Bengal to numerous waterways and to widespread inundation the provision and maintenance of communication, particularly to roads, have aspects peculiar to the Presidency.

During the last century and prior to the introduction of railways, a number of trunk roads, bridged and metalled were constructed and maintained under the supervision of military engineers, connecting the more important military and commercial centres of the region.

The development that were inaugurated during the Governor Generalship of Lord William Bentinck (1828-35) were continued and extended by Lord Dalhousie (1848-1856). "A particularly inefficient body called the Military Board, which was supposed to look after public works, was suppressed and the Department of Public Works (PWD) was constituted nearly in its existing form. The expenditure on public works which had been on the most niggardly scale was enormously increased and works of great magnitude such as Grand Trunk Road were undertaken".

With the advent of railways, however, attention was concentrated on the construction of feeder roads at right angles to them and the trunk roads, especially where parallel to the railways were in some cases allowed to go out of repair. There was a great increase in metalled feeder roads and roads of local importance.

Regarding transportation and communication in Bengal, a statement made by Military Board in 1854 that many of the roads in this part of India were constructed in the first half of the 19th century and except one or two, were mostly *Kutcha* in character. Some of these *kutcha* roads were covered with 'doobgrass' while others got inundated during the rains. The annual report on the 'Administration of Bengal Presidency for 1860-61' laid down in clear terms the policy of the Government towards development of roads. The Government was relieved, the Report said "in a great measure during the past year from the pressing necessity of providing military accommodation for troops, and has been able to give practical attention to the formation of a system of Imperial Roads throughout the province".

It is further said in the Report that "The leading features of this scheme have been to provide one main line of road atleast in each district, which shall pass through the principal town or station and be continuous that is in connection with the main lines of the next district; so that district may be connected with district and the roads be of general public advantage as well as of local benefit. At the same time the communications with adjacent provinces not under the jurisdiction of the Bengal Government have been maintained and the Imperial lines have been designed to afford the means of easy communication between the chief centres of population and to secure to every part of the country a proper outlet for its produce and ready access to the great channels or thoroughfare of commerce. The existing trunk roads and their branches form the first instalment of the projected system."

The following Table 1.1 shows that there were eleven Imperial Trunk Roads existing or under construction in Bengal extending over a length of 1,994 miles with Imperial Branch Roads aggregating in length 1,145 miles. This following table incorporating a statement of Trunk and Branch Imperial Roads existing or proposed in the Bengal Presidency in 1860-61, would give an idea of the situation in regard to road development and the direction in which the policy statement charted out the lines of advance.

It is said in the Report that all of these roads were in a more or less completed state. The Grand Trunk Road from Calcutta to the Kurrumnassa (392 miles) was the only one of any considerable length that was completed. The Assam Trunk Road on the other hand being scarcely commenced to these 3,139 miles of road must ultimately be bridged and metalled, but one-third of the entire expenditure required to complete all these roads had been incurred.

TABLE 1.1: Statement of Trunk and Branch Imperial Roads, Existing or Proposed, in Bengal

Nos.	Trunk Roads	Length in mile	Nos.	Branch Roads	Length in mile
1	2	3	4	5	6
1.	**Grand Trunk Road**				
	Calcutta to Kurrumnassa River	392	1	Howrah Branch	17
			2	Midnapore Branch via Beneoorah and Raneegunge	90
			3	Hazaribagh Branch	80
			4	Patna Branch including Dimapore Branch	95
			5	Betah Branch Road	66
					348
2.	**Madras Trunk Road**				
	Calcutta to Chutterpore Road on the Madras Frontier via Midnapore, Balasore and Cuttack	318	1	Tumlook Branch	16
			2	Puri Branch	50
			3	Nagpur Branch from Cuttack through Sambulpur as far as the Tonk River	154
			4	Cuttack to Taldangah Branch	40
					260
3.	**Darjeeling Trunk Road**				
	Peerpointee Stations East Indian Railway to Darjeeling via Caragolahghat and Purneah	174			
4.	**Berhampur Trunk Road**				
	Calcutta to Berhampur and Moorshedabed	116	1	Barasat to Barrackpore Branch Road	8
			2	Jessore Branch Road	55
					63

Contd.

TABLE 1.1 *Contd.*

1	2	3	4	5	6
5.	**Tirhoot Trunk Road** Monghyr to Beilsurah via Muzaffarpur (about)	108	1	Mizufferpore Branch	36
			2	Berh Branch	46
					82
6.	**Chittagong Trunk Road** Daoodcandy to Chittagong	126			
7.	**Assam Trunk Road** Rajmahal to Debrooghur via Dinagepore, Rungpore and Gowhatty	564	1	Dinagepore to Tylalia	72
			2	Dinagepore to Burgatchea	91
			3	Sylhet and Cherra Poonjee Road	88
			4	Durrung Branch	20
			5	Tezpur Branch	16
			6	Jaypore Branch	29
			7	Serchwah Branch	76
					392
8.	**Mutla Trunk Road** Calcutta to Matla Port	29			
9.	**Diamond Harbour Road** Calcutta to Diamond Harbour	28			
10.	**Bhagulpore and Sooree Road** Ahmedpore Station to Bhagulpore	112			
11.	Nulhutte Station to Jeagunge	27			
	Total Length of Trunk Roads	1,994		Total length of Branch Roads	1,145

In this scheme, the feeder roads had an important role as can be seen from the following extract, "to benefit fully the district traversed by the bordering on the different lines of railway and to make these lines remunerative, the Lieutenant Governor has endeavoured to create a system of local roads as feeders, which shall place all the most important towns of the district in communication with the railway".

A list of the feeders projected for the three lines of railway (the aggregate length being 664 miles) were as following Table 1.2:

TABLE 1.2: Statement of Railway Feeders, Existing or Proposed

Nos.	From what place	To what place	Length in Miles
		East Indian Railway	
1.	Elambazar	Soorool Station	9
2.	Cutwa	Burdwan Station	30
3.	Culna	Pundooah Station	17
4.	Sooty	Pakaur Station	13½
5.	Jungypore	Moradoi Station	14½
6.	Chuckye	Lucksarae Station	48
7.	Kurruckpore	Barriarpore Station	13
8.	Muddipoorah	Bhangalpore Station	60
9.	Satgatchia	Mymaree Station	7
10.	Nittanundpore	Goosharah Station	12
11.	Sasseram	Peero Station	37
12.	Nasregunge	Bhojepore Station	28
13.	Baneoorah	Panaghur Station	38½
		Total Number of Miles:	327½
		Eastern Bengal Railway	
1.	Kishnaghur	Bagoolah Station	11
2.	Santipore	Ranaghat Station	11
3.	Comercolly	Koostee Station	13
4.	Jessore	Bagoolah Station	40
5.	Bongong	Hamedpore near Chagdah	20
6.	Kotechandpore	Kishnagunge	23
7.	Farreedpore	Kotechandpore	70
8.	Berhampore	Alumdangha	55
9.	Banleah Ferry	Jeagunge	24
10.	Ishapore	Bazarkhall	8
11.	Tenadah	Chowdangha	23½
12.	Gorakala Ghat	Alendangha	31
		Total Number of Miles:	329½
		South Eastern Railway	
1.	Mutlah Road	Gurpah Station	–
2.	Comercolly	Sonarpur Station	2
3.	Rajpore	Sonarpur Station	2¼
4.	Mullong	Chapatter Station	4
		Total Number of Miles:	8¼
		Grant Total:	665¼

These roads had been projected specially as railway feeders, but there were besides the foregoing some of the existing and proposed local roads which contributed to the same purpose.

In the early decades of the East India Company's rule, public works policy was entirely concerned with the construction and repairs of military building and of some roads of military importance. Indeed, till the time of Lord Dalhousie, the authority for construction of roads and building was vested in a Military Board in each Presidency. It was as late as in 1854 that a special civil department of Public Works was set up. Buildings and roads branches of public work functions were accordingly delegated to Provincial Governments. The Provincial Governments in their turn placed most of the road mileage in the province at the care of the local bodies reserving direct responsibility for only a small fraction of it. The net effect of this lack of interest in roads was that the road system of the sub-continent as a whole languished and became extremely deficient. During the year 1899-1900 the importance of Local Bodies over P.W.D. was felt from the figure of the road mileage maintained by it. (Appendix-I). Out of the total mileage 2200 of metalled roads, 365 miles was maintained by P.W.D. and the rest by the Local Bodies. And of the total mileage of 14,287 miles of unmetalled roads, only 215 miles of roads maintained by P.W.D. rest being under the charge of Local Bodies with the constitution of a suitable organisation to look after the business of road building and maintenance, a methodical classification of existing and future roads became necessary and all roads were then classified as follows:

Class - I *Metalled*
- (a) with bridges or ferries and drained throughout;
- (b) partially bridged or ferries and drained.

Class - II *Unmetalled*
- (a) with bridges or ferries and drained throughout;
- (b) Partially bridged and drained.

Class - III Banked and surfaced, but not drained.

Class - IV Banked but not surfaced; partially bridged and drained.

Class - V	Cleared and partially bridged and drained.
Class - VI	Cleared only.

As we shall see later inspite of this declaration, throughout the period of its time the British Raj never seriously concerned with the development of rural road system which had existed in embryo in the preceding period as a part of a self-sustaining rural economy grown around local, sub-regional and regional marts.

"The deterioration of the rural road system has been at once a cause and effect of these vast changes that have taken place. As village industries fell into decay, agriculture, the only means of livelihood in the village, could no longer support a growing population. People in increasing number took to nearby towns. Roads connecting these towns with the villages were difficult and hazardous and transport was scarce and slow. The communication between villages and towns gradually adjusted themselves to the minimum". (Kalidas Lahiri, *Road Problems of West Bengal*, 1950).

In the year of 1900-1901, out of the total mileage of 4606 of metalled roads, 1,190 miles belonged to the P.W.D. (25%) while the rest was under the Local Bodies. And out of the total mileage of 34,780 of unmetalled Roads, 468 miles (1.3%) was maintained by P.W.D. and rest being under the Local Bodies (Appendix-II).

In Bengal, the roads forming main line of communication were classed partly as Provincial and partly as District Roads. The former being maintained from Provincial and latter from District funds. Provincial aid was occasionally given to the District Board for the construction of new roads specially for those intended to serve as feeders to railway. Minor roads were classed as Municipal, Local funds, military or cantonment and village roads (Fig. 1.3).

Since 1905, all business connected with Public Works (excluding Railways) had been dealt with by a Secretary under the member-in-charge of revenue and agriculture. The superior engineering establishment was divided into two services, Imperial and Provincial. The establishment employed on irrigation and on buildings and roads (including miscellaneous works) was sub-divided by Provinces and was under the Local Government. The main roads were usually incharge of the Provincial Public Works Departments and local roads were made and repaired by Municipalities and Local Boards.

The scheme of metal surfacing of all the trunk roads appears to have been relegated to a place of secondary importance. The Imperial Gazetteer of 1908 noted the situation in the following terms:

> "The total length of provincial roads in Bengal (constituted of Bengal proper, Bihar, Chotanagpur and Orissa) was 1,663 miles in 1890 – 01 and 1,659 in 1900-01, increased to 2,406 miles in 1903-04 and 2,362 in 1904-05. During the same period the length of district roads increased from 32,110 miles to 37,728 miles and 50,631 to 56,367 miles respectively, the last figure includes a great many village roads already in existence but not previously taken into account" (Vol. II).

The Imperial Gazetteer further noted that "the Grand Trunk Road traverse the Burdwan, Chotanagpur and Patna Divisions from Calcutta to the Western Frontier, with a total length in the Province of 390 miles. The Orissa Trunk Road runs from Calcutta via Cuttack to the Madras Border, the length being 320 miles. The Ranigunge-Midnapore Road has a length of 101 miles. The Ganges-Darjeeling Road runs from near Katihar to Siliguri for 124 miles. The roads are metalled. An important unmetalled road runs from Chittagong to Dandkandi, a distance of 124 miles". The construction of railways had reduced the importance of the trunk roads as the Gazetteer pointed out that some of which had been consequently made over to District Board for maintenance. In other words, the increased facilities afforded by the railways for the export and import of goods had created a demand for numerous feeder roads. The First World War obstructed the progress of all weather road construction and also of metalling of roads. Railway wagons to carry construction material were in short supply. However, the metalling and widening of some of the trunk roads continued at a slower pace, such as the Calcutta-Jassore Road, the Grand Trunk Road, and the Trunk Road in the Chittagong District.

Roads were classified to the following five distinct categories depending on their importance, management and average annual expenditure per mile:

I. Government roads maintained by the Communication and Works Department for which the average annual expenditure per mile was Rs. 171.
II. District roads maintained directly by District Board for which the average annual expenditure per mile was Rs. 62.
III. Sub-divisional roads maintained by Local Boards working under the control of the District Board. Average annual expenditure per mile was Rs. 17.

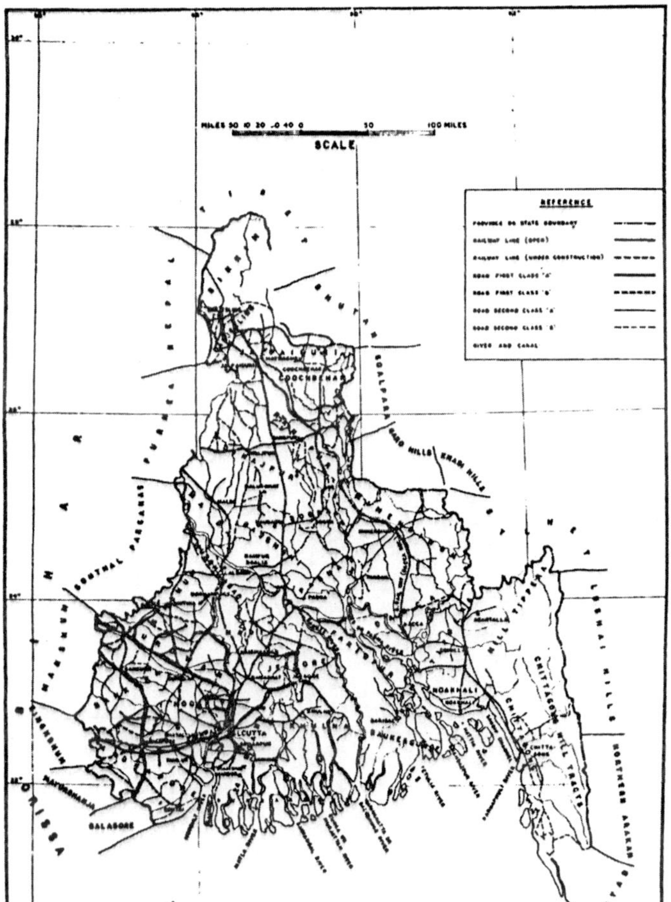

FIG. 1.3: The Presidency of Bengal Road Map (1911-1912).

IV. Urban roads maintained by Municipalities. Average annual expenditure not known.
V. Village roads maintained by Union Boards. Average annual expenditure per mile was Rs. 12.

Of the Government roads there were four main roads radiating from Calcutta which were superior to the rest and could be classed by themselves. These were the Grand Trunk Road, the Barrackpore Trunk Road, the Jessore Road and the Diamond Harbour Road.

In the Bengal as well as in the Ganga valley, the construction of all weather roads was rather expensive because all of them had to be embanked to a sufficient height above the level of ordinary floods. Any system of roads were very expensive to construct owing to the large number of rivers and canals over which bridge would have to be thrown, in those parts of the country where a system of road development would primarily be required and the amount of money that would be available from a road tax would, owing to the paucity of traffic, be totally inadequate to maintain the road in good order (Fig. 1.4).

The road development in the year of 1913 to 1926 would be revealed from the following Table 1.3:

TABLE 1.3: Road Development during 1913 to 1926

	1913-14 Miles	1923-24 Miles	1924-25 Miles	1925-26 Miles
Road Mileage				
Total Mileage				
Surfaced	2,583	3,315	3,332	3,376
Unsurfaced	13,530	15,618	15,862	15,886

Source: Basic Road Statistics, 1948.

The total expenditure on construction as well as on maintenance during the said year would also be clear from the following Table 1.4.

1.4 Report of the Indian Road Development Committee (1927-28)

By a resolution of the Council of State in 1927 a Road Development Committee was constituted with members from both the House of the Central Legislative under the chairmanship of Syt. M.R. Jayakar.

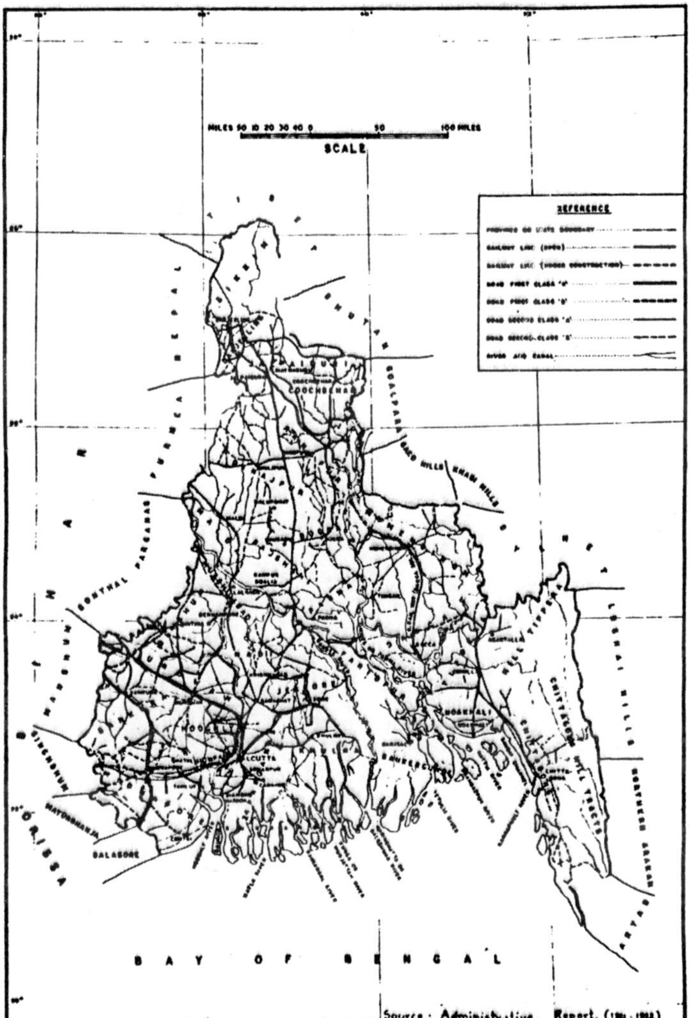

FIG. 1.4: The Presidency of Bengal Road Map (1921-1922).

This Committee in 1928, called for a change in the whole road policy of the Government. The scope and magnitude of road development in India, the Committee found, were beyond the capacity of Provincial Governments and Local Bodies. Road transport was fast becoming a matter of wider national importance; and the Committee recommended that the Central Road Fund with the proceeds of a tax surcharge on petrol in order to enable them to make annual block grants to Provinces out of this Fund for subsidising provincial works on roads. Uptil the formulation of the Post War Road Development Plan, the cost of developing an improved system of road communications in the Province was being met almost exclusively from the Central Road Fund.

TABLE 1.4: Expenditure on Construction and Maintenance during 1913 to 1926

Expenditure	1913-14 Rs.	1923-24 Rs.	1924-25 Rs.	1925-26 Rs.
Total expenditure on construction:				
Provincial Revenues	3,09,208	5,72,425	4,97,479	12,15,646
District Board Revenues	14,65,895	9,41,321	10,73,400	9,76,748
Total expenditure on maintenance:				
Provincial Revenues	8,85,326	21,43,700	22,20,454	23,86,468
District Board Revenues	19,97,571	26,55,306	25,48,310	26,14,935

Source: Basic Road Statistics, 1948.

In Bengal, the road development during the year was mentioned in the following:

	Metalled	*Unmetalled*
(i) Provincial (excluding Sikkim)	893	575
(ii) District Board (excluding village Roads)	2,513	15,447

Government was responsible for the provincial roads and district board and other local bodies for the local roads. Government provided funds from provincial revenues for the construction and maintenance of provincial roads. Contribution had in certain cases been invited from interested public bodies towards the construction of newer roads, without much response. Some provincial roads were placed in charge of district board for maintenance, funds for which were provided by Government. The district board and other local bodies maintained their own roads from their own revenues.

As found in the report of the Indian Road Development Committee 1927-28, the defects in the existing road system were:

(1) There has been at any rate until recently a lack of system and continuity in road programmes. This is the natural result of an outlook which was concentrated primarily on purely local needs, and was limited by the range of movement of the bullock cart and the provision of short feeders to railways. But with the development of motor transport there is a demand for an extended range of movement and for a coherent system which will unite broken and disconnected lengths into a continuous whole.

(2) The lack of bridges and crossings is a serious obstacle to traffic of all kinds.

(3) Road surfaces are said to be deteriorating and here again the problem is aggravated by the development of motor transport. On the one hand, motor transport demands improved surfaces; and on the other hand, its development is damaging the surface that already exist.

(4) Finally, it is generally agreed that the condition of subsidiary roads connecting village with main roads and with one another requires special consideration and relief.

The evidence received was unanimous that the road should be further developed and improved. Different witnesses stressed different points of view but the point on which there was perhaps most general insistence was the need of better communication for marketing agricultural produce.

The average cost of construction varied with the number of bridges which played an important part in a place like Bengal and on the width of the road.

It varied between Rs. 10,000 to Rs. 30,000 per mile excluding bridges exceeding 50 ft. spans.

TABLE 1.5: Details of Expenditure on Road for Maintenance and Construction in 1926-27

	Mileage to nearest Ten			Provincial expenditure Rs. 1000			Maintenance / Construction Local Fund expenditure
	Sur-faced	Unsur-faced	Total	Sur-faced	Unsur-faced	Total	Total
Arterial	890	570	1460	2004	209	2213	–
				701	53	759	
District Board	2510	15,450	17,960	–	–	–	2568
							1084
Total	3400	16,040	19,420	2004	209	2213	2568
				701	53	759	1084

The average cost of maintenance of arterial roads was Rs. 2,250 per mile.

The average cost of maintenance of unsurfaced provincial roads was Rs. 370 per mile.

No figure were available to show the average cost of maintenance of district board roads.

The position of Bengal in regard to road mileage during the year would be clear from the following table as obtained from the report:

TABLE 1.6: Road Mileage according to classes and types in 1926-27

	Provincial			Local			Both Classes		
	Sur-faced	Unsur-faced	Total	Sur-faced	Unsur-faced	Total	Sur-faced	Unsur-faced	Total
Madras	3590	530	4120	17850	2760	20610	21440	3290	24730
Bombay Presidency	5940	760	6700	2790	8180	10970	8730	8940	17670
Bengal	890	570	1460	2510	15450	17960	3400	16020	19420
Delhi	140	not stated			not stated		140	not stated	
Assam	400	3270	3670	160	5540	5700	560	8810	9370

The position of Bengal in regard to road growth, mainly surfaced roads, would be revealed from the following table:

TABLE 1.7: Surfaced mileage in the year 1913-14 and in the five years (1923-24 to 1926-27)

Province	1913-14 Miles	1923-24 Miles	1924-25 Miles	1925-26 Miles	1926-27 Miles
Madras	22544	20142	19594	20275	21440
Bombay	6628	8584	8655	8720	8830
Bengal	2583	3315	3332	3376	2400
Assam	386	550	552	554	560

1.5 Motor Transport

Motor Transport started assuming importance in the economy of Bengal only after the First World War. There were only a few thousand vehicles before the commencement of the war consisting largely of motor cars and taxis. During the war, a large number of vehicles were imported consisting largely of motor cars. Sizeable imports of commercial vehicles, i.e., buses and vans commenced only from the early twenties. From the following Table 1.8, we would have a picture of growth of motor vehicles from 1913 to 1947:

TABLE 1.8: Number of Motor Vehicles in Bengal

Year	No. of Vehicles	Year	No. of Vehicles	Year	No. of Vehicles
1913	4,058	1936	24,550	1942	25,600
1914	5,225	1937	25,303	1943	22,059
1923	14,794	1938	28,134	1944	26,206
1924	17,445	1939	23,567	1945	35,451
1925	19,751	1940	24,289	1946	31,077
1926	23,015	1941	27,598	1947	40,531
1935	25,247	—	—	—	—

Source: Basic Road Statistics, 1948.

During and immediately after the Second World War, there was a rapid expansion of goods vehicles in the country. The number of motor vehicles of all kinds imported into India was only 4,419 in 1913-14 but had risen to 25,950 in 1927-28. Average value of import of motor cars and motor cycles and parts thereof for the 5 years from

1909-10 to 1913-14 was Rs. 3,294,344 as against – Rs. 38,95,236 for 1914-15 to 1918-19. In the subsequent three years of 1919-20, 1920-21 and 1921-22 these figures were Rs. 14,178,362, Rs. 49,068,555 and Rs. 9,133,633. In 1934-35, the value of imports into Calcutta of only motor cars was Rs. 76,37,867 and in 1935-36 Rs. 77,30,598.

The following figures would reveal the condition of growth of different types of motor vehicles in Bengal 1913–47 as obtained from Basic Road Statistics (1948):

TABLE 1.9: Growth of motor vehicles in Bengal 1913-47

	Private Cars	Motor Buses	Taxis	Commercial Goods Vehicles	Motor Cycles
1913	3,199	–	136	–	723
1914	3,937	–	322	–	966
1923	10,300	–	1167	867	2445
1924	12,385	–	1430	1032	2863
1925	14,560	–	949	818	3144
1926	17,369	–	956	760	3482
1940	15,876	1974	2245	3055	417
1941	19,322	2270	2132	2833	1003
1942	16,202	2341	3090	3364	506
1943	13,477	1413	1611	4684	854
1944	13,746	2541	4111	4871	917
1945	20,984	3050	4117	6374	906
1946	13,651	3921	4536	7806	1141
1947	17,255	4636	4570	3921	1542

Motor Vehicles Act of 1914 was the first all India enactment for controlling of motor vehicles. It did not make any distinction between different types of motor nor was any attempt made to restrict their free movement.

1.6 The King's Report

By 1938, the comprehensive report on Road Development Project in Bengal by A.J. King, a special officer of Road Development Project produced by the Government of Bengal, noted "it may be said that every part of the country lies within 2 miles of an existing metalled and unmetalled road of a better class". On the face of it, therefore, it appeared that this province atleast was reasonably well served by the existing roads. The table shown in the Appendix-II would at a glance reveal the road system existed during the time (1937).

As had been reported by King that only 88 miles or 1.82 per cent of the total could be classed as high grade road of a permanent nature and suitable for carrying heavy traffic. The Government metalled roads were generally kept in a better condition than those of other classes. Of the government roads the four main roads radiating from Calcutta were superior to the rest and might be placed in a class by themselves.

These were – (i) Grand Trunk Road,
(ii) Barrackpore Trunk Road,
(iii) Jessore Road,
(iv) Diamond Harbour Road.

These roads were well kept highways being fully bridged and having a surface consisting of a layer of hardstone metal finished with either a carpet or paint of tar or bitumen.

The district metalled roads were usually of a type somewhat inferior to the intermediate grade of Government road being constructed to a lower specification and maintained in a cheaper way.

The unmetalled road in the province with a total length of 86,541 miles (approximately) vary considerably in character and many types were found, the highest being well maintained wide roads, well raised above flood level, fully bridged in respect of minor streams and of a standard comparable except with regard to the surface with that of the metalled roads while the lowest of these intended for vehicular traffic were narrow, ill kept, unbridged surface tracks which during rains were generally submerged and impassable but could in dry season be negotiated with some difficulty by highly laden country carts.

The Government unmetalled roads were small in number representing a total length of 523 miles only in the whole province of which 50 per cent was situated in Chittagong Hill Tracts, 20 per cent in Darjeeling and 10 per cent in Chittagong and Tippera and remaining 10 per cent in Howrah, Dacca, Noakhali.

District unmetalled roads and the sub-division comprising a total length of approximately 38,541 miles formed the main lines of communication within the District and constituted the bulk of the mileage of the better class unmetalled roads in the Province. These two classes of roads were very similar in character except that the more important and consequently the better kept roads were looked after directly by the district board.

The village unmetalled roads with an approximate total length of 46,698 miles were with few exception, narrow, inferior type roads, tracks and footpaths maintained at a low cost to other or with roads of higher classes.

The chief reason which made the unmetalled roads as they existed in the province incapable of regular use by vehicular traffic was the unsuitability when judged from the road point of view of the soil with which they were constructed.

The second obstacle to the regular use by vehicular traffic of the system of unmetalled roads was the presence of a large number of unbridged gaps which occurred where the roads cross streams and rivers.

Another defect in the system was the existence of stretches of road in which the embankments were too low to keep the road surface sufficiently above flood level.

A glance at the following Table 1.10 would disclose that the distribution of the metalled roads in the several districts of the Province was by no means uniform, but the system being mainly confined to West Bengal and parts of Central and North Bengal.

The continuous stretches of metalled road varied greatly in length as shown in the above Table 1.11 in which those with a length of 25 miles and over had been listed. The metalled and unmetalled roads considered together constituted a collection of roads which although considerably greater in length than was necessary to serve the country efficiently, did not conform (both as regards distribution and alignment and as regards standard of construction) to the requirement of a road system capable of efficiently serving the needs of the country and suitable to meet the requirement of traffic but offered possibilities for conversion into an improved road system of shorter length but sufficient to serve the need of the province to a reasonable degree and suitable to meet the demand of traffic expected to be carried by the system.

It is said in the report that except for the system comprising the Grand Trunk Road and the roads connected to it, the Province of Bengal had no "Road System" in the proper sense of the term even though it contained a very large mileage of roads.

TABLE 1.10: Distribution of the metalled roads

Sl. No.	District	Length Miles	Length of road to every 100 sq. miles of areas
1.	Midnapore	584	11.1
2.	Burdwan	506	18.7
3.	Bankura	476	18.1
4.	24-Parganas	336	6.4
5.	Jalpaiguri	300	10.2
6.	Darjeeling	265	21.9
7.	Birbhum	242	14.2
8.	Jessore	184	6.3
9.	Hooghly	164	13.8
10.	Nadia	117	4.0
11.	Howrah	94	18.0
12.	Mymensingh	90	1.4
13.	Murshidabad	73	3.5
14.	Rajshahi	68	2.6
15.	Dinajpore	55	1.4
16.	Khulna	47	1.0
17.	Pabna	45	2.5
18.	Malda	39	2.2
19.	Dacca	34	1.3
20.	Bakarganj	29	0.8
21.	Bogra	27	2.0
22.	Chittagong	21	0.8
23.	Tippera	21	0.8
24.	Rangpur	21	0.6
25.	Faridpur	16	0.7
26.	Noakhali	14	0.9
27.	Chittagong Hill Tracks	1	0.002

It is said in the report that "the road problem in the province is, therefore, not the simple one of merely improving (by improvement is meant providing existing roads with better and more durable surfaces and possibly strengthening, reconstructing or constructing few bridges at intervals) short lengths of existing or providing short lengths of additional road with the object of bettering a system already mostly in existence, but rather one of developing in the entire area covered by the Province a complete new road system in the development of which use is made to the greatest extent possible of the existing roads with metalled and unmetalled".

TABLE 1.11: Districtwise metalled road in length

Sl. No.	District in which located	Length in miles
1.	Burdwan, Hooghly, Howrah, 24-Parganas	1,239
2.	Jalpaiguri, Darjeeling	255
3.	Midnapore	218
4.	Bankura	158
5.	Jalpaiguri	136
6.	Midnapore	101
7.	Ditto	93
8.	Birbhum	90
9.	Rajshahi	52
10.	Midnapore	50
11.	Bankura, Midnapore	40
12.	Midnapore	38
13.	Nadia	37
14.	Murshidabad	36
15.	Pabna	35
16.	Mymensingh	31
17.	Ditto	30
18.	Dinajpore	30
19.	Midnapore	28
20.	Khulna	28
21.	Malda	27
22.	Birbhum	26
23.	Ditto	25

The Road mileage in Bengal (1937) and Authorities responsible for their maintenance, are appended in the following Table 1.12:

TABLE 1.12: Distribution of metalled and unmetalled roads

Authority responsible for upkeep	Metalled Roads (Miles)	Unmetalled Roads (Miles)	Total
(i) Provincial Government	925	523	1,448
(ii) District Boards	2,730	17,565	20,295
(iii) Local Boards	214	20,976	21,190
(iv) Union Boards	122	46,698	46,820
Total	3,991	85,762	89,753

To this account should be added the mileage of urban roads

maintained by the Municipalities. There was also a small mileage of road constructed and maintained by the Forest and Irrigation Department for administrative purposes. The gross total for the Province was approximately estimated at 92,000 miles for all classes of roads, working up to about 1.2 miles of road to every square mile of area.

The unmetalled roads, which contributed nearly 94 per cent of the total mileage, were not only unsuitable for the needs of modern traffic but were incapable of providing a means of unbroken communication throughout the year even by country carts. Of these unmetalled roads again nearly 55 per cent were those under the charge of the Union Boards, mostly village tracks of a very primitive kind.

Leaving out these unmetalled roads, the Province had in 1937 less than 5,000 miles of metalled roads. The mileage of surfaced roads of any kind was thus only about 0.06 to the square miles. Distribution of these metalled roads in the Province was also uneven. Eight districts out of twenty seven in the undivided Province accounted for 70 per cent of the total mileage of such roads.

The following Table 1.13 shows a list of important railway feeders during the time of King's (i.e. 1937).

TABLE 1.13: List of Important Railway Feeders

Sl. No.	District	Location From	Location To	Length Miles
1	2	3	4	5
		I. East Bengal Railway		
1.	Bogra & Rangpur	Sonatalu	Jumabari	4.17
2.	Bogra	"	Mokumtola	9.00
3.	Rangpur	Kamarpara	Kamarjani	10.55
4.	"	Gitadaha	Fulbari	8.17
5.	Rajshahi	Sarda Road	Charghat	5.00
6.	Malda	Samsi	Ratna	8.50
7.	Faridpur	Machpara	Sengram	6.91
8.	Jalpaiguri	Jainti	Raidah River	10.00
9.	Malda & Rajshahi	Ammurs	Tanor	12.00
10.	Rajshahi	Madhunagar	Bagmara via Tahiapur	12.20

Contd.

TABLE 1.13 *Contd.*

1	2	3	4	5
		II. East Indian Railway		
1.	Birbhum	Rampurhat	Purulia	10.50
2.	"	"	Duniagram	10.00
3.	Hooghly	Chandannagar	Bhola	6.00
4.	"	Tarakeswar	Kanarighat	4.00
5.	Burdwan	Nabadwip	Chandpur	3.00
6.	"	"	Nadanghata	7.00
7.	Birbhum	Bolpur	Khujutipara	15.50
8.	"	"	Purandarpur	16.80
		III. Bengal-Nagpur Railway		
1.	Midnapore	Jakpur	Bhatachak	2.50
2.	"	Madpur	Lacknanpur	2.00
3.	"	"	Atra	5.50
4.	"	Haur	Srirampur	2.25
5.	"	"	Kalidan	2.25
		IV. Assam-Bengal Railway		
1.	Tippera	Comilla	Dandkandi	32.00
2.	Chittagong	Hathazari	Ronzan	8.11
3.	Mymensingh	Kishoregang	Karimganj	6.57
4.	Ditto	Sararihar	Bazitpur	3.11
5.	Chittagong	Dhoon	Santirhat	0.39
		V. Bankura-Damodar River Railway		
1.	Bankura	Krishnagar	Betsi	7.00
2.	Burdwan	Bowaichandi	Akui village	2.75
		VI. Ahmedpur-Katwa Railway		
1.	Birbhum	Labpur	Ganutia	6.00
2.	Burdwan	Ramjibanpur	Kandra village	0.75
		VII. Kalighat-Falta Railway		
1.	24-Parganas	Sararhat	Naldari	6.85
2.	"	Sairakole	Usli	5.80
		VIII. Howrah-Amta Railway		
1.	Hooghly	Champadanga	Arambagh	18.00
2.	Howrah	Amta	Deora Gazipur	3.00
3.	"	Murshidabad	Basantapur	4.00
		IX. Howrah-Sheakhala Railway		
1.	Hooghly	Kumirmora	Dudkalmi	2.00
		X. Patipukur-Hasnabad Section, Including Barasat Basirhat Branch		
1.	24-Parganas	Hasnabad	Hingalganj	9.56
2.	"	Sarupnagar	Khaspur	3.16
3.	"	Kharibari	Badu	4.70
4.	"	Aminpur	Balighata Ferry	3.90

The total length of the feeder roads originally proposed by the Railway and Steamer Authorities amounted to approximately 1,861 miles, of this total length approximately 870 miles had been selected to form a part of the main scheme for improved roads while of balance – approximately 330 miles were no longer required as it had been found possibly to provide a part of the main road system.

The report concluded that because majority of roads were not only unsuitable to meet the needs of existing traffic, but also unsuitable for providing a means by which unbroken communications could be maintained throughout the year even by country carts. The factors responsible for such wretched condition of roads were listed as four:

(a) The soils with which these roads were constructed were unsuitable,
(b) There were large number of unbridged gaps. As for example, there were 650 ferries in several districts for transportation of traffic across these gaps,
(c) During rainy season, the lower section of the roads got inundated, and
(d) There was almost universal neglect of proper upkeep.

Having completed his investigations into the existing roads Mr. King next proceeded to formulate a plan for a complete and continuous road system in the province. The King's scheme took into consideration the necessity for making use to the greatest possible extent of the existing roads, both metalled and unmetalled and providing other roads to act as feeders to existing trunk and metalled roads. This scheme also avoided, as far as possible, selection of roads likely to complete with railway and steamer services.

Individual treatment was given to each district, and separate district schemes were framed. Mr. King envisaged four different classes of roads to make a complete system for the whole province on integration:

(a) The Trunk Roads to provide through communication by reasonably direct routes across the entire area of the province, connecting the headquarters of all districts;
(b) Inter-district main roads to connect headquarters of neighbouring districts by routes more direct than those

provided by the trunk roads; and

(c) & (d)The district main and the district secondary roads to provide communications further into the interior.

According to Mr. King, the Province comprised of 2,809 miles of trunk roads, 538 miles of inter-district roads and 5,621 miles of district main and secondary roads.

1.7 Road Development and Road Policy

Despite the efforts devoted to road development since the end of the 2nd World War, the road system was still inadequate in many ways. It was worth recalling that before independence, the limited aims and the state of economic development, few fields of public policy received the same degree of systematic attention from administration and engineers as to the construction and maintenance of roads.

The Indian Road Congress was established in 1934 and had functioned continuously at an advanced technical level. Problems of road development as they presented themselves in the late twenties were carefully considered by the Indian Road Development Committee.

Earlier in 1919, the Government of India Secretariat Procedure Committee and in 1920-21, the Indian Railway Committee had also recommended the constitution of one department and the Government of India to control all means of transport and emphasized that "the development of roads and railways should be directed by a single policy".

Later efforts at road-rail co-ordination had been reported by the Committee on Transport Policy and Co-ordination Government of India (1961) in the following terms.

With the onset of the economic depression in 1930 competition between railway and road transport was intensified and in 1932 Government appointed two officers K.G. Mitchell, Road Engineer and L.H. Kirkness, Railway Officer to enquire into the extent of this competition and the possibility of future co-ordination and development.

According to their report, the competition between rail and road transport was mainly in the field of passenger traffic and that also within the zone of 1 to 50 miles.

The road-rail conference which was held in April 1933, adopted a number of resolutions, advocating greater co-operation and more intelligent co-ordination of road and rail development and concerted measures to prevent uneconomic competition. One of the measures suggested was setting up of a body to ensure adequate co-ordination between the Centre and the Province. As a result, Transport Advisory Council was set-up and held its first meeting in January 1935. At its first meeting the Council adopted a concise statement of policy and a memorandum of points for further investigation. Their recommendations briefly were as follows:

(1) The funds available for development of roads should be applied largely to roads which did not duplicate existing means of transport.
(2) For the control of road traffic, legislation should be enacted aimed at greater public safety and the avoidance of wasteful competition. (This recommendation took shape in the Motor Vehicles Act of 1939).
(3) Provincial Government should create or continue the existing board and communication with advisory functions on all matters concerning co-ordination of road-rail and inland water transport.

Difficulties, however, arose subsequently regarding the implication of the word 'largely' in relation to the use of money for the development of roads which did not duplicate existing means of transport. After considerable discussion with the provinces at the 2nd Transport Advisory Council meeting held in July 1936, the Centre decided to impose the condition that not more than 25 per cent of the Road Fund allocation covering any long term programmes should be spent on road competition of railways and that subject to this percentage not being exceeded, such allocations should be applied to the development of any road included in the Skeletion Trunk Road system. It was provided that not less than 25 per cent of the allocation should be spent on feeder roads.

The problem of road-rail co-ordination recorded during the Second World War, when the entire transport system of the country was subject to heavy strain. However, in their anxiety about the situation that might develop after the war, the Government of India set up in 1943, a Technical Sub-Committee on Transport to consider the future of the road transport and road-rail relation in the country (Fig. 1.5).

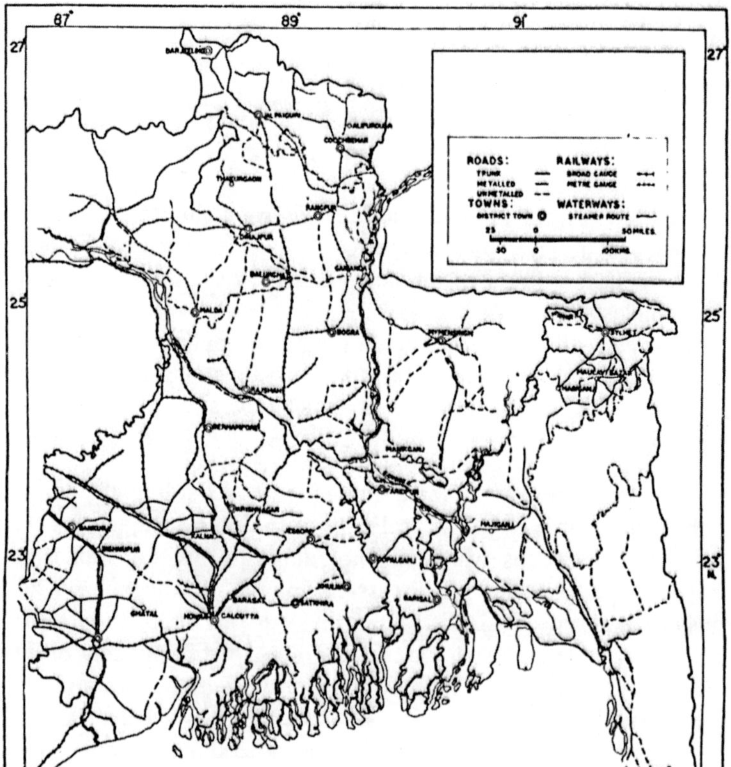

FIG. 1.5: Bengal Road Map 1946.

Their recommendations were:

(1) Goods transport on National Highways should be controlled by the Centre.
(2) The short haul goods traffic should be controlled by the Centre.
(3) As regards long distance goods transport by road, competition between road and rail should be prevented by a system of regulation, combining an expert judgment on the merits of each case on the basis of public and economic need with scientific zoning.
(4) As regards passenger transport 'the principles of maximum amalgamation of passenger service operators to form substantial concerns on main routes, and of controlled monopolies on light traffic routes should be the basis of policy.
(5) Minimum fares both for rail and road should be established by agreement.
(6) The railway should develop closer co-operation with road passenger transport and ultimately acquire a commanding interest.
(7) Within the general framework of the constitution, adjustment should be made so as to give the Province an interest in railway and Centre an adequate voice in road transport.""

Arther J. White in his article entitled "The Future of Co-ordination between Rail and Road" makes the following comment: "road improvement will doubtless be carried out at a faster pace, new motor road widenings, by-pass, wider passes, via ducts and so on. Road capacity will be increased, but the additional capacity is likely to be absorbed faster than it can be created especially in the cities. . . ."

The entire road system of the Province put to severe strain during the war years, was found wanting in material respects, simultaneously it was being felt that this vital problem of the improvement of road communications in the country could not be effectively solved on a provincial plane and that if energy was not to be dissipated on parochial objects, it was essential that road planning must have to be done on an all India basis. The Government of India assumed a direct role for the formulation and co-ordination of a comprehensive plan for the purpose.

1.8 The Nagpur Plan

In December 1943, Chief Engineers in charge of roads throughout the country met at Nagpur to consider ways and means of evolving a planned and co-ordinated system of road to meet the requirements of the entire sub-continent. They evolved a ten year road development plan to meet the country's requirement over the twenty year period from December 1943. The plan proceeded on the basis that in highly developed agricultural areas, no village should be more than 5 miles from a road, nor more than twenty miles from a main road, the average distance from a main road being 6 or 7 miles in most cases.

The task that the Conference set itself was to plan a well balanced road system for India as a whole that would anticipate the transport needs of the country for a period extending upto twenty years after the end of the war.

The plan worked out by the Conference envisaged the construction of a classified category of roads, graded according to the nature of the needs they were required to meet, national, provincial or merely local.

(a) National Highways running through the length and breath of India, connecting ports, foreign highways, capital of provinces and of large states and including roads required for strategic movements for the defence of India.
(b) Provincial Highways, the main arteries of commerce by road within a Province. They would connect up with the national highways and with the highway systems of the neighbouring provinces, join by roads of the district headquarters and other important places within the Province and then lead off into the rural areas through roads of lower categories.

District Roads were divided into two categories:

(i) Major Roads,
(ii) The other District Roads and the village roads.

The District Roads would be designed to branch off from the national or provincial highways and lead the channels of trade from them to the outlying tracts within a district.

The Village Roads would be the outer links of this network, connecting villages and groups of villages with each other, joining up with the nearest district roads or other highways and also serving as feeders to local railways or river traffic.

It will be seen that the classification adopted by the Nagpur Conference and now recognised as standard for India as a whole, is in essential particular the same as Mr. King's.

King's Plan		*Nagpur Plan*
Inter-District Main Road	–	National Highways
District Main Road	–	Provincial Highways
District Secondary Roads	–	Major District Roads
		Other District Roads

The only substantial difference between King's plan and the Nagpur plan lay in shifting of emphasis from rail-road competition. This competition was the main point of concern of King, while the Nagpur Report was more worried about strategic considerations.

A formula was worked out based on the grid and star principle by which the length of roads of each that was needed in a province was assessed. It was intended that the whole road system of the Sub-continent should be evolved in a balanced manner so that it did not suffer from over-emphasis in certain areas while communication in other adopted, was a function of diverse factors bearing on the transport needs of the country.

1.8.1 *Formula of the Nagpur Plan*

For assessing the requirement of total mileage under various categories of roads, the Nagpur Plan worked out the following formula:

Total mileage under N.H.,
P.H. and M.D.R.=

$$= \frac{A}{6} \quad \frac{B}{20} + ST - R.$$

A = Total agricultural area in square miles in the Province.
B = Total non-agricultural area in square miles.
N = Number of towns and villages having a population 2001–5000.
T = Number of towns and villages having a population over 5000.
R = Railway mileage in the area under consideration.

For the Province of Bengal the formula worked out in the following Table 1.14:

TABLE 1.14: Total Mileage under Categories of Roads in Bengal Province

Province	Agr. area in sq. mls.	Non-Ag. area in sq. mls.	No. of vill. with pop. 2001-5000	No. of towns & villages with pop. over 5000	Existing railway mileage	Road mileage requirement
Bengal	46,571	30,950	4,551	716	3,545	10,896
Bihar	38,704	31,041	2,081	290	2,775	10,051

For other district and village roads, the formula adopted was follows:

$$\text{Mileage of O.D.R. and V.R.} = \frac{V}{5} + \frac{Q}{R} + R + 2S$$

V = Number of villages with population of 500 or less.
Q = Number of villages with population of 501 – 1,000.
R = Number of villages with population of 1001 – 2000.
S = Number of villages with population of 2001 – 5000.

To this, again was to be added a certain mileage equivalent to 'D' representing the extent of agricultural and industrial developments during the next 20 years, affecting the existing density of population in the village. For the provinces of Bengal and Bihar, the formula worked out in the following manner:

TABLE 1.15: Number of villages with population

	Over 500 (V)	501-1000 (Q)	1001-2000 (R)	2001-5000	Road mileage requirement
Bengal	51,307	18,092	9,696	4,551	38,105
Bihar	47,936	12,837	5,814	2,081	25,981

As the report of Mitchell and Kirkness visualised that the sharper competition existed between the two forms with improvements of motor vehicles and better organisation of motor transport. As a solution, it was suggested that railways themselves operated road transport on routes running parallel to them. Moreover, the number of buses on any route might be restricted and the issue of time-table publication of schedules of fares and compulsory insurance might be prescribed.

The problem would be understood from the following Table 1.16:

TABLE 1.16: Conference/Committees recommendations

Year	Conference/Committee/Acts	Major recommendation
1933	Conference on rail-road competition	Set-up Board of Communication in the Province and a transport Advisory Council at the Centre.
1937	Indian Railway Enquiry Committee	Proposed : Route Licenses to vehicles to be restricted depending on adequacy of transport by rail. The Railways should have full powers to (a) run-road services (b) invest money or to enter into working agreements with road transport undertaking, and (c) to arrange road transport service through contractors.
1939	Motor Vehicles Act, 1939	Laid down that all transport to obtain permits from authorities constituted under the Act and restricted them from operating except in accordance with the conditions given in the permits.
1943	Technical Sub-Committee of the Subject Committee on Transport	Proposed that (a) goods transport on national highways should be controlled by the Centre. (b) The short-haul goods traffic should be transferred to roads. (c) The railways should develop closer co-operation with road passenger transport and ultimately acquire a commanding interest. (d) The Centre should have adequate voice in road transport. (e) A central road and road transport authority to be called the 'Indian Board' to be set-up.
1946	White Paper	Recommended tripartite companies to be set-up in which the railways, the State Government and the private operators should participate.

The King Report on Bengal was subjected to revision in the light of the recommendations of the Nagpur Conference. A special officer for road development was appointed for this purpose and a post-war road development plan was formulated by him on the basis of the report of Mr. King with modifications necessitated by the Nagpur formula. The outline of this plan was laid down and was discussed at Commissioner's Conference in each division where District Officers and representatives of the District Board were present, besides the special officer, Roads. The recommendations of these Conferences, with modifications suggested on the plan, were then placed before the government. In this way, the government came to finalise a plan in 1946, which envisaged the construction and improvement of the following categories of roads over the whole Province of Bengal during the period of 20 years beginning from 1946-47:

	Length in miles
National Highways	1,150
Provincial Highways	2,300
Major District Roads	6,200
Other District Roads	6,300
Village Roads	14,100
Total	30,100

The Nagpur report indicated the necessity of 'phasing' the entire plan into suitable periods according to a schedule of priorities assigned to different parts of the plan. Accordingly, the government of Bengal adopted a five-year programme for priority works and drew up a short plan for the period as follows:

	Length in miles
National Highways	880
Major Highways	1,785
Major District Roads	1,085
Other District Roads	181
Village Roads	140
Total	4,071

It would be interesting to compare the percentage of the total mileage of each category of roads borne on the twenty years plan to that assigned to such a category in the first five year period. Nearly 77 per cent and 78 per cent of the total length of national and provincial highways in the 20 years plan were scheduled for completion during the first five years. This percentage for the M.D.R. was 17.5 and for the two lowest categories of roads less than 3 and 1 respectively. The idea was to build up the larger framework first and then gradually to go down to the villages.

1.9 The Road Finance

It was not until 1947, after the experiences of Second World War had spot lighted Indian road transport deficiencies that positive steps were taken to set a system of national highway with Central responsibility for both construction and maintenance. At that time importance of arterial routes to national defence and national economy was recognised.

For an extensive legislative and historical background there has emerged a joint interest or partnership between the Central Government and the States. The Centre has assumed full financial responsibility for National Highway.

The growth of highway network has taken place as a result of Nagpur Plan (1943), twenty year road development plan (1958) and the three five year plans. Except from the Central Road Fund, which had a special continuing source of revenue of about Rs. 40 million per year, appropriation for highway development and maintenance were made from the general budget of the Central Government and the States. The Jayakar Committee under the chairmanship of Syt. M.R. Jayakar constituted in 1927 with members from both the Houses of Central Legislature had recommended that the Central Government should take more active interest in the development of roads by financing construction of new roads and improving the old ones.

The Government of India responded by setting up in 1929 a Central Road Fund with the proceeds of a tax surcharge on petrol in order to enable them to make annual block grants to provinces and for subsidising provincial works on roads.

Uptil the formulation of post-war road development plan, the cost of developing an improved system of road communication in the province was being met almost exclusively from the Central Road Fund. The following table which was based on the figures given by the Mitchell-Kirkness in their report, showed a comparison of expenditure incurred on road construction as apart from maintenance in various provinces in India during the period from 1923-24 to 1929-30.

TABLE 1.17: Expenditure on Road Construction and Maintenance during 1923-1930

(Rs. in Lakhs)

Year	Punjab	Madras	Bombay	Bihar & Orissa	Central Provinces	Bengal	United Provinces
1923-24	11.2	15.2	22.2	32.5	13.2	15.2	10.4
1924-25	7.8	17.4	37.7	23.1	13.2	15.7	11.5
1925-26	24.0	28.0	29.5	25.0	16.0	21.9	11.0
1926-27	35.9	22.9	23.4	16.2	21.9	18.4	14.1
1927-28	70.4	46.3	20.3	18.3	29.7	16.5	7.7
1928-29	65.5	45.8	19.4	14.9	25.3	13.8	6.6
1929-30	39.9	53.7	15.8	18.9	15.6	9.5	11.9
Total	254.7	229.3	168.3	148.9	134.9	111.0	73.2
Average per year	36.4	32.8	24.0	21.3	19.3	15.8	10.5

The table below indicates, year by year from 1930-31, the receipts from the Central Road Fund and the total expenditure on Road Fund Projects in the undivided province upto the end of 1946-47:

TABLE 1.18: Receipts and Expenditure on Central Road Fund

Year	Receipts from Central Road Fund (Rs.)	Expenditure on Road Fund Project (Rs.)
1930-31	19,30,000	4,40,849
1931-32	6,00,000	10,97,529
1932-33	22,55,521	10,28,679
1933-34	12,44,051	5,88,642
1934-35	13,20,995	7,16,717
1935-36	14,12,765	10,29,756
1936-37	17,65,547	12,93,816
1937-38	18,13,060	13,21,782
1938-39	18,46,995	20,60,163
1939-40	20,50,618	26,62,866
1940-41	20,60,801	29,45,744
1941-42	18,86,955	31,07,040
1942-43	16,10,704	8,30,316
1943-44	15,01,348	9,80,018
1944-45	14,86,240	4,47,700
1945-46	8,85,255	19,47,555
1946-47	19,78,312	8,56,534
Total	2,76,48,907	2,33,55,706

Source: Basic Road Statistics, 1948.

On the other hand, it should be noted that the first 'road user taxes' in India were the customs and excise duties on petrol from which the Central Road Fund was created in 1929. The annual yield from these taxes went on rising sharply as revealed in the following figures:

1925 - 26	Rs.	97 lakhs
1933 - 34	Rs.	434 lakhs
1945 - 46	Rs.	1,701 lakhs.

Other taxes like motor vehicle tax and fees, the revenue from provincial government was as follows:

TABLE 1.19: Revenue Taxes from 1939-1947

	Revenue from taxes Lakhs of Rs.	Revenue from fees Lakhs of Rs.
1938-39	16.99	4.88
1939-40	16.83	1.28
1940-41	17.89	4.97
1941-42	15.45	1.73
1942-43	13.99	1.78
1943-44	13.36	2.00
1944-45	16.99	2.98
1945-46	18.70	3.46
1946-47	25.68	3.52

Other taxes on road users imposed by the Government of India like the revenue and protective custom duties on imported motor vehicles, bicycles, and parts thereof, excise duties on tyres, receipt under the Indian Motor Vehicles Acts, etc. were also entirely merged into the Central Revenue. Inspite of the King's plan, the report of the Jayakar Committee and the Nagpur Plan, the roads were being in the need of funds.

Grants from the Central Road Fund had been mostly utilised in improving and modernising the surfaces of important roads which had to bear considerable motor traffic.

The responsibility of the Central Government till it decided to accept full responsibility of National Highway from April 1, 1947, ended by allocating financial resources to the province from the Central Road Fund. The authorities mostly responsible for roads were the District Boards, the Local Boards and the Union Boards. It is obvious that none of the local bodies was in a position to support a road development programme of any consequence.

Between 1936-37 and 1940-41 as for example, the average yearly expenditure on roads by union boards of Bengal stood at a more 7.7 per cent of their total receipts or Rs. 15 per mile for construction and maintenance of 50,000 miles of village roads under their charge. The situation was slightly better for the boards but far below the requirement. The annual road expenditure of the district boards of budget or in other words 'the District Boards' average expenditure per mile on its 40,000 miles of roads thus amounted to a little more than Rs. 100 per year.

Prior to the inception of the Central Road Fund the following was the picture of road expenditure in Bengal:

TABLE 1.20: Road Expenditure in Bengal

Year	Bengal (Rs. in lakhs)
1923-24	15.2
1924-25	15.7
1925-26	21.9
1926-27	18.4
1927-28	16.5
1928-29	13.8
1929-30	9.5
Total	111.0
Annual Average	15.8

The Road Fund Schemes, as hitherto, were first formulated by the Provincial Board of Communications and then on approval by the Standing Committee on Roads of the Government of India, were taken up for execution. The Government of Bengal formulated and put into execution two regular programmes for road development in the province, the first and the second Quinquennial Programmes. A third programme was also presented to the Government of India when the war began. Altogether about 550 miles of roads and a few bridges and causeways were constructed to modern standards out of the Central Road Fund allocations. From the above table it appeared that at no time during its rule in India did British Raj seriously consider the development of roads as a priority in its administrative policy framework. The entire burden of road expenditure was placed on the scanty resource of local bodies which in actuality meant that road development never became a really urgent and imperative issue for the administration.

Inspite of the broad suggestions for road development, made in King's Report, no one can miss its main forms on the problem of rail-road competition. In fact, the concern over this competition was not so much for devising the most suitable combination of transport systems needed for the country, as for protecting long haul transport system of railway against the short haul transport system of roads. It is common knowledge that roads in Bengal provided means of local movement and sustained, local, sub-regional and regional markets, whereas railways, designed as covers of the country's foreign trade, concentrated only on the big cities and ports and never really fostered internal commerce. The local roads, in particular, since long before the arrival of the Europeans, have been playing a significant role in maintaining connectivity at local levels and developing local economics.

2

DEVELOPMENT OF ROADS DURING THE PLAN PERIODS (1951-1974)

In our country, roads are the major means of transportation and communication. For strong economic growth and overall prosperity of the nation, the development of roads is inevitable and it can be said that the progress of a nation is directly proportional to its road development activities. In west Bengal, before independence, road development work was very much limited. During that time, the foreign rulers constructed some roads but those were primarily to consolidate their own rule in the country rather than serving the greater interest of the people. The roads were never designed to help the proper economic growth of the nation.

The road plans were prepared to serve the interest of the people as a whole. Along with all-round development activities in the country, roads were constructed to keep pace with them to achieve the proper growth rate. The basic approach to planning road development in West Bengal should be to build an extensive network upto village level so that every concentration of population may be brought within easy access of an integrated system of roadways.

Development of roads in Bengal was rather slow in pre-partition period. The plateau rivers Mayurakshi, Ajay, Damodar, etc. were prone to heavy floods during rainy season and hence difficult to bridge. The rivers of Bangladesh were very large and only small rivers were bridged.

In West Bengal compared to demand the facilities were limited. The huge urban agglomeration along the Hooghly river, the bias of the economy upon foreign trade, the general decay of the port of Calcutta and desperate efforts to resuscitate it have jointly prevented the state to obtain regional balance in this regard.

2.1 Aims and Objectives of the Plans

Just after partition there were 1,900 kilometres of well maintained Government roads, 3,325 kilometres of District Board roads and 3,700 kilometres of generally poorly maintained Municipal roads. After independence, roads were classified as National Highway, State Highway, District Board roads and other minor roads and specifications were laid out for them.

The first elaborate plan on this line is the 'Nagpur Plan', where all India norms for road development is attempted in this well-known Nagpur Report in 1943. These norms are old and closely related to the colonial economic system.

A comparison of this norm with the pattern of achievement in West Bengal is worthy of consideration. In the following Table 2.1 the data is presented in self-revealing manner.

TABLE 2.1: Achievement of Roads in West Bengal

Type of Road	Road length (in kilometres)							
	Nagpur Norm 1943	At independence 1947	1951	1956	1961	1966	1969	1974
National Highway	947.20	656.00	815	1101	1273	1280	1476	1476
State Highway	1707.20	160.00	670	1063	1402	1491	2331	2351
Major District Road	4724.80	12.80	13	1183	2219	2651	3800	3903
Other District Road	4512.00	126.40	1009	1088	1984	3624	2829	4007
Village Road	9358.40	—	—	201	417	1056	1115	1315
Total	21249.60	955.20	2507	4642	7295	10102	11551	13052

The above Table 2.1 clearly shows that in West Bengal, the entire policy of road development at the time of independence, was heavily stressed on the possibility of attaining high centralisation.

The road development programmes in the first two plans were formulated in the perspective of the post-war road development plan know commonly as the 'Nagpur Plan' which was drawn up as back as 1943 as mentioned earlier. With the programmes undertaken in the first and second plans, the target as envisaged in the Nagpur Plan should have exceeded both in regard to surfaced and unsurfaced roads. The First Five Year Plan (1951-1956) with an allocation of

Rs. 13.85 crores for State roads emphasized on the Calcutta — Delhi and the Calcutta — Bombay highway with funds available from the Centre. The aim was to link the districts and sub-divisional headquarters. Road construction was not easy as transport of construction materials often posed problems in the riverine state with numerous waterways. In the second plan (1956-1961) with the state's outlay of Rs. 14.80 crores, the emphasis was still on more kilometerage of roads rather than on bridges. Despite the considerable expansion of the road kilometerage over the last thirty years, the road network remains deficient in certain respects, such as unbridged river crossings, substandard surface, narrow carriageway etc. The road development programmes for the third plan were formulated in accordance with the broad objectives laid down in the twenty year road development for the period 1961-1981 which had been drawn up by the Chief Engineer of the State and the Central Government. The year 1961 marked the beginning of a new chapter on road development in India as the target of the Nagpur Plan, which aimed at increasing the kilometerage of surfaced roads from 210,000 kilometres to 333,000 kilometres was fulfilled, though not statewise. Despite substantial progress made in rural development over the last 18 years, the road system has still large deficiencies. Besides inadequate road length, the existing roads in many areas have sub-standard surface, narrow width and weak bridges.

A number of roads originally meant for light traffic now require to be strengthened for much higher intensities of traffic which has developed or is anticipated to develop. Many economically backward regions and hilly areas have poor communication and a large number of villages still lack road links with market towns, and in metropolitan cities the development of the road system have fallen far behind the growing requirement of increased traffic. Review of the Fourth Plan shows that the performance of the state sector was not worth the effort given. The departmental projects required allocation of Rs. 42 crores, but the allotment was reduced to Rs. 14 crores. Therefore, with the drastic financial reduction, none of the projects originally designed for the fourth Plan could be undertaken. In the fifth plan period due emphasis would be laid on spatial phasing of network development between the rural roads and the link routes. Such phasing will more quickly open up the backward areas and will provide accessibility to newer areas wherefrom road building materials could be economically obtained and this will finally make the road building more independent of materials brought from distant places. During the three Annual Plans (1966–1969) and the Fourth Plan (1969–1974), the outlay for roads was poor (Fig. 2.1). The position in the fifth plan is better but still far from satisfactory. The Table 2.2 below shows the outlay of roads in West Bengal as compared to the total plan outlay, and Table 2.3, road bridges constructed and envisaged:

TABLE 2.2: Outlay on Roads during different Plans

Plan	% of total Plan Outlay
Ist.	19.10
2nd.	10.70
3rd.	7.00
Annual Plans	5.40
4th.	4.60
5th.	3.30

TABLE 2.3: Number of Bridges over 100 Metres

Plan	Nos. of Bridges
Ist.	8
2nd.	11
3rd. & Annual	29
4th.	12
5th.	4 + 4 Nos. under construction.

Source: Bureau of Applied Economics & Statistics.

Improvement of communication is essential for development. Road communication, in particular is of very great importance in West Bengal, where the deltaic soil and long wet season keep large areas cut off from the centres of commerce and industry for a considerable period of the year. Great stress has therefore been laid on road constructions in the successive plans of the State.

Due to the increased economic activity in the region, good roads as well as transport facilities registered a demand of high priority. It is the roads which provide means of inter-district and intra-district movement and tend to sustain regional marts and development efforts of trade centres even in the remotest corner of the region. While the railways connect the important locations and touch fringe areas only, road transport serves as a feeder to the railways in positive ways.

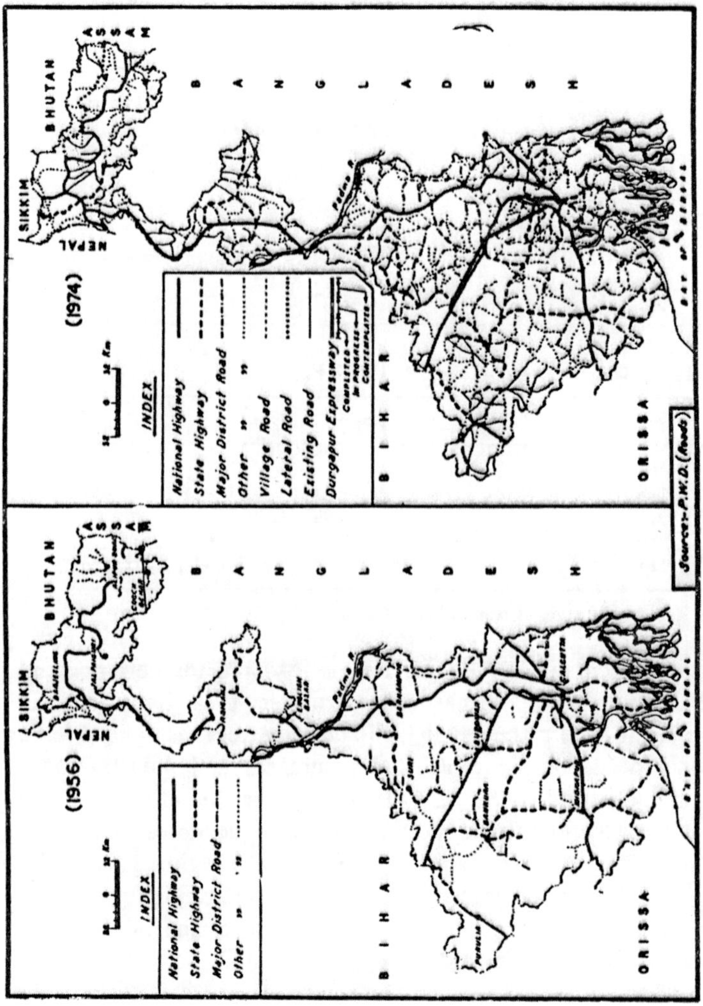

FIG. 2.1: Road map of West Bengal (1956, 1974).

The main emphasis of the five year plans was laid upon long distance roads. The first five year plan in general connected passages for long distance points of the State and National Highways. The work-load was comparatively heavy in constructing and making new openings. The Second Five Year Plan concentrated on relatively short distance roads, the Third Five Year Plan mainly on arterials and fourth five year plan, on rural roads. The rural roads were constructed to link the important locations, e.g., trade and business centres, industrial bases and places of tourist interest. Apart from these, there are short and long roads, narrow and unmetalled, giving access to numerous inner most parts of villages and markets. These are mainly villages and district board roads and are maintained by either village panchayats or district boards. The State and National Highways, and the extra-municipal road systems are being maintained and constructed by the Public Works Department of the State Government.

The growth of roads in length and number depends largely on inhabited localities, markets, important towns, overall density of population and on the momentum of economic development. From the data we can study the existing situation. With the help of some cartographic depictions, development of roads in West Bengal under the plan periods have been analysed.

To consider the actual geographical position of roads in the region, application of the location quotient has been attempted to measure the spatial differences in road development in West Bengal. Road residual has been used to calculate the relationship between road, population and area.

2.2 The First Five Year Plan (1951–1956)

The aim of the First Five Year Plan was to link the districts and sub-divisional headquarters.

At the end of the First Plan, P.W.D. roads accounted for only 12.5 per cent of the total road length while the district board had 77.8 per cent of the total road length under its maintenance and municipalities maintained only 11.9 per cent of the total road lengths in West Bengal. The total length of roads as maintained by different agencies in 1956 would be clear from the following Table 2.4:

TABLE 2.4: Road Development during the years 1951-1956

Districts	Road length in kilometres maintained by		
	P.W.D.	District Board	Municipality
Burdwan	339	2742	247
Bankura	335	1500	108
Birbhum	131	1275	110
Midnapore	630	3037	275
Howrah	75	1590	280
Hooghly	213	1817	322
24-Parganas	772	8455	1332
Calcutta	—	—	737
Nadia	364	1572	288
Murshidabad	264	2589	303
West Dinajpore	95	637	71
Malda	116	766	67
Jalpaiguri	381	726	27
Cooch Behar	128	877	47
Darjeeling	561	527	183
Purulia	238	—	—
Total :	4642	28108	4397

Source: Bureau of Applied Economics & Statistics.
Executive Engineer, P.W.D. (Roads).

The above Table 2.4 shows that major portion of roads in West Bengal was maintained by district board. But when surfaced and unsurfaced roads were dealt separately, it was found P.W.D. maintained largest percentage of surfaced roads in West Bengal while district Board had largest proportion of unsurfaced roads under its upkeep. P.W.D. bears the main responsibility for the development of roads in West Bengal since Independence.[1]

District board roads serve as links to areas of production and market centres. They mainly serve the needs of the rural population connecting rural settlement with each other, also connecting nearest district board roads and river ghats, and are more important from traffic point of view (Fig. 2.2).

The programme of road development under the First Plan envisaged the construction of 4800 kms. of roads, including National Highways. At the end of the First Plan 2451.2 kms. were fully developed and 2400 kms. of district board roads were taken over by the Government.

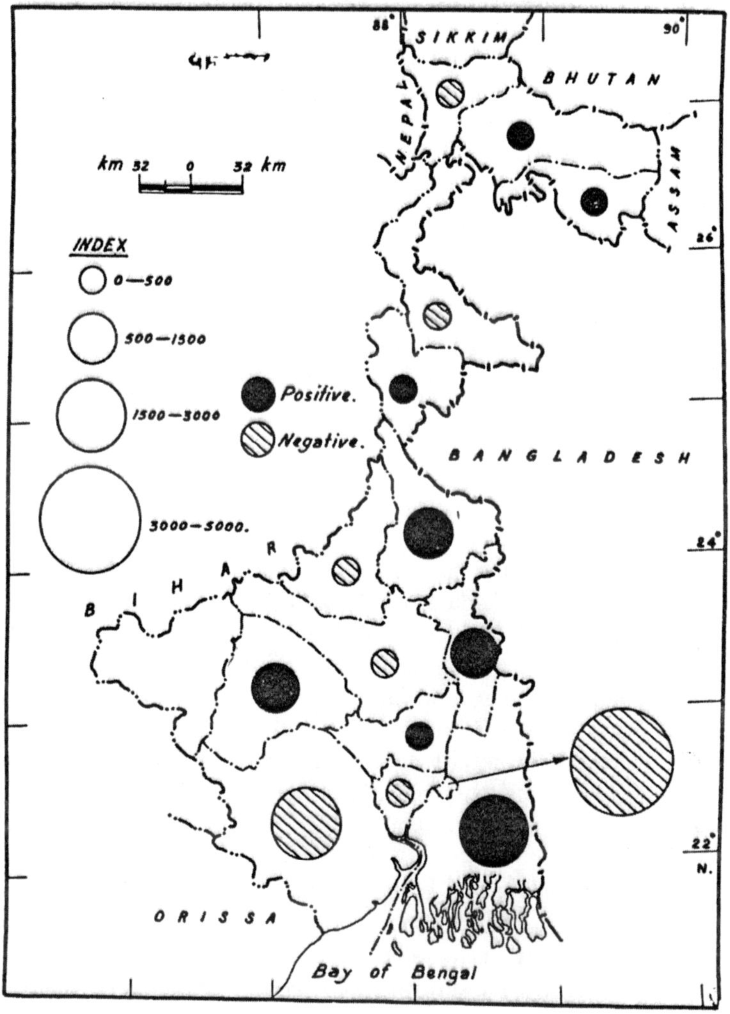

FIG: 2.2: Road Residual (Population/total road length), 1956.

In 1956, the total length of roads under P.W.D.[2] was 4642 kms.

2.2.1 *Regional variation in road development during first plan*

Coming to the regional variation in West Bengal, there was much disparity between different parts in the distribution of the total roads. It was shown in the map that there were nine density categories in West Bengal easily distinguishable starting from 0 to 280 kms. per 1954.46 sq.km. having 40 kms. as an interval. There were huge areas not having a single kilometre of road in the extreme southern Sundarban region with the exception of Sagar Island where road density was low.

A very low density of 0.40 kms. per 1954.46 sq.km. was found in patches specially towards the border of the State, namely Jaipur and Jhalda of Purulia District, Raniband and Raipur of Bankura District, Tufanganj and Alipurduar of Cooch Behar District, Suri, Muhammadbazar and Dubrajpur of Birbhum District, Darjeeling town of Darjeeling District and whole of Malda and West Dinajpur District . Northern Sundarban region, namely, Basirhat, Hasnabad, Kulpi, Mathurapur, Canning and Sandeshkhali also represented low growth of roads (Fig. 2.3).

The only area of comparatively high density, i.e. 280 km. per 1954.46 sq.km. was observed in and around Calcutta, covering parts of Hooghly, Howrah and 24-Parganas.

In Bankura during the First Plan, 257.6 kms. of Highways within the district were macadamised. In 1951 there were 802 village roads in the Sadar and 181 in the Birbhum subdivision of the district. Village roads were a pressing necessity in the district.

Midnapore, the second largest in the State in area, which was 13619.5 sq.km. in 1951, the population of the district was 3,359,022 in 1951, whereas the total length of roads was 3942 kms. Density of population in Midnapore was 246.71 persons per sq.km. whereas the density of road was 28.94 km. of road per 100 sq.km. of area (Fig. 2.4).

Howrah has today a complex industrial base spreading over a rather narrow and highly congested strip of land along the Bhagirathi which incidentally profoundly influences the industrial economy of West Bengal. During the first plan the district made no significant progress in the construction of roads as the emphasis was on the maintenance of the existing roads. Howrah is connected with the rest of the country by National Highway No.2 to the north and National Highway No.6 to the west. Other important roads in the city are G.T. Road, Benaras Road and Howrah-Amta Road. There were almost no worthwhile roads within the urbanising areas during the year. Most of the other miscellaneous roads were scattered without pattern or long term usefulness and they were mostly unmetalled.

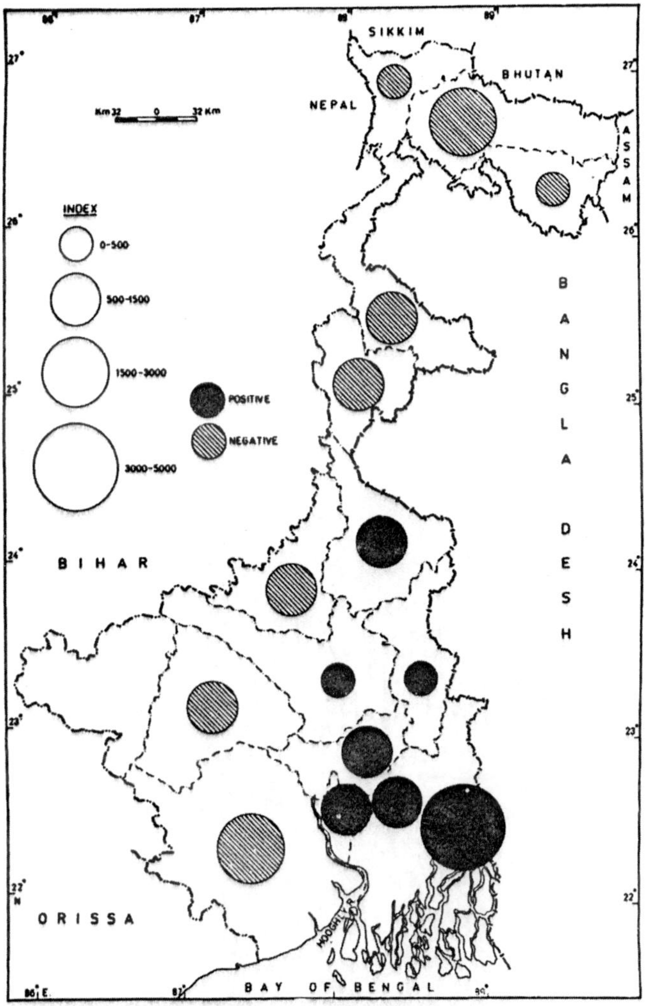

FIG. 2.3: Road Residual (Area/total road length), 1956.

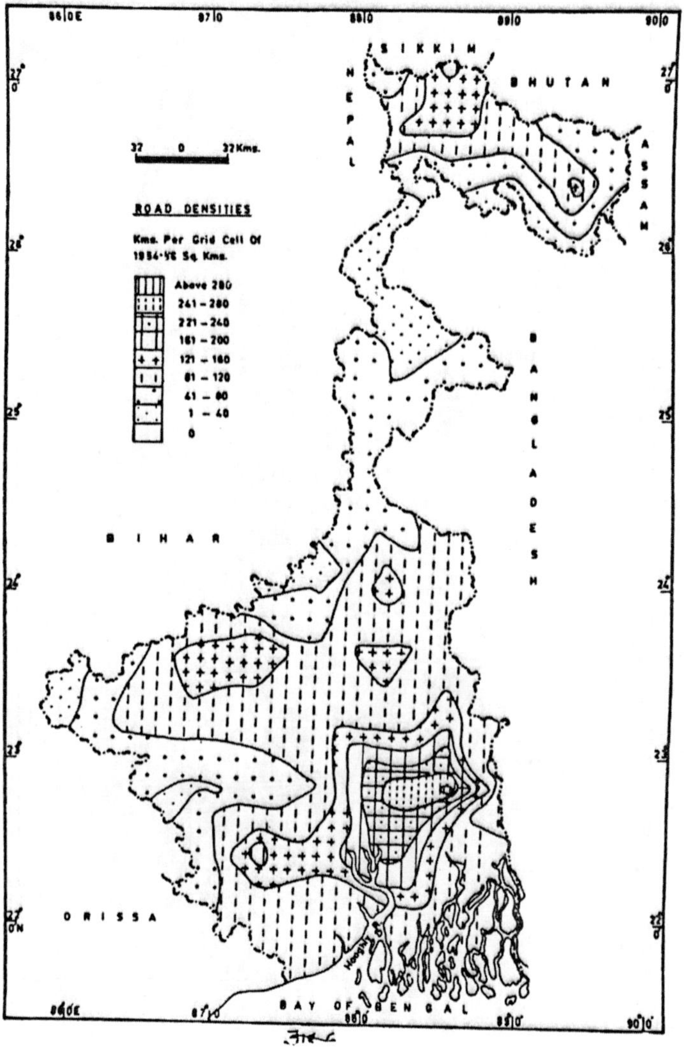

FIG: 2.4: Road Density (1956).

24-Paraganas the largest district in the State where the total length of roads was 8818 kms. and the total area of the District was 14,601.7 sq.km., while the population of the District was 4,609,309 in 1951, which signified that the growth of the roads kept pace with the growth of population and development. Calcutta on the other hand is a city of first magnitude, a true metropolis. It is a city with a world outlook in its great sea port, a city of commerce and manufacture, the focal point of a huge regional network of transportation and communication. An increase in population did not match with the necessary increase in developed land and also in road length. The formidable space difficulties of the Metropolitan District had been a powerful constraint on the development of a transportation system.[3]

The less developing districts from the point of view of road development, were Darjeeling, West Dinajpur, Malda and Cooch Behar. These districts had no good, all weather roads.

The road development programme of the First Five Year Plan was therefore devoted mainly to connecting all the district and sub-divisional towns with one another and with the State Capital. The road length in 1951-52, the first year of the First Five Year Plan was only 3.4 thousand kms. and in 1955-56 the last year of the First Plan it was 7.3 thousand kms. (Fig. 2.5).

2.2.2 *Completion of roads in the first plan*

The following roads were completed during this period:

National Highways — new constructions, and improvement of 455.6 kms. during the First Five Year Plan period (1951-56).[4]

(i) Calcutta — Delhi National Highway (No. 2 length 243.2 kms. in West Bengal).
(ii) Calcutta — Bombay and Calcutta — Madras National Highways (Nos. 5&6). These highways have the same alignment within the state, length 126 kms.
(iii) Patna — Gauhati National Highway (No. 31) length in West Bengal is 289.6 kms. passed through North Bengal connecting Dalkhola, Siliguri and Cooch Behar.
(iv) Siliguri — Gangtok National Highway (No.31A) length in West Bengal 56 kms. Connects Sivok (on the foothills of Himalayas in Darjeeling district) and Gangtok, capital of Sikkim.

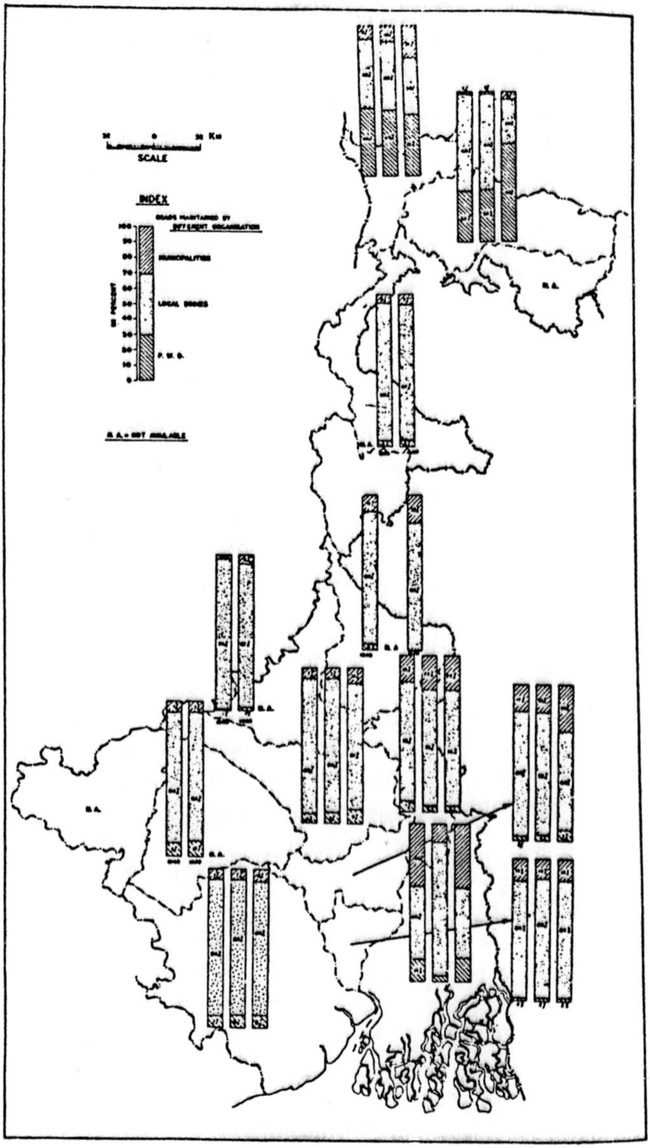

FIG: 2.5: Percentage Bar Chart showing percentage of road length maintained by different organisations (1948, 1953, 1955).

(v) Calcutta---Siliguri National Highway (No.34) length 298.2 kms., passes through 24-Parganas, Nadia, Murshidabad, below Ganges and then crossing the Farakka Barrage, move up to Siliguri through Malda and West Dinajpur.

(vi) Calcutta — Bongaon National Highway (No.35) length within the State is 72 kms., connecting Barasat and Bongaon and proceeding to the border between India and Bangladesh.

The State Highways' total length was 1145.6 kms., out of which new construction and improvement of 768.8 kms. were included in the First Five Year Plan:

(a) Darjeeling — Haldibari State Highway — in the district of Darjeeling, Jalpaiguri and Cooch Behar via Siliguri.

(b) Gajole — Balurghat State Highway connecting Malda, West Dinajpur via Bansihari town.

(c) Birbhum — Midnapore State Highway through Birbhum, Burdwan, Bankura and Midnapore districts running from Moregram on the Bhagirathi in Murshidabad district to the Orissa border via Suri, Durgapur, Bankura, Kharagpur, Midnapore and Nadia.

(d) Berhampore — Kakdwip State Highway connecting Murshidabad and 24-Parganas district via Krishnanagar, Barasat, Calcutta and Diamond Harbour.

(e) Berhampore — Suri State Highway connecting Murshidabad, Birbhum districts via Kandi.

(f) Chinsura — Bankura State Highway connecting Hooghly and Bankura districts via Tarakeswar, Arambagh and Bishnupur. From Bankura the route took up an elbow bend and continued upto Bombay.

The road development programme in the State also included the construction and improvement of 2211.2 kms. of major district roads, 2016.6 kms. of village roads and number of bridges.

More emphasis laid on road development during this period would be clear from the following Table 2.5.

2.3 The Second Five Year Plan (1956-1961)

At the end of the Second Five Year Plan more emphasis was laid on P.W.D. roads, as a result, the total length of surfaced roads under its maintenance increased from 4642 kms. in 1956 to 7295 kms. in 1961, i.e. 57 per cent increase. The total length of surfaced and unsurfaced roads under the district board however decreased from 26594 kms. in 1956 to 26255 kms. in 1961. With the exception of Bankura, Cooch Behar, Darjeeling, Jalpaiguri and Purulia, the total road lengths of all other districts increased comparatively more than that of the First Five Year Plan period (Fig. 2.6).

TABLE 2.5: Allotment and Expenditure under the First Five Year Plan (1951-56)
(Rupees in lakhs)

	Allotment	Expenditure	Percentage
Transport	1553.59	1510.26	97.2
(i) Roads	1383.16	1337.67	96.7
(ii) Road Transport	170.43	172.59	101.3
(iii) Ports and Harbour	—	—	—

Source: West Bengal Statistical Handbook, Bureau of Applied Economics & Statistics.

Municipal roads showed a remarkable expansion in the districts of Hooghly and Calcutta. Position of West Bengal in regard to road development during the end of the Second Five Year Plan would be understood from the following Table 2.6:

TABLE 2.6: Road Development during the Years 1951—1961

Districts	Road length in Kilometres maintained by		
	P.W.D.	District Board	Municipality
Burdwan	658	2685	251
Bankura	305	1252	107
Birbhum	516	1472	134
Midnapore	879	2839	318
Howrah	197	1547	285
Hooghly	442	1593	565
24-Parganas	1023	6411	1384
Calcutta	—	—	806
Nadia	443	1538	494
Murshidabad	485	2552	309
West Dinajpore	400	1302	69
Malda	251	748	72
Jalpaiguri	569	713	44
Darjeeling	605	488	188
Cooch Behar	268	—	48
Purulia	254	1115	58
Total:	7295	26255	5132

Source: Bureau of Applied Economics & Statistics.
Executive Engineer, P.W.D.

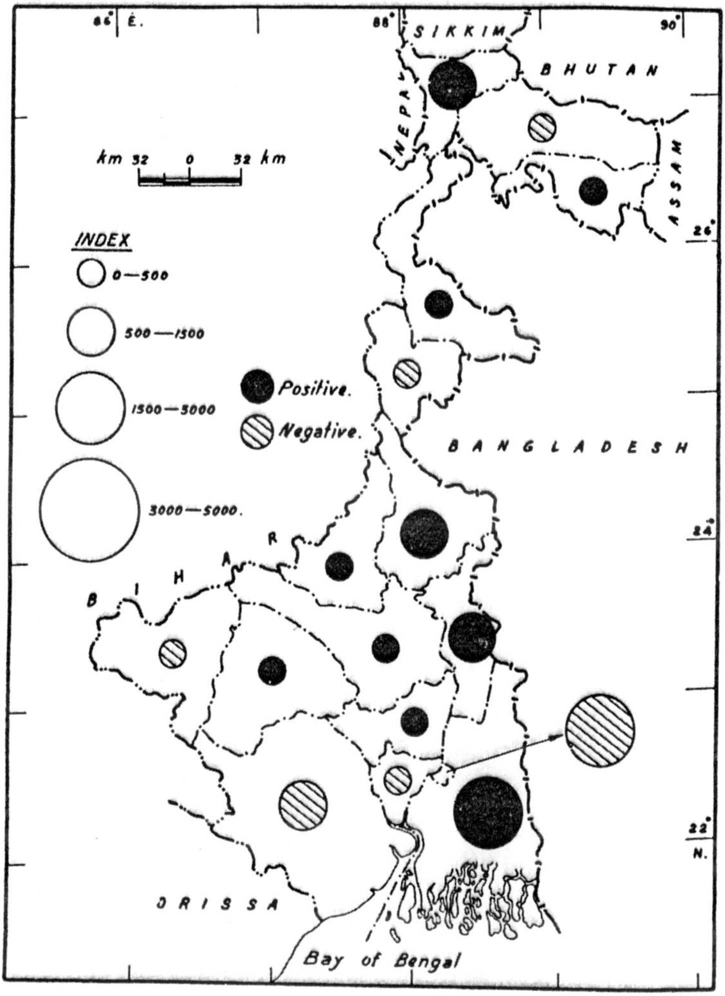

FIG. 2.6: Road Residual (Population/total road length), 1961.

Length of P.W.D. surfaced roads[5] increased much more than that of 1956, indicating more importance was given to the construction of P.W.D. surfaced roads during the Second Five Year Plan. All categories of P.W.D. roads, e.g., National Highways, State Highways, Major District roads, Other district roads and village roads were developed extensively (Fig. 2.7).

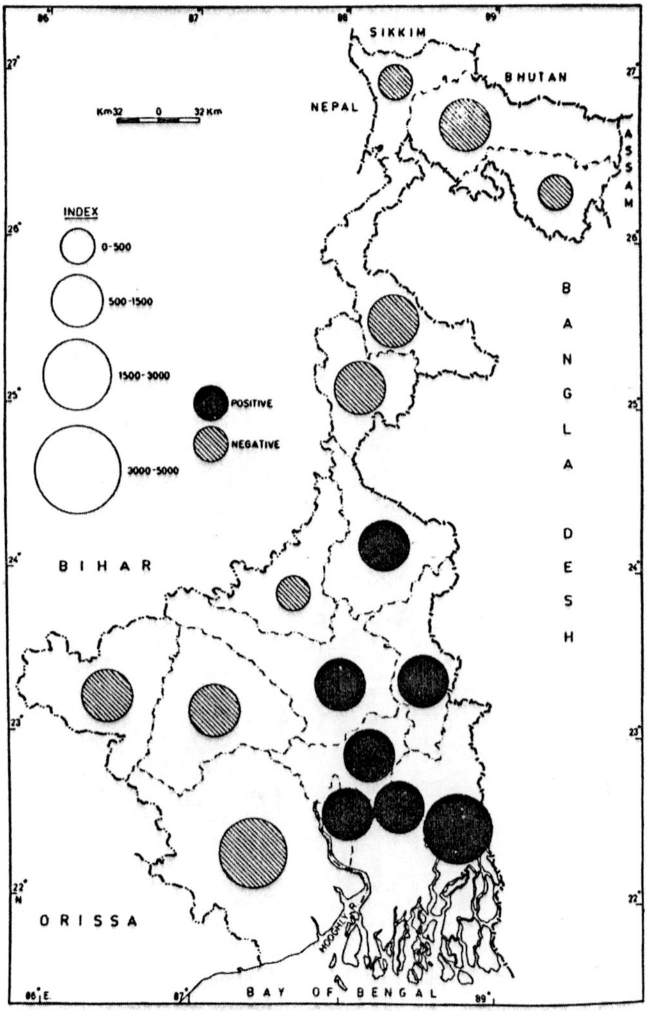

FIG. 2.7: Road Residual (Area/total road length), 1961.

TABLE 2.7: Total Length of Surfaced P.W.D. Roads

(In kilometres)

Category of Road	1951	1956	1961
National Highway	815	1101	1273
State Highway	670	1069	1402
Major District Roads	13	1183	2219
Other District Roads	1009	1088	1984
Village Roads	—	201	417
Total:	2507	4642	7295

Source: Executive Engineers, P.W.D. (Roads).

The Second Five Year Plan period provided for the construction and improvement of 5760 kms. of roads including 2240 kms. carried over from the First Plan for completion. The total length of new roads taken up was therefore 3520 kms. of which 288 kms. were transferred to the territories. About 3200 kms. of roads were completed and the remaining 2720 kms. were left in various stages of progress. This part was carried over for completion during the Third Plan. In the first three years (1956-1959) of the Second Plan, about 1920 kms. of State roads and 160 kms. of National Highway were completed to surfaced stage in addition to those at various stages of construction. About 32808 metres of bridge were also completed during this period. Some 480 kms. of surfaced roads were also completed in 1959 upto final surfacing stage. In 1960, 640 kms. of metalled roads and 107.2 kms. of village roads were built. In 1961, 72 kms. of National Highway, 333 kms. of other district roads and 639 kms. of village roads were developed (Fig. 2.8).

The target under the Second Plan envisaged work on 5760 kms. of roads with the purpose of extending the road network to connect all the thana headquarters with a developed system of road. At the end of the period, the total road length under maintenance of P.W.D. stood at 7295 kms. only 57 per cent increase took place from 1956.

The Forest Directorate Development Scheme for communication in the Second Plan envisaged the construction of 17.6 kms. of roads in the hilly terrain in the north and improvement of existing forest roads; only 12.8 kms. of roads were built and remaining 4.8 kms. were carried over for the Third Plan.

During the said plan period, the road length in the State increased by 4.4 thousand kms., showing a rise of about 60 per cent.

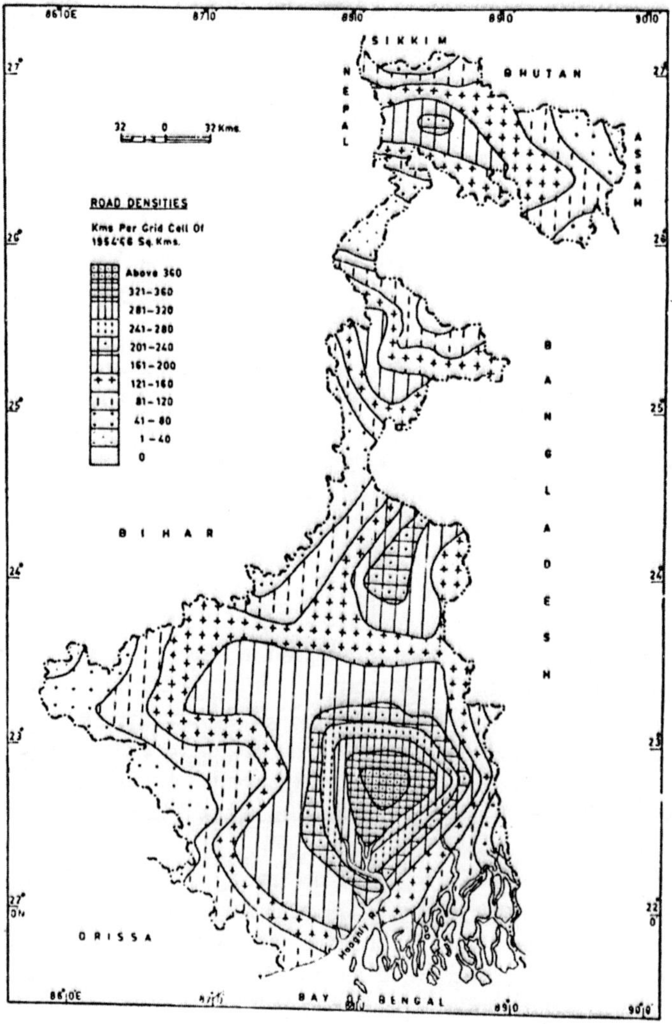

FIG. 2.8: Road Density (1961).

2.3.1 *Regional variation in road development during second plan*

During this period, like 1951-1956 plan period, road development was not even in character, there was much disparity between different parts as shown by the distribution of total roads (Fig. 2.9).

There were some significant patches of low road density like Kalimpong and Siliguri in Darjeeling District, northern West Dinajpore, eastern corner of Cooch Behar District, eastern and western Malda, eastern corner of Purulia District around Jhalda, Sandeshkhali, Hasnabad, parts of Sagar Island in 24-Parganas.

On the other hand, high density areas were significantly dominant around Calcutta, parts of Howrah, 24-Parganas and Hooghly where the high degree of urbanization depend largely on road transportation.

During the Second Plan Period, an important turning in the road development in India was initiated by revising the old Nagpur Norm. The Nagpur Norm was revised in 1957 for a twenty year development plan (1961-1981) to incorporate the basic objectives of planned economic development of India. According to 1957 Norm, West Bengal should have 58,720 kms. of road in 1981 consisting of 1884.8 kms. of National Highway, 4236.8 kms. of State Highway, 13294.4 kms. of Major District Roads, 17905.6 kms. of Other District Roads and 21510.4 kms. of Village Roads.[6]

2.4 The Third Five Year Plan (1961-1966)

The highlight of the Third Five Year Plan is, that the end of the Plan Period the total length of roads in West Bengal became 41,708 kms., i.e. only a 7.8 per cent growth took place from that of the Second Plan. Two hundred kilometres of municipal roads were added while Zilla Parishad[7] Roads were reduced. It was found during this period that P.W.D. was taking charge of many zilla parishad roads.

Total P.W.D. roads increased to 38.5 per cent while, zilla parishad roads did not increase and municipal roads to 3.8 per cent which clearly signified the importance of P.W.D. in regard to road expansion during this plan period also.

During the Third Plan, a task of building 2720 kms. of roads carried over from the Second Plan and building a new length of 1520 kms. of roads, taken in hand but the latter one was not completed within this period. Construction of bridges as included in the

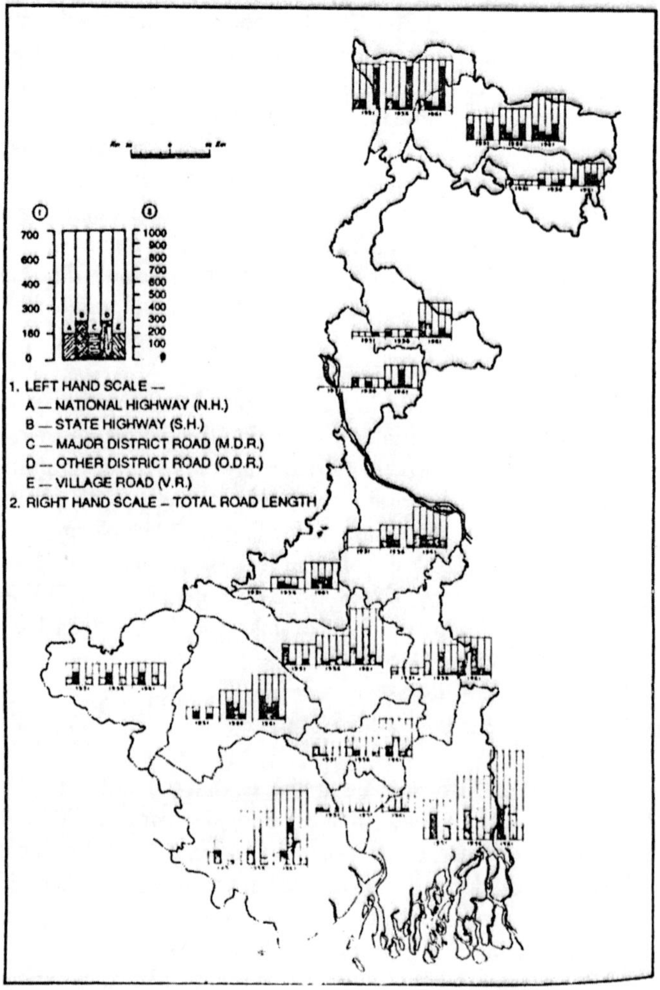

FIG. 2.9: Distribution of surfaced roads (P.W.D.), 1951, 1956, 1961.

programme with the restriction that, programme of road and bridge construction would be phased according to availability of funds. This programme was based on a consideration of priorities and included a number of district roads which were selected after the recommendation of the respective District Development Councils. The financial allocation for the period for road construction and improvement was Rs. 22.35 crores. Moreover, the deficiencies in achieving the planned targets in the First and Second Plans and the cost of upgrading the roads wherever necessary were also taken into consideration while formulating the Third Plan (Fig. 2.10).

TABLE 2.8: Road Development during the Years (1961-1966)

Districts	Road length in kilometres maintained by		
	P.W.D.	District Board	Municipality
Burdwan	823	2483	279
Bankura	631	1303	105
Birbhum	643	1373	133
Midnapore	1093	3405	353
Howrah	240	1521	323
Hooghly	727	1568	551
24-Parganas	1465	6702	1436
Calcutta	22	–	808
Nadia	627	1457	437
Murshidabad	705	2491	319
West Dinajpore	570	1092	26
Malda	371	823	67
Jalpaiguri	702	623	107
Cooch Behar	393	–	68
Darjeeling	730	481	202
Purulia	382	930	58
Total:	10124	26252	5272

Source: Bureau of Applied Economics & Statistics.

Calcutta was benefitted by expansion of 22 kms. of State Highway in this period and Hooghly and Birbhum by 3 kms. and 5 kms. correspondingly. Other district roads were also extended extensively in different parts of West Bengal.

In the two years of the Third Plan, the total road length increased 7by 0.4 thousand kms. Table 2.9 shows the length of extra municipal roads maintained by State Government.

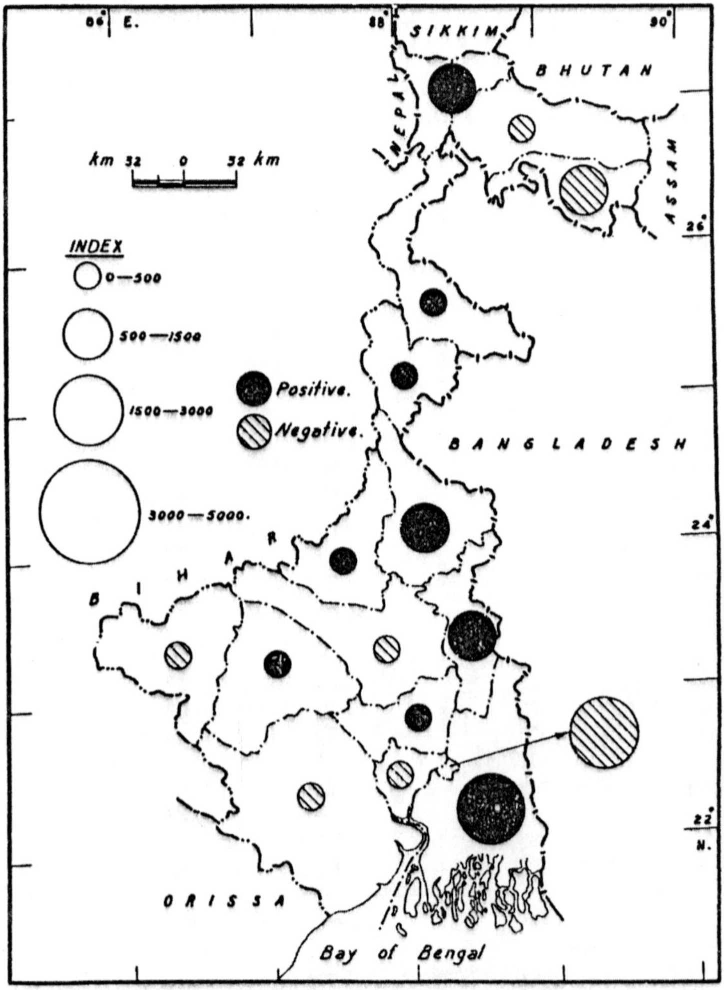

FIG. 2.10: Road Residual (Population/total road length), 1966.

In comparison to unsurfaced roads, surfaced roads recorded a rapid increase in length during the entire period.

Road length per 100 sq.km. of area was 3.9 kms. for the State in 1951-52 which was increased to 13.8 kms. in 1962-63 (Fig. 2.11).

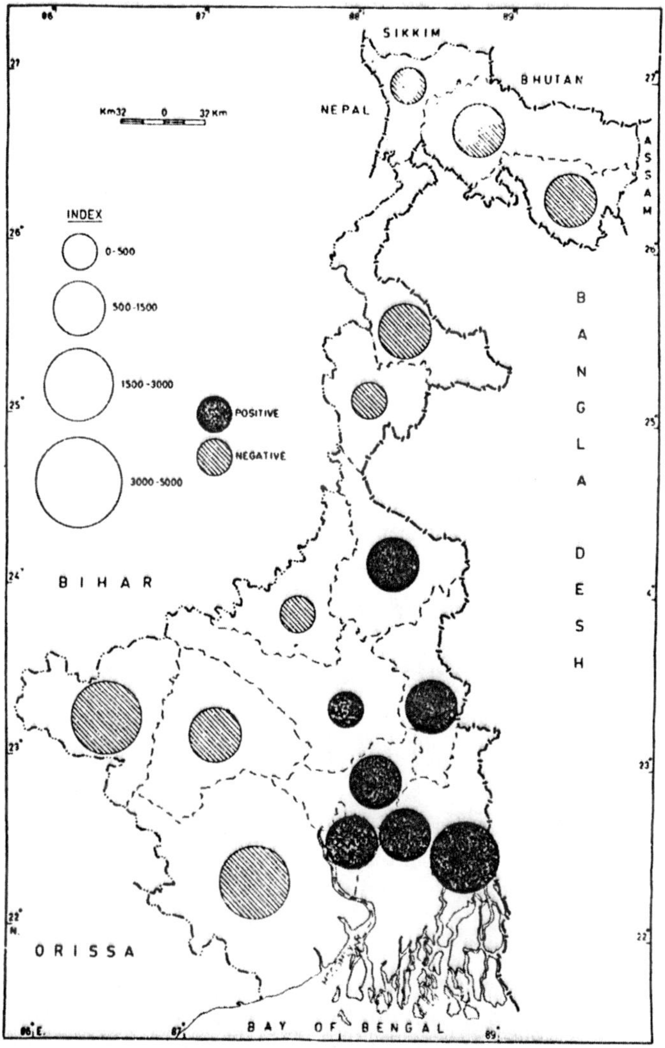

FIG. 2.11: Road Residual (Area/total road length), 1966.

TABLE 2.9: Roads Maintained by Municipalities

Types of Road	In thousands of kilometres				
	1951-52	1956-57	1959-60	1960-61	1962-63
Surfaced	2.2	6.8	8.9	9.2	9.8
Unsurfaced	1.2	2.3	2.2	2.5	2.3
Total	3.4	9.1	11.1	11.7	12.1

Source: Basic Road Statistics, 1964.

2.4.1 *Regional variation in road development during third plan*

During this period, there was much disparity between different parts as shown by the density map (Fig. 2.12). There were fourteen density categories distinguished in West Bengal starting from 0 to 480 kms. per 1954.46 sq.kms. of area.

Low density of roads were still marked in Burdwan, Bankura, Nadia, eastern Murshidabad, eastern and western Malda, Cooch Behar, Darjeeling and Jalpaiguri. Calcutta and its neighbouring areas presented high density of roads.

The average density of road in West Bengal was 0.47 km. per sq.km. at the end of this period, as compared to 0.44 km. per sq.km. in 1961.

2.4.2 *Completion of roads in the third plan*

During this period emphasis was laid on construction of bridges and roads of proper standard as also on linking roads.

In this period, the National Highway No.6 (Calcutta — Bombay) was opened to traffic. The National Highway No. 2 bypass was constructed between Vivekananda bridge and Grand Trunk Road which has eased up congestion on G.T. Road. The work on the two roads was taken up late in 1962 by the special Road Organisation, for a total estimated cost of Rs. 12 crores financed partly from the loan assistance received from the International Development Authority.

A 1,036m. long bridge (Sarat Setu) shortened the Calcutta — Kharagpur route by 80 kms. for motorists who had to make a long detour via Arambagh.

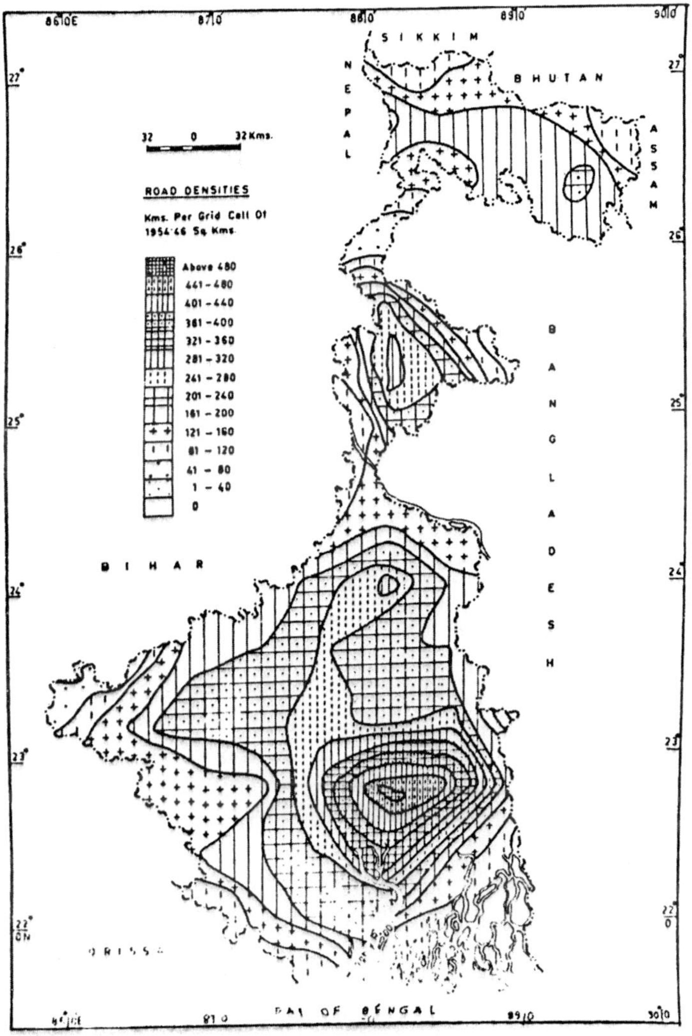

FIG. 2.12: Road Density (1966).

Work on the construction of subways for buses and pedestrians between the Howrah Bridge and the Railway Station was commenced on 1964 and completed in 1974.

The Durgapur Express Highway, another important addition to the inter-district roadmesh of the Howrah District was taken up during the Third Five Year Plan. The road connecting Durgapur with Dankuni and Bally, ran parallel to the Howrah-Burdwan chord railway line and crossed the G.T. Road near Palsit polarisation of industry at one hand and Calcutta conurbation on the other, thus highlighting the need for early completion of the Durgapur Expressway.

While during the First and Second Plans proper emphasis was not allocated for maintenance due to shortage of funds, construction of major bridges and roads of proper standard and linking of the villages took high priority during the period. So far, 115 bridges of length varying from 100 ft. to over 1000 ft. were built.

2.5 Annual Plans (1966-1969)

Since 1950, Planning Commission had drawn up the Five Year Plans. The First three Plans were for the periods 1951-56, 1956-61 and 1961-66. After the Third Plan, there was an interregnum of three years from 1966-67 to 1968-69. The situation created by the Indo-Pakistan conflict, two successive years of drought, devaluation of the currency, inflation and erosion of the resources available for planning purposes, delayed the finalisation of the Fourth Plan. Between the Third and Fourth Plan, three Annual Plans were formulated within the framework of the draft outline of the Fourth Plan.

The state of economy and the non-availability of the financial resources for plan purposes limited the size of development outlay during this period. At the end of the three Annual Plans the total road length in the State increased to 45,767 kms. P.W.D. surfaced roads increased by 14.3 per cent and municipal roads by 13 per cent from 1966.

The total length of National Highway at the end of the three plan periods was 1476 kms., a 15.3 per cent increase from 1966. Significant expansion was noticed for the major district roads and State Highways. Other district roads decreased to 795 kms. from 1966 to 1969. Major district roads increased by 43 per cent from 1966 to 1969.

It can be explained as that the other district roads were turned into or classed as major district roads by the P.W.D. during this period.

This is one of the reasons why major district roads were developed more than other roads during the said period.

The road development at the end of the three annual plans is shown in the following Table 2.10:

TABLE 2.10: Road Development during 1966-69

Districts	Road length in kilometres maintained by		
	P.W.D.	Local Bodies	Municipality
Burdwan	1257	2493	316
Birbhum	746	1388	102
Bankura	765	1373	135
Midnapore	1553	3649	426
Howrah	528	1446	322
Hooghly	922	1606	566
24-Parganas	2110	6762	1840
Calcutta	22	—	809
Nadia	814	1293	521
Murshidabad	868	1634	320
West Dinajpore	831	1030	82
Malda	472	825	87
Jalpaiguri	891	635	105
Darjeeling	732	426	265
Cooch Behar	1291	—	69
Purulia	560	829	49
Total:	14362	25389	6014

Source: Bureau of Applied Economics & Statistics.
Executive Engineer, P.W.D.

2.5.1 *Regional variation in road development*

Only three districts of West Bengal namely, 24-Parganas, Hooghly and Nadia had adequate road length to support the population and in relation to area (Fig. 2.13 & 2.14).

As a result of planning, roadways developed extensively in the Hooghly district and regular services of motor trucks and buses established direct connection between the remote and inaccessible areas and the urban and trading centres within the district as well as in the surrounding areas. Now the district can claim 947.7 kms. of roads per 1000 sq.km. of area thus having the third highest density in the State, after the cities of Calcutta and Howrah.

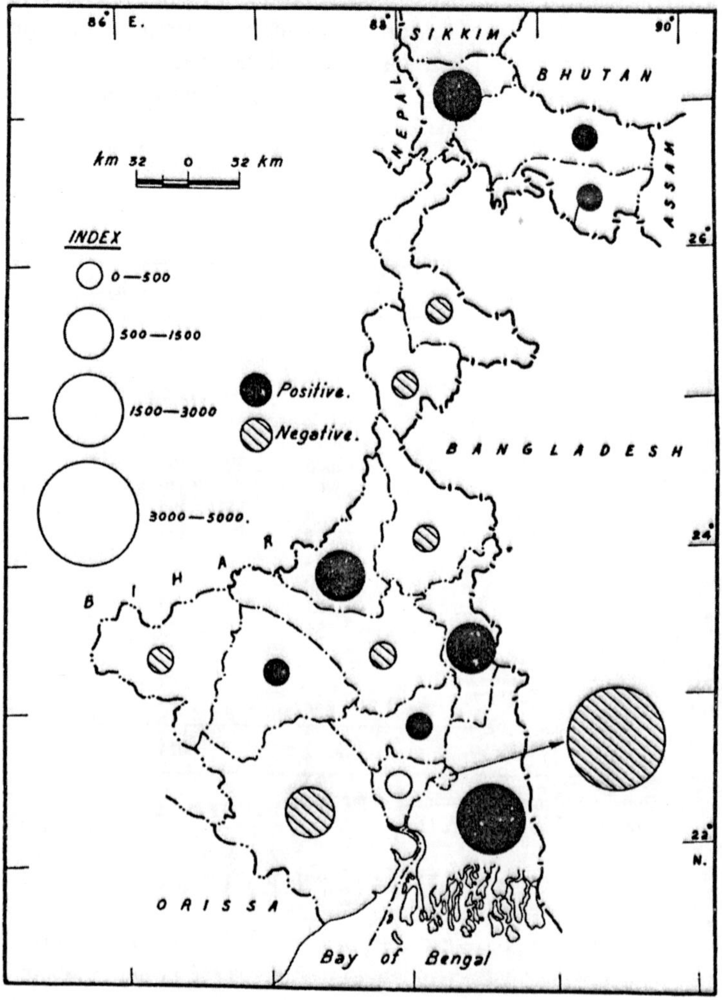

FIG. 2.13: Road Residual (Population/total road length), 1969.

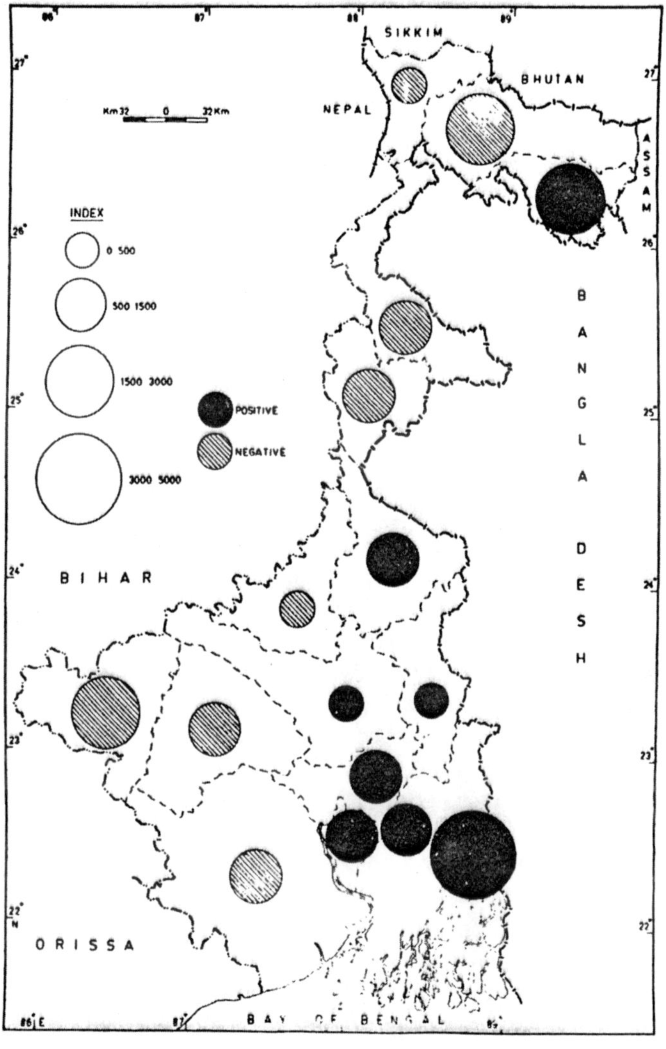

FIG. 2.14: Road Residual (Area/total road length), 1969.

Most of the village roads were maintained in Nadia by municipalities. These were generally *kutcha* roads mostly with 4.87 metres embankment. Most important of them were sometimes provided with cement concrete and improved culverts so that they might serve as fair weather road Mention should be made of 24-Parganas District with 14,601.7 sq.km. of area and 6,280,915 population; it was one of the self-supported districts from the point of view of roads. With its large area, the district had 10,711.9 kms. of roads, the largest share of roads in comparison to other districts during this period.

The Calcutta Metropolitan District is the urban hub of a vast hinterland which had a population of approximately 145 million in 1961. The Metropolitan district has drawn to it by far the greatest part of the urban population in West Bengal, more than 30 per cent of the total population of the Eastern Region and 42 per cent of the urban population of the four States of West Bengal, Orissa, Bihar and Assam. In the recent past, road development work progressed at extremely slow pace, 8 kms. of major new roadway was added in the C.M.D. during the first three plan periods (Fig. 2.15).

West Dinajpore, Jalpaiguri, Malda, Darjeeling and Cooch Behar remained still backward and of these Malda and West Dinajpore had very poor development of roads. In West Dinajpore, local bodies maintained 53 per cent of roads, while P.W.D. 42 per cent and the remaining roads by municipality. In the preceding plan period P.W.D. maintained 19 per cent, Zilla Parishad 7.8 per cent and Municipality 3 per cent of the roads. Birbhum and Bankura districts did not progress much in roads.

2.6 The Fourth Five Year Plan (1969-1974)

The Fourth Five Year Plan commenced on 1st April, 1969. In formulating the objectives of the Fourth Plan, important considerations, such as, economic and social goals, people's need, balanced growth in the country, present and future traffic etc., were taken into account alongwith cost-benefit analysis. Four important aspects of road development which need special attention in formulating future plans, are provision of roads related to:

(a) Major industrial, mining and other development projects,
(b) Rural markets,

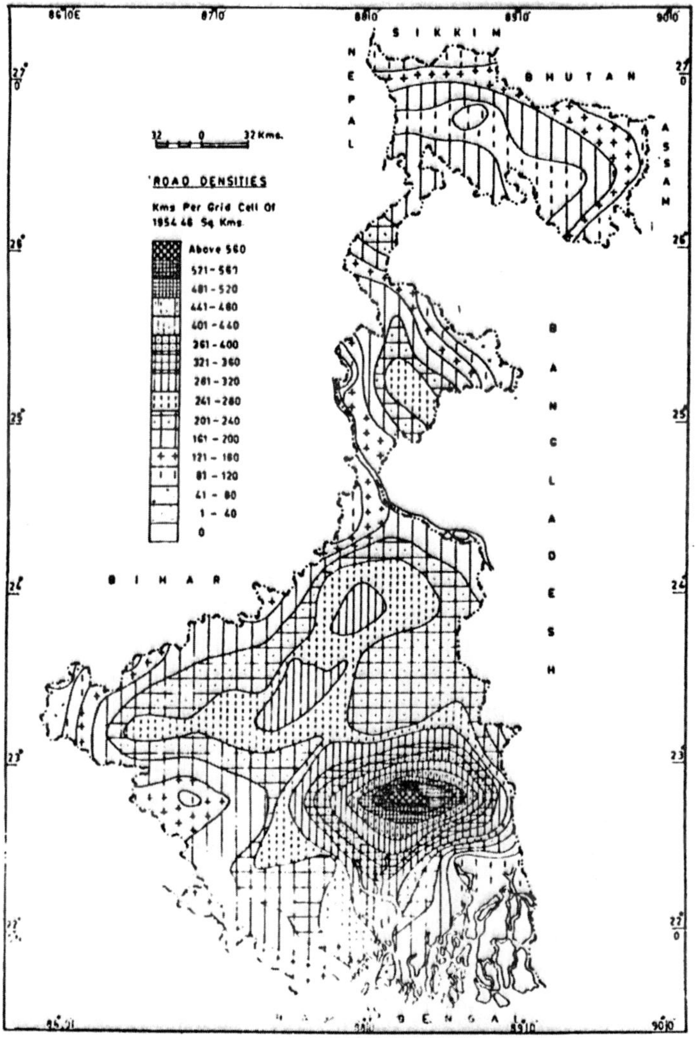

FIG. 2.15: Road Density (1969).

(c) Development of backward areas and regions including hill areas and coastal areas, and
(d) Metropolitan City areas and large cities and their environments.

It must also be necessary to make adequate provision of funds for maintenance of existing roads, otherwise the roads will become unusable. The formulation and execution of the development programmes would call for strengthening of organisation at all levels. At the time of the formulation of the Fourth Plan it was recognised that despite the substantial progress made in road development since the commencement of the Five Year Plans, the completion of the missing links will not only eliminate the detour in some cases but will also help in quicker transport of people, commodities and perishable goods. The Fourth Plan also envisaged construction of 14 major bridges, whose absence is impedimental to the transport system of the State. The Plan provided for 960 kms. of roads on account of:

(a) The missing link in the present network,
(b) The roads required to serve international border areas, inter-State communications, industrial concentrations, heavy conurbation and tribal and undeveloped areas,
(c) The need to have short distance feeder roads, and
(d) The need to provide bypasses around congested localities.

There were certain major bridges of national importance for which Central assistance was provided in the Fourth Plan, e.g. the second Hooghly bridge in Calcutta over the Hooghly River at Princep Ghat and the additional crossing at Kalyani would cost Rs. 18.08 crores of which Rs. 11.24 crores was spent in 1966-71. In the First Three Plans and the three Annual Plans, the Centre had spent a sum of Rs. 134.86 crores on road development, of which West Bengal had a sum of Rs. 50.21 crores on road development. During the Fourth Plan, the Centre estimated the expenditure as Rs. 822.4 crores of which West Bengal's share would be Rs. 14.6 crores.

The total length of roads maintained by different organisations was estimated at 56,562 kms. in 1974. Districtwise data of Gram Panchayat was not available. The length of extra-municipal roads maintained by P.W.D. in West Bengal at the end of 1973-74 was 15,562 kms. of which 13,652 kms. was surfaced roads and 2,028 kms.

was unsurfaced roads.

During this period there was no construction of National Highway but State Highway increased by 20 kms. There was considerable development of other district roads, an increase of 42 per cent from 1969, major district roads increased by 3 per cent and village roads by 18 per cent.

Development of roads maintained by different Organisations in different districts of West Bengal are given below Table 2.11:

TABLE 2.11: Road Development during 1969-74

Districts	Road length in kilometres maintained by		
	P.W.D.	Local Bodies	Municipality
Burdwan	1371	4142	329
Birbhum	868	1306	106
Bankura	930	1469	216
Midnapore	1655	4095	625
Howrah	547	1426	308
Hooghly	1065	1427	349
24-Parganas	2112	6631	2201
Calcutta	22	—	820
Nadia	822	1319	607
Murshidabad	911	2476	355
West Dinajpore	846	762	116
Malda	517	816	87
Jalpaiguri	1061	774	173
Darjeeling	843	416	209
Cooch Behar	1383	2173	68
Purulia	609	1008	61
Total:	15.562	30,240	6,630

Source: Bureau of Applied Economics & Statistics.
Executive Engineer, P.W.D.

With the exception of Birbhum and Darjeeling all the districts of West Bengal had new surfaced roads in 1973-74, of which highest kilometres of roads (76 kms.) was added in Cooch Behar. Cooch Behar received special attention during this Plan period among all the districts in the north.

The following table would give a vivid picture of surfacing type of National Highway and State Highway in West Bengal as on 31st March, 1974:

TABLE 2.12: Surfaced Highways in West Bengal

Districts	National Highway (Surfaced) in kms.				State Highway (Surfaced) in kms.			
	Cement con-crete	Black topped	Water bound maca-dam	Total	Cement con-crete	Black tapped	Water bound maca-dam	Total
Burdwan		154		154	3	25		28
Birbhum					30	138		168
Bankura						211		211
Midnapore		106		106	4	128		132
Howrah		71		71		142		142
Hooghly		110		110	2	125		127
24-Parganas		111		111	1	564		565
Calcutta						22		22
Nadia		108		108	13	15		28
Murshidabad	32	106		138	28	61		89
West Dinajpore		165		165		128		128
Malda		76		76		150		150
Jalpaiguri		207		207		67		67
Darjeeling		102		102		264		264
Cooch Behar		61		61		43		43
Purulia		67		67		187		187
Total:	32	1444	Nil	1476	81	2270	Nil	2351

Source: Executive Engineer, P.W.D. (Roads).

All the districts of West Bengal possessed black topped National Highway. Cement concrete State Highway, however, existed in Burdwan, Malda, Howrah, Hooghly, Purulia, West Dinajpore and Calcutta. Municipal roads in West Bengal increased by 15 per cent from 1969. Surfacing of major district roads, other district roads and village roads during the period would be understood from the following Table 2.13.

2.6.1 *Regional variation in road development*

Regional disparity would be clear from the density map (Fig. 2.16) comprising of seventeen categories of road density ranging from 0 to more than 640 kms. per 1954.46 sq.km. Deltaic Sundarban forest region still depicted negative density of road.

TABLE 2.13: Surfaced and Unsurfaced Major District Roads & Others in West Bengal (1974)

District	Road length in kilometres			
	Cement concrete	Water bound Macadam	Unsurfaced	Total
Burdwan	1015	73	101	1189
Birbhum	545	6	149	700
Bankura	588	37	94	719
Midnapore	1077	207	133	1417
Howrah	294	8	32	334
Hooghly	642	28	158	828
24-Parganas	1328	38	70	1436
Nadia	634	27	25	686
Murshidabad	630	7	47	684
Malda	284	7	—	291
West Dinajpore	483	20	50	533
Jalpaiguri	665	5	117	787
Darjeeling	364	—	113	477
Cooch Behar	450	13	816	1279
Purulia	226	6	128	355
West Bengal	9225	482	2028	11715
Total:	18450	964	4061	23430

Source: Executive Engineer, P.W.D.

Low road density still existed in the areas of western Purulia, south-eastern Midnapore, eastern and northern Murshidabad, northern Darjeeling and eastern Cooch Behar (Fig. 2.17).

Physical obstruction acted as a constraint in these above-mentioned areas.

In fact, the high density region did not expand to a large area in the State but was only limited to highly urbanised and industrialised sector of West Bengal, namely, the Calcutta conurbation area (Fig. 2.18).

In other words, Calcutta's supremacy in regard to roads clearly revealed in the map and it shows that transport played a very important role in giving Calcutta a separate geographical entity in West Bengal.

2.6.2 *Road developments during the period*

Since roadways have penetrated into the regions more deeply than railways, length per sq.km. of roads was much higher than railways. But Government roads constituted only a portion of the entire road system.

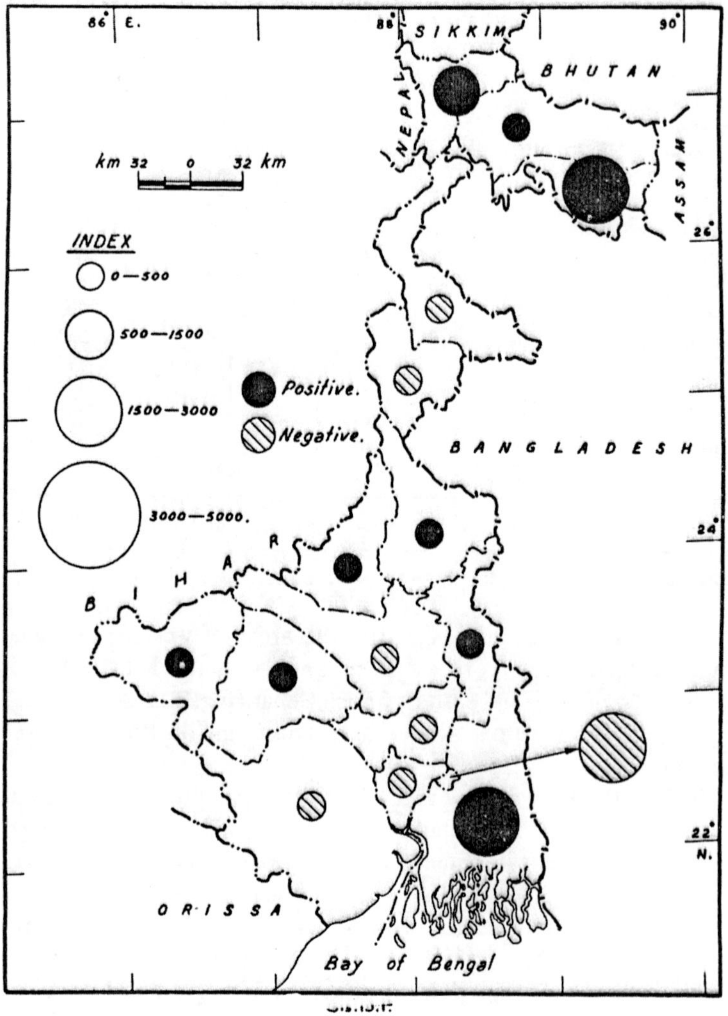

FIG. 2.16: Road Residual (Population/total road length), 1974.

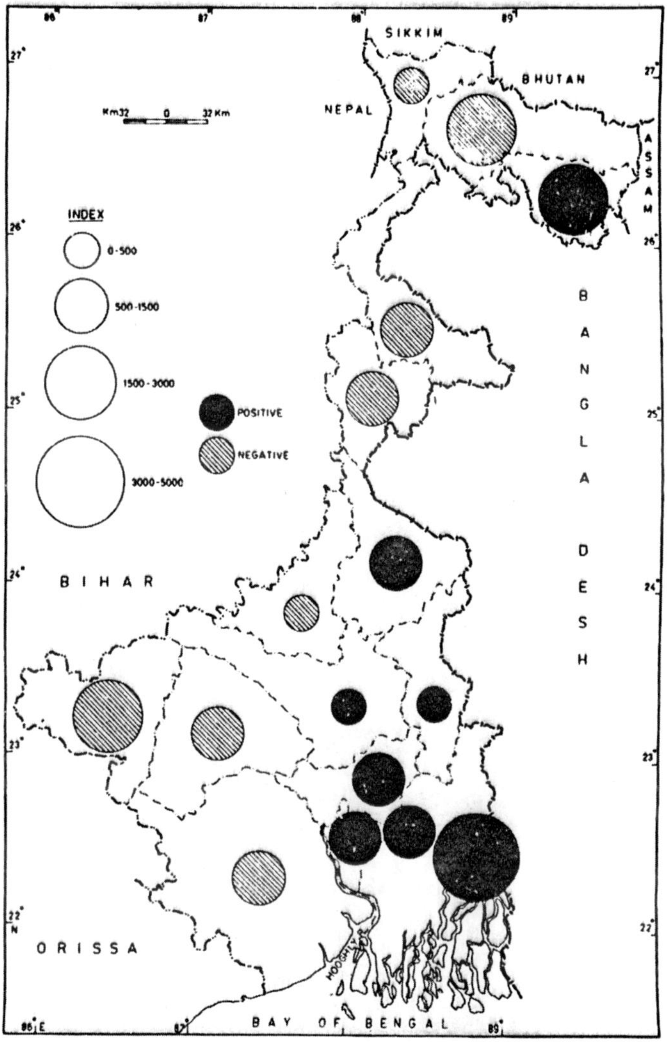

FIG. 2.17: Road Residual (Area/total road length), 1974.

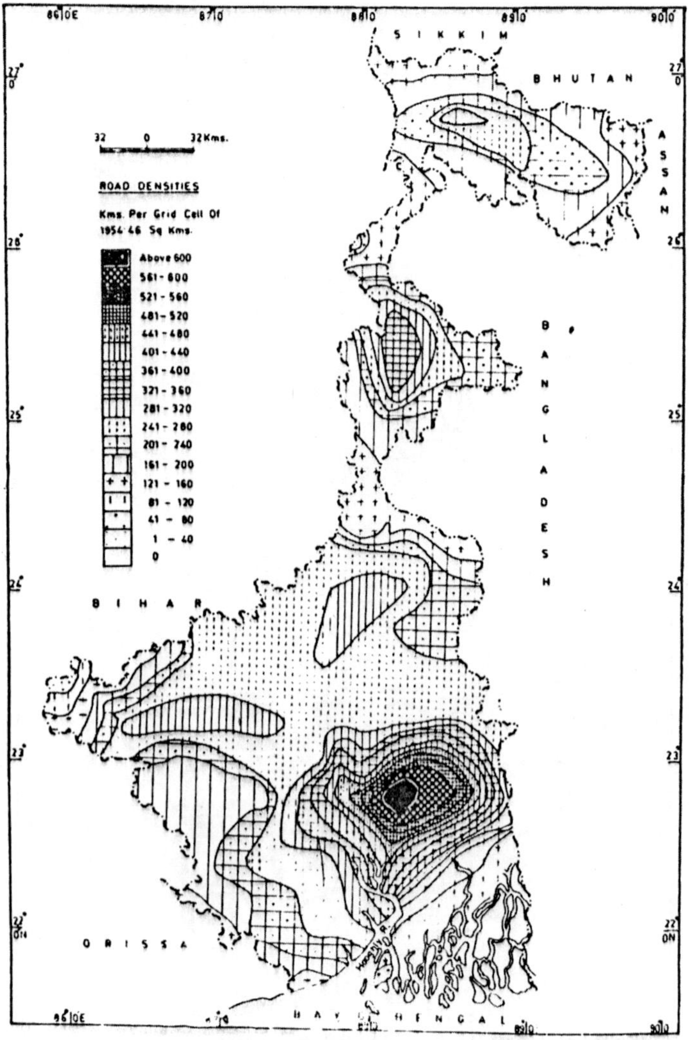

FIG. 2.18: Road Density (1974).

Road development projects in Howrah District included the Durgapur Expressway and the bypass between Bally and Adi Saptagram, however, the latter was only built. The Durgapur, Asansol, Howrah and Calcutta conurbations have led to a serious congestion of traffic on the Grand Trunk Road. It was said that "the Durgapur Expressway was projected as the only answer to this problem". A survey of road transport conducted by the Ministry of Transport in connection with the economic assessment of the Durgapur Expressway reveals that over 75 per cent of all traffic originating from or terminating in the Asansol-Raniganj-Durgapur area move eastward or south-eastward away from the area along the G.T. Road. Goods Vehicles account for more than half of the total vehicular traffic along this road.

There is no doubt that more village roads are needed as the present village roads are not adequate, but the Fourth Plan envisaged construction of only 73.6 kms. of such roads. All the districts except Howrah did have larger length of village roads during the said plan period. Some areas in the western region of the State like Purulia and parts of Bankura have very little to look forward to during the Fourth Plan. The economic possibilities of these regions have not been fully tapped either for their extreme backwardness or for the poor state of transport in these areas. Under present day circumstances, only a rapid road development can remove this deficiency (Fig. 2.19).

In Nadia, Fourth Plan laid emphasis on roads which would serve industrial concentrations, potential centres of economic growth and underdeveloped areas. P.W.D. has converted many village roads into district and State highways giving them to metalled crust 3.66 metres wide on embankments, the width of which will vary from 7.32 to 9.75 metres. In Calcutta, a very low percentage (6%) of city space was used for roads indicating the inadequacy of streets and avenues. This was further aggravated by the low standard of maintenance, unsatisfactory traffic control and highly mixed traffic, such as, passenger cars, trucks, trams, hand carts, rickshaws, pedestrians, etc. Pressure of over increasing population, unplanned growth of the city, paucity of open spaces, mode of transportation, together with the concentration of business and administrative centres in the central business area were some of the factors making the situation of Calcutta more critical (Fig. 2.20).

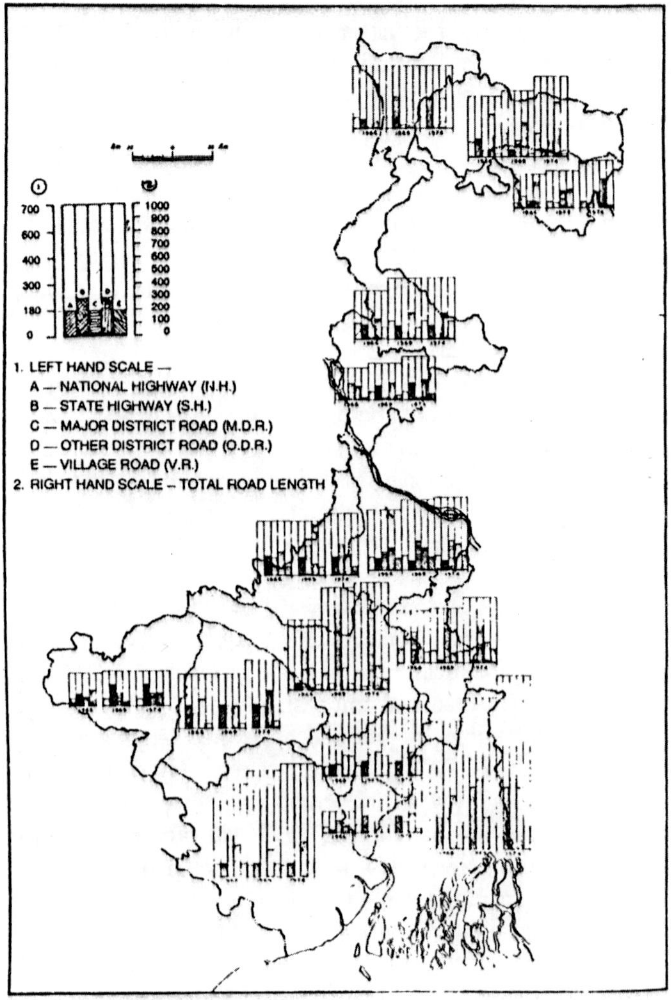

FIG. 2.19: Distribution of surfaced roads (P.W.D.), 1966, 1969, 1974.

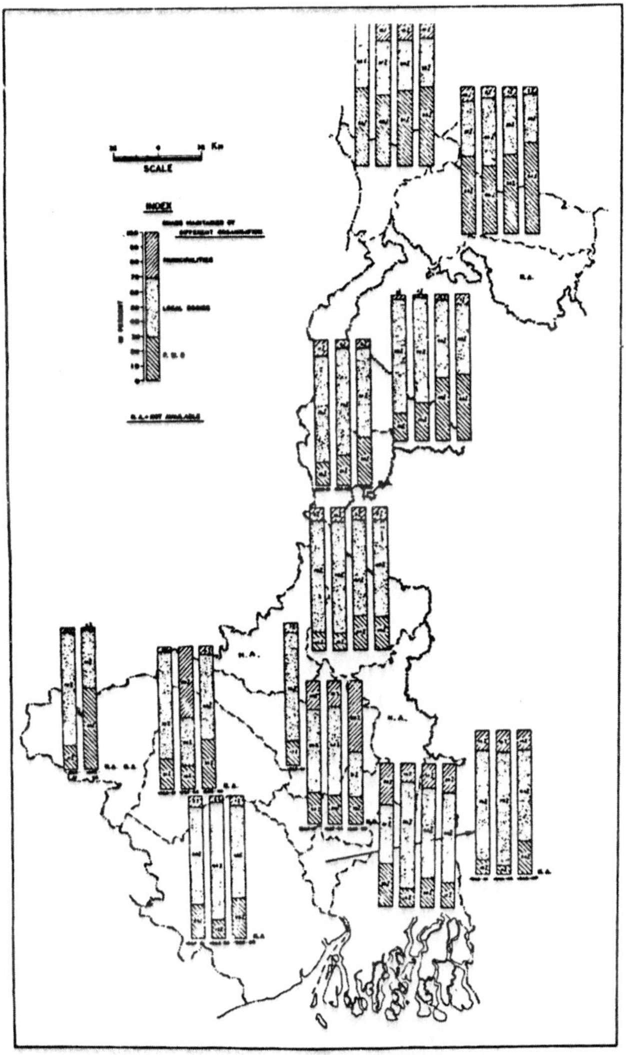

FIG. 2.20: Percentage Bar Chart showing percentage of road length manitained by different organisations (1960-61, 1965-66, 1968-69, 1971-72).

At present, there are 481.6 kms. of such type of critical roadways in the overall system; 185.6 kms. in Calcutta and Howrah and 296 kms. in the remaining Metropolitan District. In fact, there has been no appreciable change or improvement in the city's roadways system for the last hundred years (Report of Calcutta Metropolitan Development Authority, Traffic and Transportation in Calcutta, 1979).

Among the northern districts, Cooch Behar progressed in roads, its progress next to 24-Parganas and Howrah. Cooch Behar with 3.8 per cent of area of West Bengal had 7.1 per cent of roads of the total roads in 1974.

The development of roads in West Bengal would be clear from the following Table 2.14:

TABLE 2.14: District-wise Distribution of Roads

Districts	Percentage of roads to total roads				
	1956	1961	1966	1969	1974
Burdwan	8.98	9.09	8.59	8.88	8.11
Birbhum	4.08	4.21	4.88	4.88	4.46
Bankura	5.25	5.37	5.15	4.96	5.12
Midnapore	10.64	10.21	11.63	12.29	12.49
Howrah	5.25	5.13	4.99	5.01	4.47
Hooghly	6.35	6.58	6.82	6.76	6.15
24-Parganas	28.50	22.31	23.16	23.40	21.44
Calcutta	1.99	2.04	1.99	1.81	1.65
Nadia	6.00	6.26	6.04	5.74	5.38
Murshidabad	8.52	8.47	8.43	6.16	7.33
West Dinajpore	2.17	4.48	4.05	4.24	3.37
Malda	2.56	2.71	3.02	3.02	2.78
Jalpaiguri	3.06	3.35	3.43	3.56	3.93
Darjeeling	3.43	3.24	3.39	3.10	2.87
CoochBehar	3.22	2.92	1.10	2.97	7.10
Purulia	-	3.61	3.28	3.14	3.28
Total	100.00	100.00	100.00	100.00	100.00

Road development was uniform in Midnapore, Jalpaiguri and Purulia while Cooch Behar made considerable expansion from 2.79 per cent in 1969 to 7.1 per cent in 1974. Table 2.15 gives the growth of total road length in urban area (1961-1969) in West Bengal.

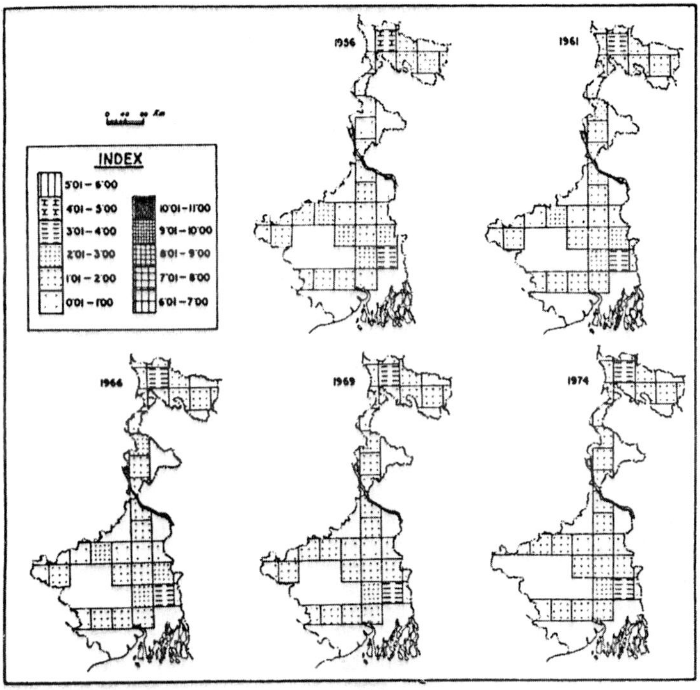

FIG. 2.21: Spatial differences in road development (National highway).

TABLE 2.15: Urban Roads

	Road length in kilometres		
	1960-61	1965-66	1968-69
West Bengal	4593	4593	4615
India	46361	83974	87839

Source: Basic Road Statistics.

In comparison to India as a whole, West Bengal has progressed very slowly in road building. Only 22 kms. of roads were added in 1968-69 in West Bengal. But the regional achievement in regard to road density was satisfactory. According to the statistics of 1973-74 the road length per 100 sq.km. of geographical area was 64 kms. in West Bengal as against 36 kms. in the country as a whole. The total length of roads maintained by different organisations in West Bengal was estimated at 56,562 kms. in 1974. The length of extra municipal roads maintained by P.W.D. in West Bengal at the end of 1973-1974 was 15,562 kms. of which 13,934 kms. were surfaced and 2,028 kms. as unsurfaced (Fig. 2.22).

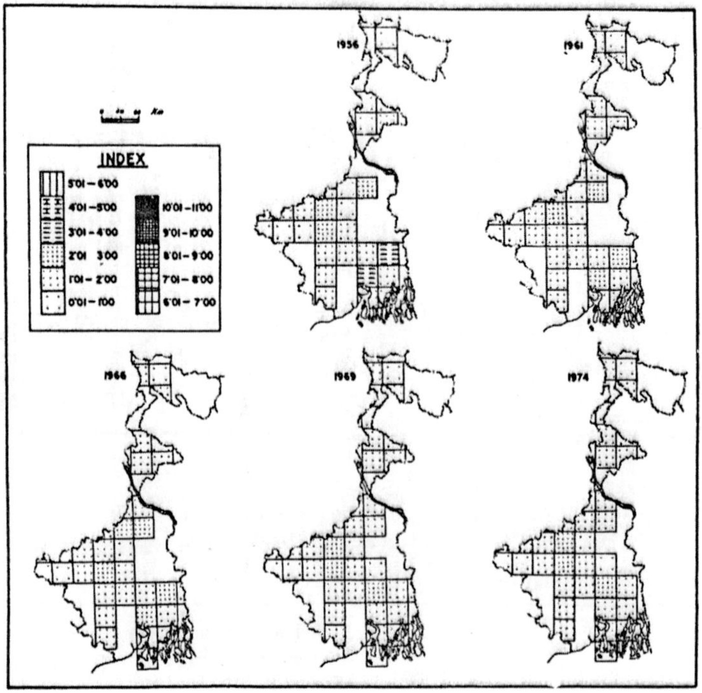

FIG. 2.22: Spatial differences in road development (State highway).

A brief account of the Road Activities carried out by P.W.D. and P.W. (Roads) Departments were given below — (Roads Improvement, 1951-1974):

National Highway

Grand Trunk Road	(N.H. 2)
Calcutta — Siliguri	(N.H. 34)
Patna — Gauhati	(N.H. 31)
Siliguri — Gangtok	(N.H. 31A)
Calcutta — Bongaon	(N.H. 35)
Calcutta — Bombay	(N.H. 6)

Central Sector Works (under construction)

Belghoria Expressway
Calcutta — Haldia Expressway (N.H.41)
Calcutta — Durgapur Expressway (proposed)
Widening of N.H. 34 (Calcutta to Farakka).

State Highways:

Barrackpore Trunk Road
Siliguri — Jalpaiguri Road
Siliguri — Darjeeling Road
Barakar — Purulia — Ranchi Road
Calcutta — Diamond Harbour — Kakdwip — Namkhana Road
Panagar — Illambazar — Suri — Massanjore Road
Raniganj — Midnapore Road
Kharagpur — Digha Road
Raniganj — Bansihari — Balurghat Road
Gajal — Baniadpur Road
Saptagram — Tribeni — Kalna — Katwa Road
Bishnupur — Sonamukhi — Rangamali Road
Purulia — Hura — Rajagram Road.
Baidyabati — Tarakeswar Road
Salkia — Chanditala — Chapadanga Road
Arambagh — Kotalpur — Bishnupur Road
Lateral Roads and Hill Roads in the districts of Darjeeling and Jalpaiguri.

Road Under Construction

— Mirik Simana Basti

West Bengal Road No. 31 from Shukia Pakri to Nagri Tea Estate.

Bridges

	Length	
	in ft.	in metres
Tarsen bridge, Hashimara	1426	434.64
Teesta bridge, Jalpaiguri	1995	608.07
Sankosh bridge, Jorai	1139	347.17
Kaljani bridge, Alipurduar	434	132.28
Jaldhaka bridge, Dhupguri	1375	419.10
Upper Jaldhaka bridge, Nagrakata	996	303.58
Cossye bridge, Midnapore	1419	432.51
Talla bridge, Calcutta	2100	640.08
Majerhat bridge, Calcutta	460	140.21
Belghoria bridge, Calcutta	1750	533.40
Ichamati bridge, Basirhat	530	167.64
Lish, Ghish, Chel, Neogra and Ral bridge in Jalpaiguri district		

Extension of Teesta bridge — (1400 ft) (Jalpesh Setu).

Krishali Setu, Swamika Setu, Rupnarayan bridge, Ajoy bridge, D.L. Roy Setu, Sarada Setu, Ramkrishna Setu, Rammohan Setu, etc.

Major and minor bridges and culverts under maintenance of P.W. (Road) and P.W. Department (Fig. 2.23).

TABLE 2.16: Bridges in West Bengal

Year ending as at 31st March	Number of major bridges	Total number of bridges & culverts
1966	396	3,900
1967	396	4,000
1969	396	4,150
1974	403	4,532

Source: Public Works Department.

Table 2.17 gives an insight into the manner in which planners have shifted the emphasis from road construction to other sectors of developments with a misconceived idea that investment on roads is non-productive.

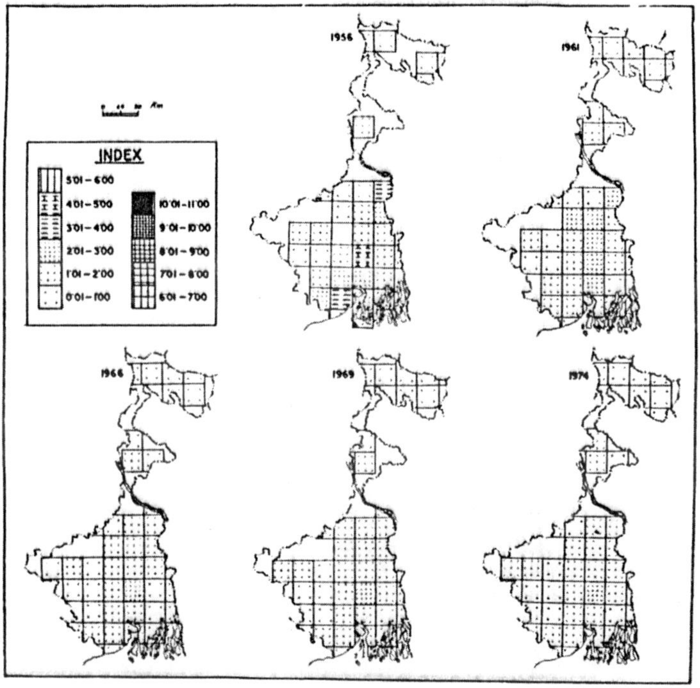

FIG. 2.23: Spatial Differences in Road Development (Major district road).

The late Dr. B. C. Roy said at the 15th Session of the Indian Road Congress at Calcutta — "There is a misconception that road construction is not a productive proposition. I can think of few state undertakings that will be more productive in the long run". (*Statesman*, dated 19th December, 1977).

Today, many areas in the State, particularly in the hills and the tribal belts of Purulia, Bankura and Midnapore, are still without roads. Fertilizers, pesticides, seeds and other essential items are not readily available to them. No development is possible without proper communications and, therefore, there should be priority for roads in the core sector, for balanced development (Fig. 2.24 & 2.25).

TABLE 2.17: Picture of Road Development Activities in West Bengal (1974)

Name of the district	Total area in sq.km.	Total population	Total length of pucca roads completed till March'74 in km.	Km.per 100 sq.km.	Km. per 1000 of population
Burdwan	7028	3,916,174	1197	17.03	–
Birbhum	4550	1,775,909	715	15.67	–
Bankura	6881	2,031,039	799	11.67	–
Howrah	1471	2,417,286	507	34.47	–
Hooghly	3145	2,872,116	879	27.95	0.306
24-Parganas	13796	8,449,482	2004	14.52	0.237
Calcutta	104	3,148,746	22	21.15	0.007
Midnapore	13724	5,509,247	1315	9.58	0.239
Nadia	3926	2,230,270	770	19.61	0.345
Murshidabad	5341	2,340,204	857	16.04	0.291
Malda	3713	1,612,657	510	13.73	0.316
West Dinajpur	5206	1,859,887	726	13.94	0.390
Darjeeling	3075	781,777	730	23.73	0.934
Jalpaiguri	6245	1,750,159	939	15.04	0.536
CoochBehar	3386	1,414,183	554	16.36	0.400
Purulia	6259	1,602,875	400	6.39	0.249

Source: Statesman, 19th December, 1977.

TABLE 2.18: Development Expenditure of West Bengal

	Development in lakhs of Rupees					
	1951-56	1956-61	1961-66	1966-69	1969-74	Total
Development of State Roads	1,212	1,405	2,183	1,045	294	6,703

Source: Economic Review, 1973-74.

Expenditure on state roads were highest in the Third Plan for the construction of arterial roads and lowest in the Fourth Plan due to the unavoidable circumstances as mentioned earlier (Fig. 2.26).

2.7 Fifth Plan (1974-1979)

It is one of the part of the Fifth Plan to develop roads in rural sector under Minimum Need Programme for which a provision of Rs. 20 crores is allotted by the Centre to the State for construction of link roads to villages which will be then directly connected alongwith the construction of rural roads.

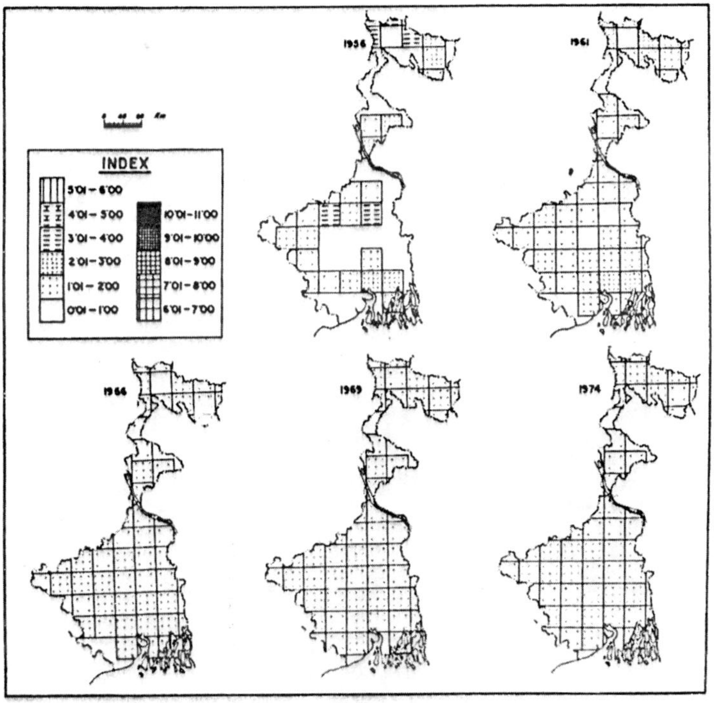

Fig. 19.IV.

FIG. 2.24: Spatial Differences in Road Development (other district roads).

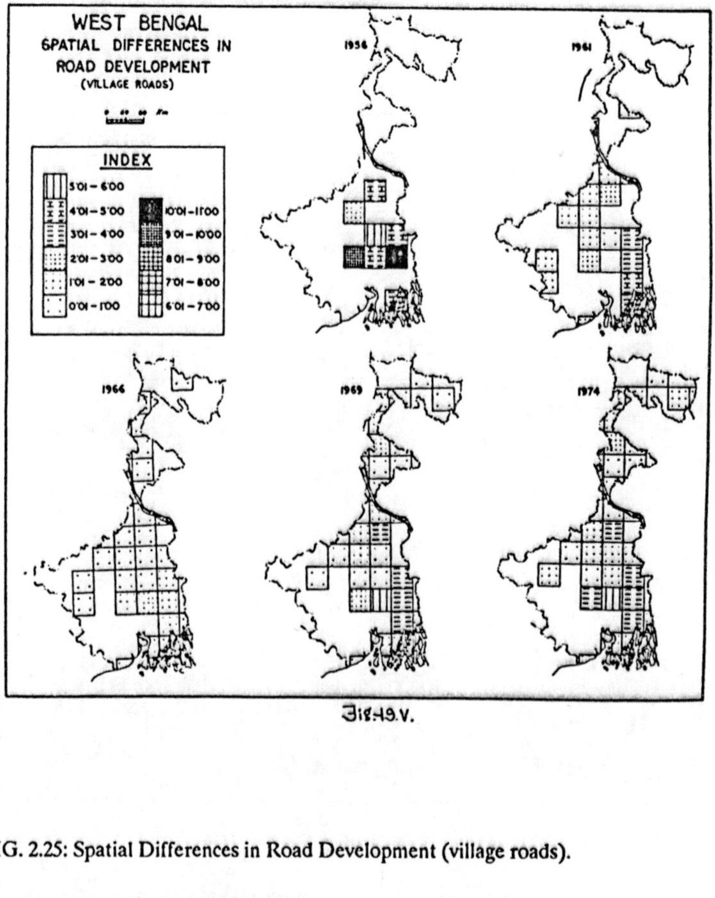

FIG. 2.25: Spatial Differences in Road Development (village roads).

Mr. Jyoti Basu, Chief Minister, West Bengal said that when the need for communication increased, the allocation for road development was reduced from 19 per cent in the First Plan to 3.2 per cent in the Fifth Plan.

Even the target for the construction of 1,800 kms. of National Highways according to the twenty years road plan was not fulfilled. The Chief Minister said that special emphasis would be laid on the construction of rural roads and development of existing roads.

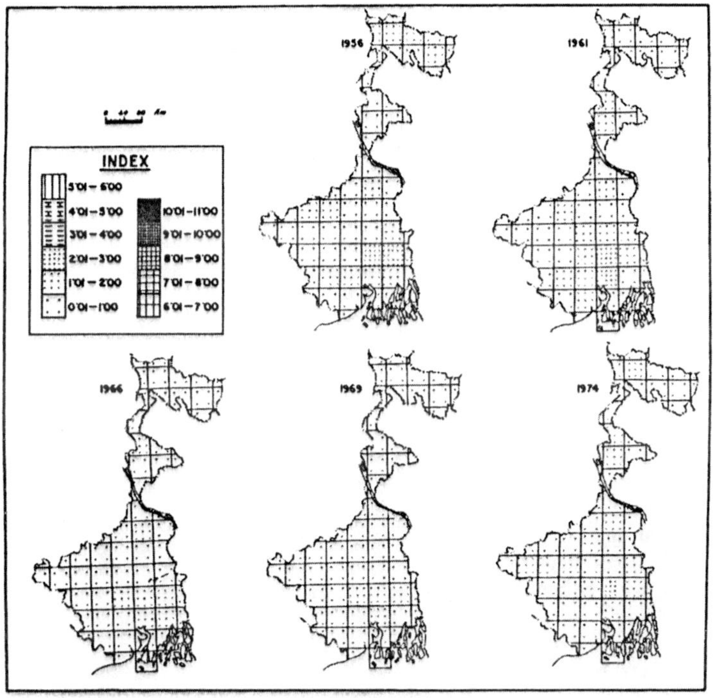

FIG. 2.26: Spatial Differences in Road Development (type mix of the roads).

2.8 Constraints of Road Development

Although the need for road development has long been realised, certain factors have prevented speedy construction of roads in the State. Despite flat topography and gentle relief, except in the extreme north, road construction in West Bengal from the engineering point of view, has presented quite a problem. One reason is that the State is criss-crossed by a large number of rivers. Non-availability of road building materials has also been a constraint, because the soft alluvial soil has rather limited load bearing capacity and, therefore, rugged roads are to be constructed, and frequent maintenance is also necessary because of the soil aggravated by the rain. Only in the districts of Birbhum, Bankura, western parts of Burdwan and Midnapore, the local laterite soil is suitable for easier road construction.

2.9 Disparities in Road Network

State disparities in road network in terms of road kilometerage on population and on area can be observed in the below Table 2.19:

TABLE 2.19: State Surface Roads

Sl. No.	States	Surfaced Road Mileage (kms)		
		Per 100 sq.km. of area		Per 100,000 Population
		1965-66	1969-70	1969-70
1.	Andhra Pradesh	10.4	13.4	85.3
2.	Assam	5.8	6.8	45.5
3.	Bihar	13.9	14.1	43.4
4.	Gujarat	8.6	10.0	73.4
5.	Haryana	0.0	16.3	71.8
6.	Himachal Pradesh	1.7	4.0	66.2
7.	Jammu & Kashmir	1.50	1.90	90.2
8.	Kerala	29.00	54.6	100.00
9.	Madhya Pradesh	6.3	6.7	71.2
10.	Maharashtra	11.2	15.2	89.7
11.	Mysore	22.2	25.4	187.0
12.	Nagaland	1.6	2.0	67.1
13.	Orissa	8.3	8.3	58.3
14.	Punjab	29.0	24.4	90.7
15.	Rajasthan	5.3	6.1	81.6
16.	Tamilnadu	33.6	37.5	118.7
17.	Uttar Pradesh	11.6	12.4	41.3
18.	West Bengal	21.4	21.5	42.6
19.	All India	11.00	12.8	73.00
20.	Mean	11.00	12.8	73.00
21.	Standard Deviation	10.17	13.34	33.98
22.	Covariance	92.53	104.24	46.55
23.	Range	32.1	52.7	145.7

Source: Indian Journal of Regional Science, Vol. V, No. 1, 1973 — The Problem of Inter-Regional Disparities (The Indian Background), Om Prakash Thakur, pp.98-99.

The statistics of West Bengal in regard to surfaced roads per sq.km. area show an above average growth, while in regard to population it did not keep pace with the road growth of 1974-75. According to the latest available figures West Bengal ranked highest in regard to total roads length followed by Uttar Pradesh. Total kilometerage of roads in West Bengal is 1,17,938 kms. in 1974-75 of which 28,639 kms. is surfaced and 89,299 kms. is unsurfaced.

2.10 Summary of the Discussion

Road network expanded after Second World War, during the post-war recovery many areas have new roads.

Continued growth in urbanisation, population and per capita income triggered phenomenal growth in the road services and the construction of new roads. Since a trunk road system had been established around 1950, much of the new growth consisted of rural secondary roads.

The earliest roads were built from the small centres, but road expansion gradually declined as rail traffic becomes a source of support for communication. The expansion and upgrading of the network around major urban places went hand in hand with the development of commerce as road connections to the outlying trade areas were improved. Many villages were connected to a central place. Much of the development between 1950 and 1969 came about through national development strategy. New feeder roads were constructed to provide access to agricultural lands, medical clinics, educational institutions and markets.

Rural roads development also took place in anticipation of and in response to agricultural development.

Major trunk road additions were not important, since the basic framework had been laid, but several important linkages were constructed to improve accessibility to areas which had economic potential but poor connections to ports or other trading centres. Closer examination of the road network of West Bengal affords deeper insight into the factors that affect the spatial diffusion of roads at a time when interconnection is a prominent motive for transport development.

Effects of difficult terrain, unequal distribution of resources, railway competition, and the like on the distribution of roads may be regarded as being partly subsumed by the population and area variables. Much of the impact of these factors on the transportation system is expressed through their relationship to the population pattern. As expected, total population accounts for more of the variation in total road kilometerage than area accounts for, obviously there is a greater need for transportation for a given population in a large unit than in a small one. As population increases in an area, the demand for transportation is intensified; as new transport lines are built into the area, an increase in population is encouraged, which in terms calls for still more transportation. However, the residual maps provided intuitive evidence of the lag and lead nature of transport development.

2.11 Position Today

According to latest available statistics of 1976, total roads in West Bengal is 1,38,165 kms. of which 1,07,651 kms. is surfaced and 30,514 kms. as unsurfaced or in other words 78 per cent of the total roads is still unsurfaced.

Total kilometerage of extra municipal roads under P.W.D. at the end of 1977 is 16,283 kms., the same being 14,025 kms. at the end of 1974 (Appendix III A).

NOTES

1. A map of percentage bar chart showing the total percentage of roads under the supervision of the different agencies.
2. The P.W.D. road lengths (districtwise) shown in the Appendix III and in a road map showing P.W.D. roads categorywise in all districts of West Bengal.
3. Road-population ratio for the rural areas will be high, for urban area will be low.
4. *West-Bengal: Land and People*, Bimal Chandra Sinha (1956) pp. 88-89.
5. Only black-topped and cement concrete surfaces have been shown as 'surfaced Roads'. Executive Engineer, P.W. (Roads).
6. With 17 of the said twenty year Plan already spent, West Bengal still requires to build 41,600 kms. of roads.
7. During this plan, District Board has been transferred to Zilla Parishad and the Gram Panchayats and the two authorities together known as Local Bodies.

3

DEGREE OF ACCESSIBILITY BY ROAD

The purpose of the study is to know the degree of accessibility of roads in West Bengal, as accessibility is one of the most important aspects of the network analysis. In the words of Forbes (1964) 'Accessibility is the term which generally implies to the ease of getting to a place'. The availability of transport facilities or the ease of accessibility plays an important role in the economic development of an area. In fact, the life blood of a region circulates through it's arteries of roads. Accessibility indicates the importance of a place, particularly the ease with which one can travel from one place to another. No place is inaccessible and the places are not of equal difficulty. Accessibility has a direct relation with the distance to be covered, greater the distance less the accessibility and vice-versa (other things remaining same – ceteris paribus). This is an index to measure the degree of transportation development in a region or the effectiveness of transportation cover.

Accessibility may be physical or static, and relative. Physical or static accessibility of a place can be measured in relation to the physical distance from a transportation artery. Accessibility with reference to the time and cost of travel in between a regional central place and the places lying within its sphere of influence is relative accessibility.

The present chapter deals with the distribution of the accessible and inaccessible areas measured in terms of the physical distance from a transportation artery with accent on the inaccessible areas because these areas need transportation development in the future. In constructing the accessibility maps, 5, 10, 15 kilometres isodromes[1] have been drawn along roads to show the degree of accessibility. (Figs. 3.1, 3.2 and 3.3).

As already mentioned, no place can be said to be totally inaccessible. However, the objective of the Nagpur Plan states that "in a highly developed agricultural area no village should be more than 2 miles (3.2 kms.) away from a road nor more than 5 miles (8

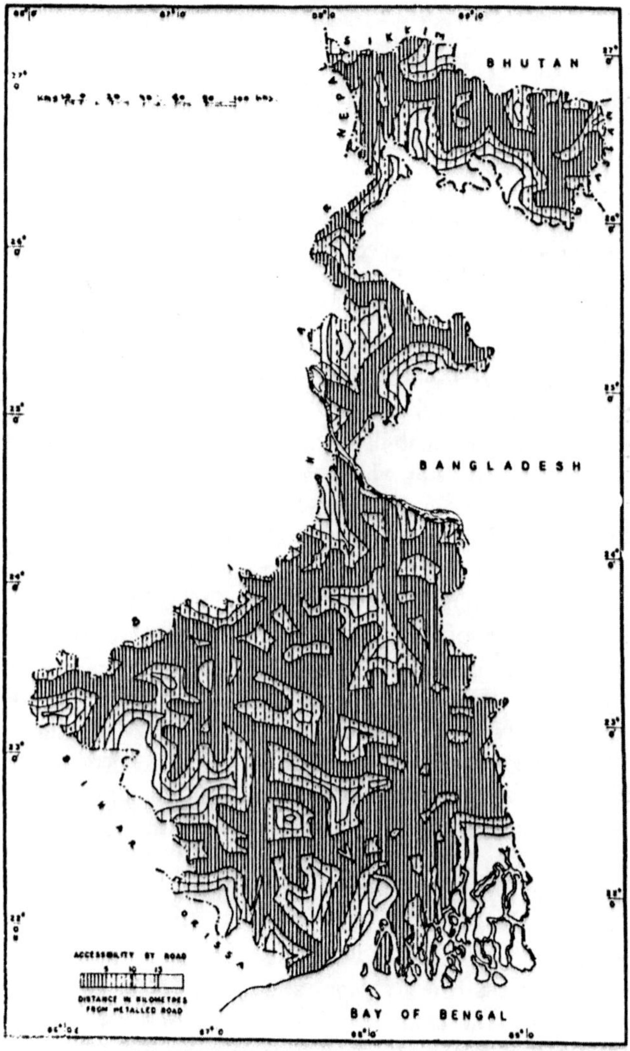

FIG. 3.1: West Bengal Accessibility by Road 1956.

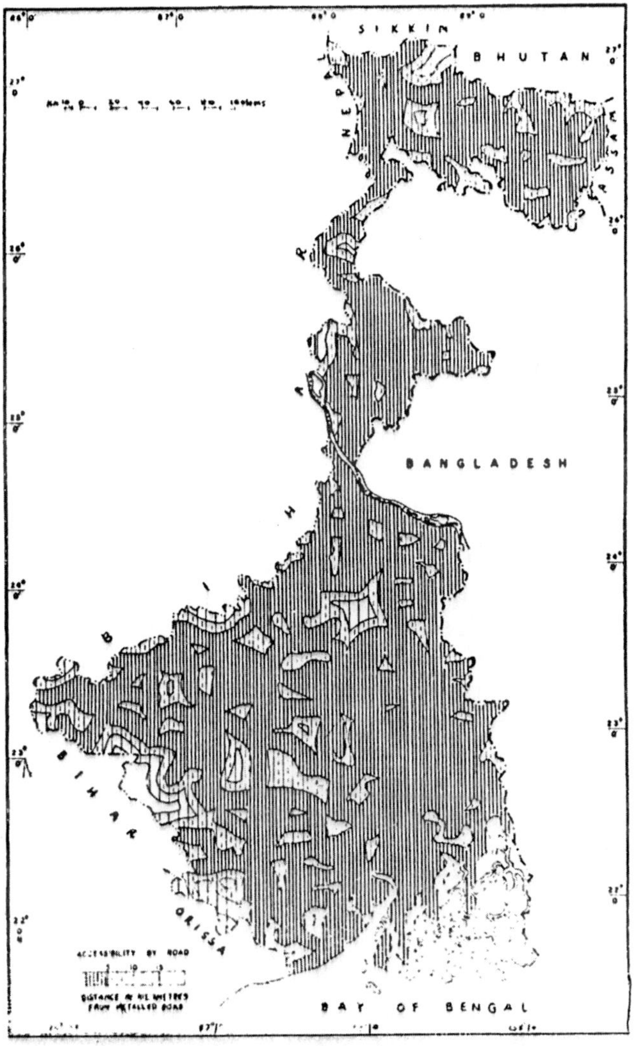

FIG. 3.2: West Bengal Accessibility by Road 1966.

kms.) from a main road. Similarly, in a non-agricultural region no village should be more than 5 miles (8 kms.) from a road nor more than 20 miles (32 kms.) from a main road" (Report of the Chief Engineer on Road Development Plan for India, 1961-81, New Delhi, 1958, p.6). But later at the end of the Fourth Five Year Plan the norm was changed and for the Fifth Plan a completely new norm has been introduced to launch direct attack on poverty. All villages having population size of more than 1,500 persons are required to be connected by all-weather roads. The total demand of roads is likely to be generated if we admit this norm, will vary according to the geometrical model of network we adopt.

Since all over the country Nagpur norm is still preferred, this study, also based on Nagpur norm, regards 8 kilometres distance as the optimum.

The degree of road accessibility was studied for three years 1956, 1966 and 1974 and it was found that 80 per cent (approximately) of areas regarded as inaccessible in 1956, were classed as accessible in 1974. This would be apparent from the road accessibility map (Fig.3.1).

An increased density of network has rapidly improved the accessibility of locations in an area. Table 3.1 shows a comparative picture of accessibility in different regions. From the point of view of accessibility, West Bengal could be divided into five regions based on percentage of total area within 5 kms. of road. The regions were grouped according to their degree of accessibility based on existing accessibility pattern, i.e. 1974.

Very good accessible regions, viz: Howrah, Nadia, Hooghly, Burdwan and Murshidabad, from the very beginning of the Five Year Plans, showed better accessibility by roads. The road density was also high in these regions (Fig. 3.2).

These district are situated in the Gangetic plains with rich alluvial soils. The land is flat suitable for easier road constructions. Nadia is situated in the moribund deltaic tract. Howrah was formed by the interaction of the Damodar and the Hooghly. The south-eastern margins of Howrah and the mouth of the Rupnarayan are still active which continue along the eastern coast line of Midnapore.

Nadia and Howrah surpassed all others in 1974 as regard to accessibility and scored the highest in the State (Fig. 3.3). Here about 90 per cent of the area lie within 5 kms. of roads. Howrah showed rapid growth in accessibility since 1966. This growth was closely related with road development.

TABLE 3.1: Degree of Accessibility by Road

Name of the District	Total area in sq. km.			% of total area within 5 kms.			% of total area 5 kms. to 10 kms.			% of total area 10 kms. to 15 kms.			% of total area Beyond 15 kms.		
	1956	1966	1974	1956	1966	1974	1956	1966	1974	1956.	1966	1974	1956	1966	197
Bankura	6883.44	6855.8	6881	50	73	78	[illegible]	20	18	10	7	4	10	—	—
Birbhum	4543.37	4514.4	4550	57	75	83	26	19	13	11	6	4	6	—	—
Burdwan	7031.85	7007.4	7028	59	75	86	23	15	10	18	10	4	—	—	—
Hooghly	3141.93	3139.3	3145	75	80	89	20	16	11	5	4	—	—	—	—
Howrah	1471.64	1450.7	1474	73	84	90	22	13	10	5	3	—	—	—	—
Midnapore	13619.51	13606.3	13724	45	59	72	35	27	22	13	9	6	7	5	—
Murshidabad	5424.75	5367	5341	55	73	86	29	15	9	11	9	5	5	3	—
Nadia	3955.45	3908.5	3926	73	82	90	25	18	10	2	—	—	—	—	—
24-Parganas	13708.35	14601.7	13736	43	64	74	14	12	8	5	4	2	25	20	14
Purulia	6234	6234	6259	32	54	68	34	25	23	15	10	6	19	10	3
W. Dinajpur	3586.63	5340.2	5206	48	69	78	36	25	18	14	6	4	2	—	—
Malda	3646.46	3605.1	3713	36	69	77	37	25	20	13	6	3	14	—	—
Jalpaiguri	6159.8	6171.7	6245	59	71	78	28	23	19	10	6	2	3	—	—
Cooch Behar	3455.32	3403	3386	37	60	79	22	19	17	19	10	—	21	11	—
Darjeeling	3003.6	3254.1	3037	49	69	77	34	22	14	14	9	9	5	—	—

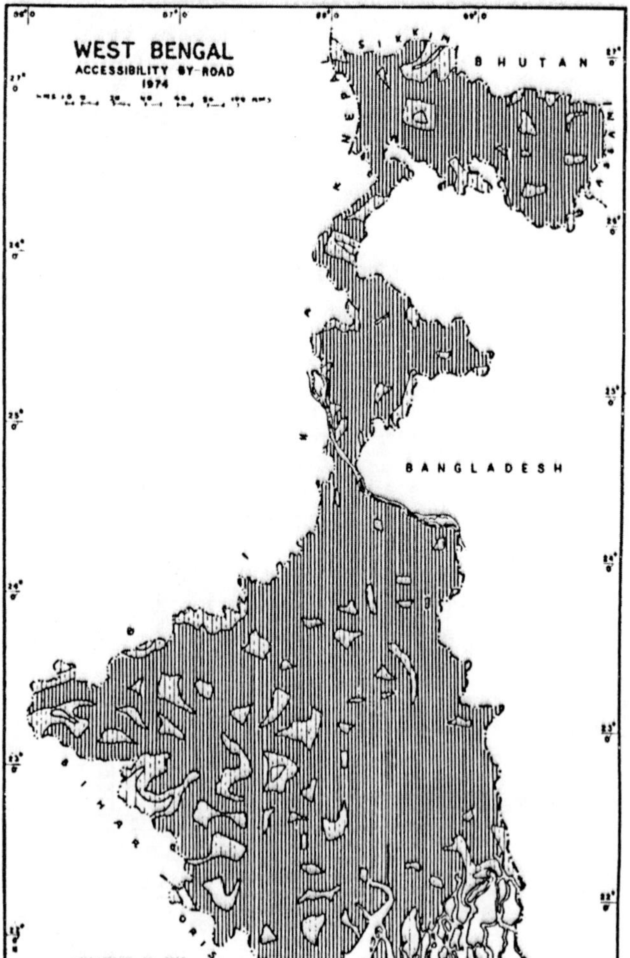

FIG. 3.3: West Bengal Accessibility by Road 1974.

TABLE 3.2: Regional Accessibility Pattern

Percentage of total area within 5 kms. of road	Degree of accessibility	Name of the district
70%	Very poor accessibility	Purulia
71% – 75%	Poor accessibility	Midnapore and 24-Parganas
76% – 80%	Fair accessibility	Bankura, West Dinajpore, Jalpaiguri, Malda, Cooch Behar and Darjeeling
81% – 85%	Good accessibility	Birbhum
86% – 90%	Very good accessibility	Howrah, Nadia, Hooghly, Burdwan and Murshidabad

TABLE 3.3: Road Density in different Regions

Name of the District	Road Density		
	1956	1966	1974
Howrah	0.051	0.165	0.344
Nadia	0.092	0.160	0.196
Hooghly	0.068	0.230	0.280
Burdwan	0.048	0.117	0.170
Murshidabad	0.049	0.131	0.160

One of the factors which differentiates Howrah from the other districts, is it's highly urbanised character with urban population 32.4 per cent in 1951, 40 per cent in 1961 to 42 per cent in 1971. Howrah cannot be thought of as a city in its own right, as it is so completely tied to the economy, social structure and physical form of Calcutta and it's Metropolitan District and it can be said that it exerts independently only in the political sense of its administrative boundaries. Within the Calcutta Metropolitan District, growth was concentrated in Calcutta. Regarding population density, Howrah ranked second in West Bengal with 1625 persons per sq. km. in 1971. This was very high in comparison to population densities of cities outside India, nonetheless considerably lower than that of its sister city Calcutta.

Howrah is an industrialised district where the industrial base is dominated by the engineering industry. The textile industry contributes 20 per cent of the industries approximately and chemical industry is ranked next. Though economically Howrah has enjoyed better condition than Nadia, being a border State, Nadia was given special attention for extension of roads which is indicated by the present high accessibility of the region. The development of roads was not however very rapid, only 72 per cent increase in 1966 to 22 per cent in 1974. The First Plan extended the road network in Nadia to connect all police station headquarters but could not provide adequate funds for maintaining road standards, improving the bridges and providing missing links. The Third Plan investment was therefore directed primarily to improve the quality of roads, bridges and culverts. The Fourth Plan laid emphasis on roads which would serve areas of industrial concentrations, potential centres of economic growth and underdeveloped areas.

Hooghly district possesses 89 per cent of its area within 5 kms. of road. Hooghly ranks next to Howrah, with road density about 0.28 kms. per sq. km. in 1974. Areas lying beyond 10 kms. of road were not found to be existing since 1966. It obviously points directly towards road expansion. Still it is insignificant as there is only 21 per cent increase from 1966 to 1974. Areas within 5 kms. to 10 kms. of road was still observed in 1974 about 11 per cent.

In Burdwan there are good number of village roads and 119 metalled roads connecting the headquarter and other towns with the interior of the district. It has one National Highway (G.T. Road) which passes through the district for a distance of 233.6 kms. linking Burdwan with Calcutta. Due to the presence of coal, Burdwan is well industrialised with greater concentration of industries around Durgapur and Asansol, and the high accessibility keeps pace with the rapid industrialisation in this region. Only parts of Salanpur, Tanuria and Balaban near extreme border of the Burdwan District have 4 per cent of areas beyond 10 kms of road.

Murshidabad, on the other hand, with a road density of 0.16 kms. per sq. km. in 1974 had only 5 per cent of area beyond 10 kms. of road in 1974. In Murshidabad the Calcutta-Darjeeling Highway first run east of Bhagirathi from south to north upto Berhampur and then it crosses the river and continues north to Farakka. Many strategic State Highways branch out from it and go eastwards to the border of Bangladesh.

Birbhum was the only district which can be categorised as good accessible region having 85 per cent of area within 5 kms. of road during 1974 inspite of the low rate of road development which was only 13 per cent from 1966 to 1974. Recently, as a result of intensive action, roadways have developed extensively in Birbhum. The isolation of all areas have been eliminated and the district has now well connected with different parts of the State as well as adjoining areas. A metalled road connects the district, originating from G.T. Road, from Suri crossing the Ajoy River at Illamabazar.

Bankura district in the southern parts of West Bengal and all the northern districts, i.e., Jalpaiguri, Darjeeling and Cooch Behar and the two central districts, Malda and West Dinajpore, were classed as fair accessible region having 75 per cent to 80 per cent of area within 5 kms. of road.

Of all the above-mentioned districts, Cooch Behar was given special attention for extension of surfaced roads in 1974, and road development was very weak in Darjeeling since 1966. As a result, Cooch Behar shows better accessibility than the other fairly accessible regions in 1974, about 79 per cent of it's area lying within 5 kms. of road. But 17 per cent area still remained beyond 10 kms. of road during the same year.

Darjeeling comprised of little area approximately 14 per cent beyond 10 kms. of road in 1974. In comparison to these regions, others however presented unimpressive accessibility, such as West Dinajpore possessed 18 per cent of area beyond 10 kms. of road.

Malda	–	20% of area beyond 10 kms. of road.
Jalpaiguri	–	19% of area beyond 10 kms. of road.
Bankura	–	20% of area beyond 10 kms. of road.

Purulia upland extending east of Bankura has typical rolling landscape alternating with jungle covered swells and flat alluvial valleys. A slightly rolling laterised country side continues farther east beyond Sonamukhi. This landscape however impedes road construction. Midnapore and 24-Parganas having 70 per cent to 75 per cent of area within 5 kms. of road were classed as poor accessible region. These regions though the largest in the State, the growth of road was not balanced with it and a large tract of inaccessible area was found. Mention should be made of Sundarban region of 24-Parganas, which is so criss-crossed with canals, ponds and small islands, having 29 per cent of the total area of the district represented 14 per cent of inaccessible area in 1974 and 25 per cent in 1956.

Midnapore did not have inaccessible area like 24-Parganas and only 6 per cent of area remained within 10-15 kms. of road in 1974 but no area beyond 15 kms. of road.

The development of roads would be clear from the following road density in Table 3.4:

TABLE 3.4: Road Density

Name of the District	Road Density		
	1956	1966	1974
Midnapore	0.046	0.080	0.096
24-Parganas	0.056	0.100	0.145

It appears from the above table that 24-Parganas did possess better system of roads than Midnapore inspite of very low rate of road growth in these two districts, only 20 per cent in Midnapore and 37 per cent in 24-Parganas from 1966 to 1974.

Purulia was the only district represented as very poor accessible region having 68 per cent of area within 5 kms. of road.

Purulia is definitely a resource rich district. Lack of adequate transport facilities is one of the reasons which made Purulia a backward district of the State. Road density was 0.038 per sq. km. in 1974. Purulia presented 23 per cent of area within 5-10 kms. of road, 6 per cent within 10-15 kms. of road and 3 per cent of area beyond 15 kms. of road. The potentiality of Purulia can be attributed next to Durgapur, but the rich deposits of resources can only be utilised when proper emphasis on road expansion is given by the Government.

In West Bengal, the importance of agricultural activity imposes on the transportation system a demand for widespread network of roads capable of serving the kind of dispersal activity that is inherent with agriculture. Although West Bengal has the highest road kilometerage per unit area when all types of roads are considered, it has less road kilometerage per 100,000 population than India as a whole and stands third after Tamilnadu and Kerala in surfaced road kilometerage per unit area.

To meet the demand of the State's expanding economy it is not only necessary to extend the road kilometerage but also to rectify the general deficiencies in the existing road network.

NOTE

1. Isodromes are lines with similar road distances. The isodromes can be divided into two groups, actual isodromes drawn on the basis of the existing road connections and aero-isodromes drawn on the basis of homogeneous transport area, i.e., irrespective of whether there are roads or not, direct lines between places as the 'Crow flies'.

4

SPATIAL STRUCTURE OF TRANSPORTATION NETWORK
Some Measures of Nodal Accessibility

By the term transportation network, we generally mean a set of geographical locations interconnected in a system by a number of routes.

This study of transportation network consists of two parts. The first part is concerned with the quantitative analysis of transport network with the various methods of connectivity measurements. The second part is concerned with an aggregate measure of transport facilities (network) of nodes.

The purpose of the study is confined to the examination of the different forms and structure of transportation networks and to evaluate them as entire system, rather than as individual routes within the system.

For achieving this, various factors of the network as a graph are considered. Network as a graph has two subdivisions – degree of connectivity and degree of nodal accessibility. The degree of connectivity is indicated by alpha index (α), beta index (β), gamma index (γ) and diameter (π), while the degree of nodal accessibility is determined by nodal connectivity, route factor, road capacity, road degree, aggregate travel distance, distance to nearest Class I town. Nodal connectivity is indicated by direct connectivity, indirect connectivity and total accessibility. The determination of the aggregate measures of transport facilities (network) of nodes will be apparent in Table 4.1.

PART - I

4.1 Network as a Graph

At present graph theory is used by geographers to describe the spatial structure of transportation networks. The network of transport happens to be a very real feature of the geography of an area from the point of view of human interaction and is an important indicator of the level of its development.

TABLE 4.1: Network as a Graph.

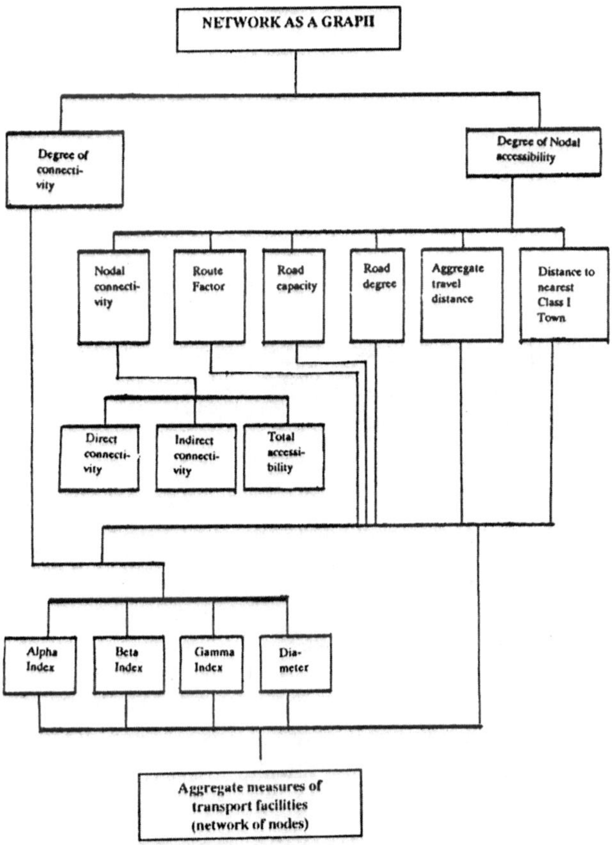

In this part, some elementary concepts of graph theory have been introduced, to explain some basic structural properties of networks. Application of graph theory in the analysis of transportation network has been attempted in many studies beginning with Eular in 1736 and Konig in 1936.

In the study of transportation in West Bengal, application of graph theory provided the author with satisfactory results. The boundary of the network which may be regional and/or administrative, act as a constraint in the system.[1]

Topological transformation of all the roads are converted into points called nodes (vertices). A node is defined as a point of origin or destination, a significant town enroute, or a junction of two or more edges. An edge is a link between any two nodes.

4.1.1 *Degree of connectivity*

Since the expansion of transport linkages between nodes is directly related to increase in the demand for transportation facilities for moving goods and people, the degree of connectivity of a transport network is indicative of the complexity of the spatial order that imposes on the region it serves. The intensely developed network system should exhibit the greatest number of inter-connections.

The degree of connectivity is measured by the following indices which are direct application of topological concepts of the network efficiency. The definitions of the indices to measure the degree of connectivity are given below:

Alpha Index

As defined by K.J. Kansky, alpha measure is an adjusted form of the cyclomatic number. It can be defined for planer graphs

$$\alpha = \frac{\text{actual circuits}}{\text{maximum circuits}} = \frac{e\text{-}v+1}{2v\text{-}5} \quad (4.1)$$

Where e is the number of edges, v is the number of vertices. Alpha index is expressed in percentages.

Beta Index

It expresses in the numerical form, the ratio of the number of edges (e) or routes in a system, to the number of vertices (v) or nodes in that system,

$$\beta = \frac{e}{v} \quad (4.2)$$

Transportation networks having complicated structure have higher values of β and simple structure have lower values. The Beta index will give a measure of connectivity regardless of the size of the area involved.

Gamma Index

By K.J. Kansky, the gamma index is simply the ratio between the edges and vertices of a given transportation network. The relation between edges and vertices are expressed in a slightly different form than the previous two indices (α and β). Assuming a network is abstracted as a planer graph, the addition of each vertex to the system increases the minimum number of edges by three, and the gamma index becomes –

$$\gamma = \frac{e}{3(v-2)} \tag{4.3}$$

Network connectivity as measured by gamma index, indicates the degree by which the network deviates from an inter-connected graph and approximates in maximally connected graph.

Diameter

The index for measuring the shape of a network is diameter (it is also a weak index for measuring transportation network)

$$\pi = \frac{c}{d} \tag{4.4}$$

where c = total length of the transportation network
d = network's diameter.

Diameter (π) is an index for measuring the shape of a network by counting the number of edges in the shortest path between the most distant vertices.

Two of the most commonly employed graph theoretic measurements of connectivity are the gamma and alpha indices which are also applied to find out the efficiency of the given network. All measures used in the present study are directly derived from graph theory. Two general classes of measures will be found in the study, which are,

(1) measures of transportation networks in their entirety,
(2) measures of individual elements of transportation network.

4.1.2 *Graph theoretic measures of whole transportation network*

The given topological network of West Bengal (Fig. 4.1) consists of nineteen vertices defined by size criteria, i.e., towns with 50,000 population and above (based on the census year 1971), alpha, beta and gamma indices are calculated to measure the degree of connectivity for this network.

When the Value of beta index is between 1 to 3, it could be termed as complex network. Higher values in the beta index are produced by a complicated structure, with a high number of edges. Therefore, the increasing connectivity of the graph will be accompanied by a decreasing number of vertices, and the β index will assume higher numerical value (Kansky, p. 18). Thus, the index increases in magnitude as the ratio of the number of edges to the number of vertices increases.

In the case study, number of nodes in the given network are nineteen and number of edges are twenty-five. Therefore, the beta index is $e/v = 25/19$ i.e. 1.32 which reflected slightly complex network form. This value may indicate higher degree of inter-connections or may exhibit the beginnings of the development of inter-connections.

In the given network the gamma index is found to be $e/3(v\text{-}2) = 25/3(19\text{-}2) = 0.49$. In terms of maximal connectivity, the network is 49 per cent connected (for convenience in interpretation, the numerical value may be expressed as a percentage of connectivity).

Because of the greater number of edges relating to those necessary for minimal connectivity, the network has maximum circuits 33 and the minimum circuits is found to be 7, so the alpha index is (7/33X100) i.e. 21 per cent so this network circuit is 21 per cent of the maximum.

It can be deduced that the highways were not designed to provide a number of alternate connections to cities within the State. The results obtained can be summarized as:

Alpha index	=	0.21
Beta index	=	1.32
Gamma index	=	0.49

Since these indices are based on the particular topology as selected, the indices will vary according to the network chosen. In this particular case, it could be said that it was nearly maximal connected network.

Based on the gamma and alpha indices, the network pattern is designated as grid pattern which is identified as a transitional state of network growth between Spinal pattern and Delta pattern. Spinal pattern shows minimal connectivity while Delta pattern shows maximal.

The actual dimension of the network can be measured by diameter index written as a ratio c/d., (eq. 4.4) where c is the total mileage of the given transportation networks and d is the total mileage of the networks diameter (Kansky, 1963).

In the given network the total kilometerage c is 2481 kms. There were eight edges between the two distant nodes, Cooch Behar and Basirhat. So, there is no unique diametre but eight alternative paths that fulfil the minimum diameter retention and the mean length of the eight diametre path is 873 kms., so that the shape index is c/d = 2481/873 = 2.84.

This value of diameter index revealed complicated transportation network which in fact reflected higher degree of development.

4.1.3 *Degree of nodal accessibility*

In this study the position of individual node in relation to total transport system has been analysed. All the measures for determining nodal connectivity has been applied and then the total accessibility of each node in relation to others in the given system was determined. In examining nodal accessibility, six indices have been selected, which are nodal connectivity (direct connectivity, indirect connectivity and total accessibility), route factor, road capacity, road degree, aggregate travel distance and distance to nearest Class I town.

Nineteen vertices or nodes are selected on the basis of total population above 50,000 and correspondingly twenty-five links or edges are drawn on highways. All the measures are computed from the given topological map (Fig. 4.1).

In this analysis emphasis is made on the identification of the spatial structure of the component node and the linkage association of the transport network; so that linkages and flows between centres, or nodal hierarchy in terms of their functions and accessibility to the rest of the network, can be known.

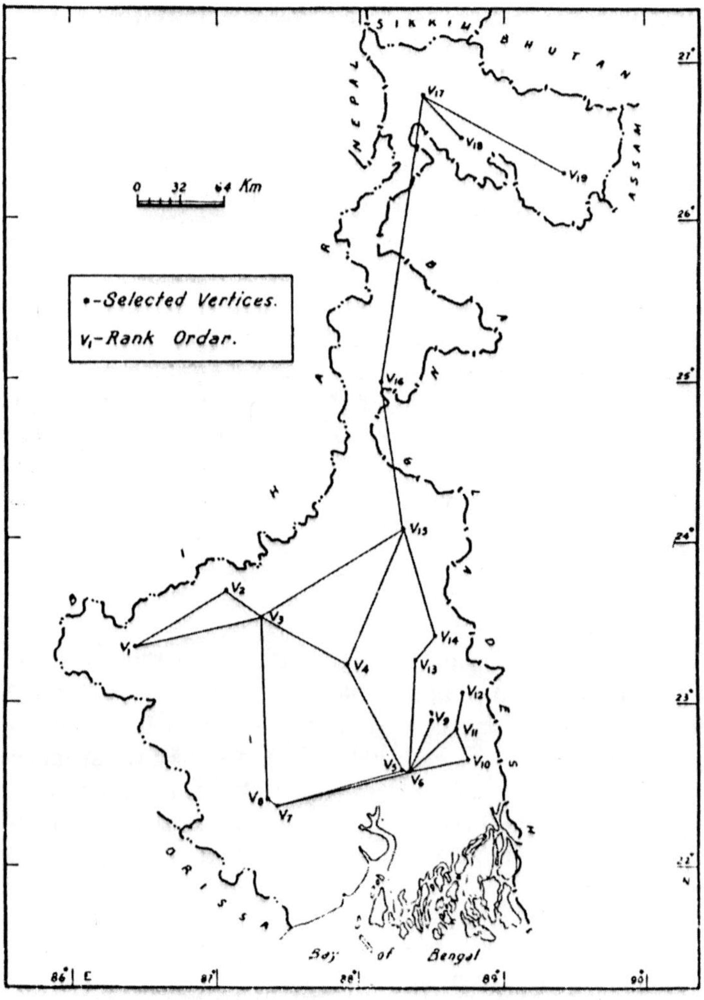

FIG. 4.1: Selected Vertices of Road Network (1974).

4.1.4 *Nodal Connectivity*

The first indicator of nodal accessibility is nodal connectivity which includes direct connectivity, indirect connectivity and total accessibility.

(i) *Direct Connectivity*

The abstraction of a network can be represented as a matrix where the horizontal rows are identified as a set of origin and vertical columns of the matrix are defined as a set of destination nodes. The number of rows and columns in the matrix would each correspond to the total number of nodes in the network. This matrix representation which has proven most useful in theory types of network analysis is known as connection matrix. Connection matrix indicates direct connectivity between vertices. But there is some limits to this analysis, since only inside connections are considered in this analysis. If there are some distortions due to artificially imposed boundary of the region, the point near the boundary will have low connectivity, i.e., low connectivity within the system and then outside connections may become more important but are not taken into account.

The given network has been abstracted as a graph and this graph is then represented in a 19 X 19 matrix in which the cell entries record the presence or absence of linkages between pair of nodes in the network. If a linkage exists between any pair of nodes, a value of 1 is entered in the appropriate cell and if no direct linkage exists, then a value of zero is recorded in that cell. Therefore, this matrix signifies only the direct connections between a pair of nodes.

Each row sum equals to the total number of linkages (direct) from a given centre in that row to the set of other centres in the network and is thus degree of a node measured. The degree of a node would be identified from the connectivity matrix given in the appendix (Appendix IV).

The nodes are ranked hierarchically in terms of the magnitude of direct connections in Fig. 4.2, and in the following Table 4.2.

From the above Table 4.2 it is apparent that Calcutta has scored the highest degree of direct connections than the rest of the nodes in the system. The six direct connections of Calcutta are with Howrah (which is the nearest node), Basirhat, Habra, Nadia, Santipur and Kharagpur. The location of Calcutta inside the system has greatly influenced the connectivity score.

TABLE 4.2: Direct Connectivity

City	Number of direct Connections	Rank
Calcutta	6	1
Durgapur	5	2
Berhampore	4	3
Burdwan	3	4
Howrah	3	4
Kharagpore	3	4
Habra	3	4
Santipur	3	4
Siliguri	3	4
Purulia	2	10
Asansol	2	10
Midnapore	2	10
Naihati	2	10
Basirhat	2	10
Krishnanagar	2	10
Englishbazar	2	10
Bongaon	1	17
Jalpaiguri	1	17
Cooch Behar	1	17

Durgapur with 5 direct connections is the next important, linking directly with Burdwan, Purulia, Asansol, Midnapore and Berhampore. Both of these nodes (Calcutta and Durgapur) are the most important urban centres.

Berhampore comes third in the State, having direct linkages with Durgapur, Burdwan, Krishnanagar and Englishbazar scoring four only.

Some of the important urban nodes having three direct connectivity are Burdwan, Howrah, Kharagpur, Habra, Santipur and Siliguri. Though these nodes are urban as well as industrial centres, yet they have low direct highway connections to the rest of the system.

Asansol being an industrial centre should have more direct connections but being situated in the border of the system reflected low connectivity compared to the inside nodes.

With the exception of Bongaon, Jalpaiguri and Cooch Behar having a very poor degree of direct connectivity, only one, the rest of the nodes have only two direct connections. Poor direct connectivity of Bongaon, Jalpaiguri and Cooch Behar may be due to their location in the extreme end of the network.

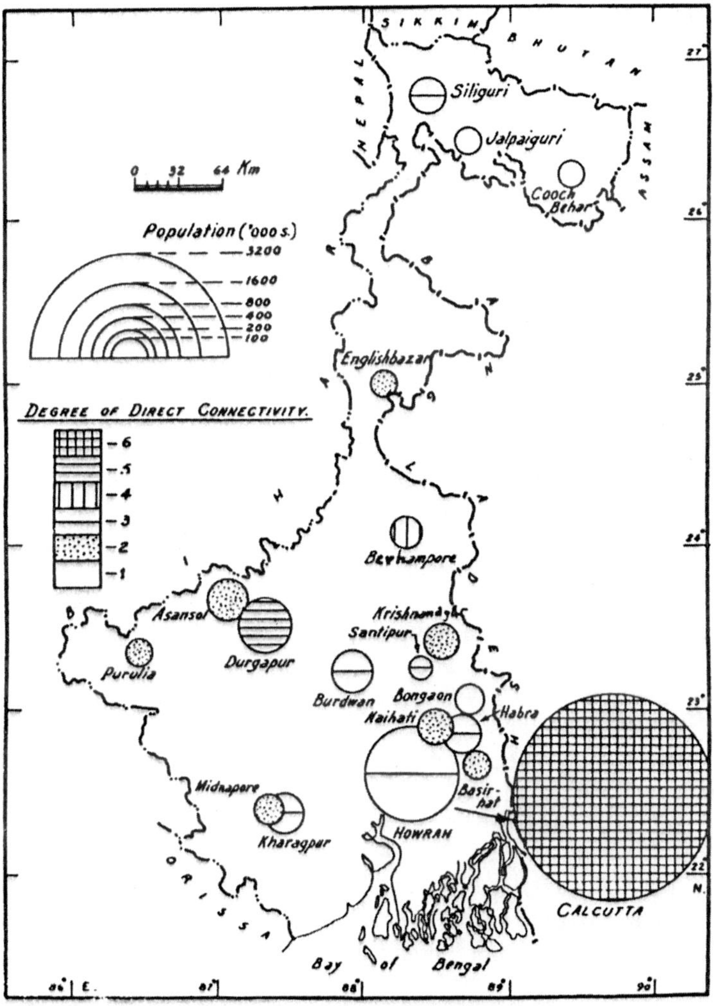

FIG. 4.2: Grouping of Nodes Based on Direct Connectivity (1974)

It is thus evidenced that since Calcutta is a metropolis, hence, the most accessible centre, or in other words, it can be said that higher accessibility has led to a great metropolitan hub. While predicting the accessibility and the type of the city, it should be kept in mind that only direct connectivity cannot provide us with the real picture. Calcutta is no doubt the best connected node but other nodes are also accessible through indirect means.

Calcutta's total accessibility to industrial belt cities like Durgapur and Asansol must also be taken into account. By the direct connections between these centres, the relative importance of Calcutta is exemplified and is, therefore, poor indicator of hierarchy. To assess in the proper perspective what, therefore, is needed is to measure both the direct and indirect connections, so that the total accessibility can be known thus giving the ideal ranking of the nodes in the given network.

A system though completely connected may have many places between which there is only one direct link. This does not mean that these places can be reached through that link only, it is quite possible that they may be reached by one or more intermediate vertices, i.e. via some indirect routes from other places.

(ii) *Indirect Connectivity*

Indirect connection matrix C^n is obtained by raising to nth power the original connection matrix, when n is the number of linkages between node i and node j. The number of indirect routes of n-linkages connecting any two vertices in the system is determined, from the elements of the matrix C^n. Every node will have a path connection to all other nodes when the value of n is equal to the diameter of the network (the minimal number of links between the two most distant nodes in the network).

The most distant nodes in the given network are Bongaon (V_{12}) and Cooch Behar (V_{19}) for which the number linkages is eight, therefore the original connectivity matrix is to be raised to the power eight, to obtain the indirect connectivity.

(iii) *Total Accessibility*

Total accessibility is obtained from matrix T — Total Connectivity Matrix, by summing up the row and column elements of C^n matrix, which record both the direct and indirect paths between the nodes of the network. The total accessibility is also called unweighted accessibility.

The summation of the row elements represents the accessibility of a given node to other nodes in the network. The summation of the column elements represents the accessibility of a node to the network.

Based on this matrix *T* [Total Connectivity Matrix — Appendix-IV-A], nodes are ranked in terms of their relative position (accessibility) on the network. The higher the value of the row sum, the greater the accessibility of the node (Fig. 4.3). The following Table shows the hierarchy of cities based on total accessibility score:

TABLE 4.3: Total Accessibility Score

Node	Total accessibility score	Rank
Calcutta	22398	1
Howrah	15335	2
Durgapore	15084	3
Kharagpore	14329	4
Burdwan	13304	5
Berhampore	12620	6
Santipore	12475	7
Habra	10950	8
Naihati	10649	9
Basirhat	10168	10
Midnapore	9048	11
Krishnanagar	7718	12
Purulia	6817	13
Asansol	6817	13
Englishbazar	4557	15
Bongaon	3301	16
Siliguri	1806	17
Jalpaiguri	621	18
Cooch Behar	621	18

The total accessibility score for the given network shows high accessibility for Calcutta and Howrah. As already mentioned, the accessibility of a location on a network is strongly influenced by the structure of the network. Calcutta is top most in both connectivities (direct and indirect) and hence it is undoubtedly the highly accessible centre in the given network, which also reflected the same in reality. By direct or by indirect routes Calcutta surpassed all other nodes in the system.

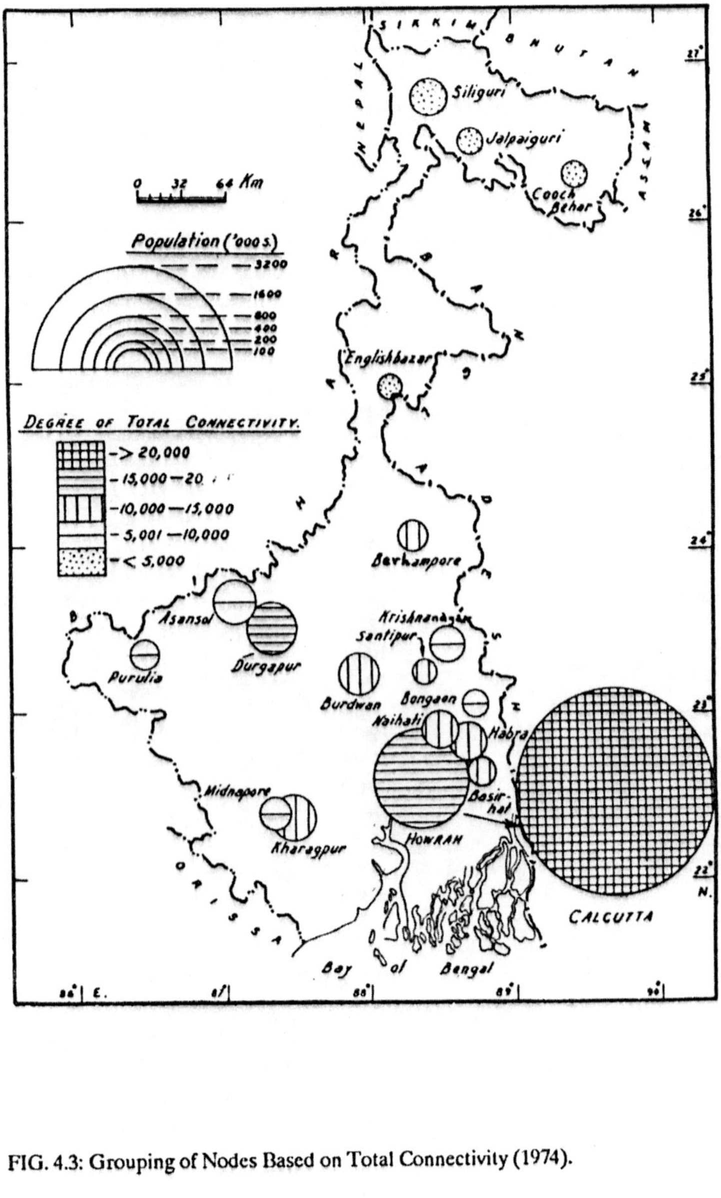

FIG. 4.3: Grouping of Nodes Based on Total Connectivity (1974).

Howrah has ranked fourth in respect of direct connectivity but stood next to Calcutta when total connectivity is considered. This shows that Howrah can be reached by indirect routes or in other words Howrah is connected more by indirect routes rather than the direct ones thus explaining the higher level of total connectivity. Calcutta is the largest node in West Bengal and Howrah is the second largest node and this study verifies this fact.

Calcutta-Howrah Urban Complex, by far, is the most central place because it is not only the converging point of almost all the major roads and railways in the Eastern region of India, but is also a busy international airport and seaport. Population and transport service-wise there is no immediate competitor of Calcutta-Howrah Urban Complex and, therefore, it has been accepted as the level I in total accessibility.

Durgapur is marginal, compared to Howrah regarding total accessibility and comes after Calcutta and Howrah in respect of direct connectivity.

Kharagpur, one of the largest Railway Junctions comes after Durgapur.

Total accessibility in Bongaon is favourable but direct connectivity is very poor due to its extreme location in the system.

Siliguri, on the other hand, is directly connected with three centres but ranked very low in total accessibility, because of its position in the extreme corner of the network, till it is one of the most important transport node in the north. Since whole West Bengal is considered in the network, the picture of Siliguri is therefore distorted.

In the system, Calcutta ranked as the most accessible city, on the other hand, Jalpaiguri and Cooch Behar ranked as the least accessible cities which could be partly explained by their location in the extreme end of the system.

4.1.5 *Route factor*

Another approach for measuring the connectivity of nodes is Route Factor or Tortuosity Ratio. With the advancement in such studies several indices have been evolved to measure the efficiency of networks either in their entirety or particular components of them.

The Tortuosity Ratio is the ratio between the route distances to the direct origin — destination distances. This origin — destination distance which is also known as straight line distance, is frequently used in the evaluation of transport network. The success and efficiency of a transportation network to some extent can be measured by comparing the direct distance between pairs of nodes and the shortest actual distance between them on a network. "Straight line alone determine the time, effort and cost of movement between two points, but it is common experience that the route distance between the two points may be considerably greater than the straight line distance. The ratio of route distance to straight line distance is termed as the route factor" (Alan Hay, pp. 38).

Most attempts to measure deviousness are based upon the concept of the route factor.

To obtain the route factor in the given network two sets of aggregate travel distances are computed for each node, one based on actual route distance and the other on straight line distance.[2] The ratio between the two values indicate whether the individual node may be reached by more or less devious routes.

It is noticed that certain higher order centres tend to be connected by the shortest possible routes between each other, whereas many smaller order nodes have devious routes in their connection with the rest of the system.

The tortuosity ratio or route factor values are based on:

$$Tr = \frac{AD}{DD} \quad (4.5)$$

where Tr is the tortuosity ratio,
AD is the aggregate actual road distance, and
DD is the aggregate travel distance based on direct or straight line distances.

The following Table 4.4 shows the ranking of the nodes based on route factor ratio.

Basirhat and Englishbazar have least deviousness as signified by their route factor ratio near to one. Since the straight line distances are measured irrespective of physical constraints, while route distances are measured by taking into considerations the physical obstructions, the route factor ratio will be more than one, and if the value of the ratio is nearer to one the node will have less deviousness. As the ratio increases, the deviousness will also increase. The big urban centres show high route factor ratio, e.g., Calcutta, Durgapur and Kharagpur which indicate that deviousness are more in reaching these centres. The major urban centres are located near large rivers, hence caused deviouness.

TABLE 4.4: Route Factor Ratio

Nodes	Aggregate Route Distance (kms)	Aggregate straight line distance (kms)	Route Factor	Rank
Englishbazar	4522	4220	1.07	1
Basirhat	4046	3711	1.09	2
Habra	3857	3423	1.12	3
Siliguri	7295	6451	1.13	4
Bongaon	4394	3711	1.18	5
Berhampore	3712	3137	1.18	5
Asansol	4444	3689	1.20	7
Cooch Behar	9914	8151	1.22	8
Santipur	3759	3088	1.22	8
Purulia	5615	4565	1.23	10
Krishnanagar	3915	3190	1.23	10
Jalpaiguri	8341	6668	1.25	12
Calcutta	3771	2999	1.26	13
Howrah	3706	2943	1.26	13
Burdwan	4056	3139	1.29	15
Durgapur	4673	3388	1.34	16
Midnapore	5413	3979	1.36	17
Naihati	4296	3089	1.39	18
Kharagpur	5243	3634	1.44	19

West Bengal has got large number of rivers and rivulets with unbridged gaps and missing links which act as a constraint in the system, increasing the route factor. The average route factor of the network works out to be 1.21

Holroyd[3] calculated average route factor for a network of regular geometry as 1.21, and it is applicable for both square and hexagonal networks. Since average route factor obtained is 1.21, it shows the network is of regular geometry.

Calcutta and Howrah have route factor value between the maximum and minimum in the network, i.e., ½ (1.07 + 1.44) = 1.255.

4.1.6 *Capacity of roads*

Capacity of roads is also of consideration, because the number of lanes, width, nature of surface etc. of the roads affect the flow capacity of routes.

TABLE 4.5: Road Capacity

Type of Road	Highway Capacity (India as a whole) Maximum Capacity in P.C.U. per day
Single lane Road (3.66 M or 12′-0″ wide surface)	1,000
Two lane Road (6.71 M to 7.32 M. or 22′-0″ to 24′-0″ wide surfaced)	4,000
Four lane divided road each having two lanes (13.4 M and 14.63 M or 44′-0″ and 48′-0″ wide surfaced)	
(a) where slow moving animal drawn vehicles are permitted	12,000
(b) where slow moving animal drawn vehicles are not permitted	16,000
(c) where slow moving vehicles are not permitted and access is controlled and crossing are at grade	25,000

Note: P.C.U = Passenger Car Unit
Source: Chief Engineer, Road Wing, Ministry of Transport, Government of India.

In West Bengal, the road capacity as measured by P.W.D. (Roads) are given in Table 4.6.

TABLE 4.6: Road Capacity in West Bengal

Type of Road	No. of vehicles/day exceeding 30 Cwt unladen weight	Approximate equivalent Tons of traffic/day
National highway	1500 – 4500	12,000-36,000
State highway	450 – 1500	4,000-12,000

Source: Executive Engineer, P.W.D. (Roads), West Bengal.

From the above Table 4.6, the average equivalent tons of traffic/day works out to —

National highway — 24,000

State highway — 8,000

In this study the above values are multiplied by the local degree or road degree to derive the weight carrying capacity for each of the nodes.

For example, if a particular node has a road degree of 5 composed of 2 National highways and 3 State highways, then the capacity available is:

National highway — 2 X 24,000 = 48,000
State highway — 3 X 8,000 = 24,000

Road capacity = 72,000
equivalent tonnes of traffic/day.

Road capacity of the different nodes are shows in Table 4.7.

TABLE 4.7: Nodal Road Capacity

	Road Capacity	Rank
Calcutta	1,44,000	1
Kharagpur	72,000	2
Durgapur	72,000	2
Berhampore	64,000	3
Habra	56,000	4
Siliguri	56,000	4
Naihati	48,000	5
Basirhat	48,000	5
Santipur	48,000	5
Krishnanagar	48,000	5
Englishbazar	48,000	5
Asansol	32,000	6
Howrah	56,000	4
Burdwan	32,000	6
Midnapore	32,000	6
Bongaon	24,000	7
Jalpaiguri	24,000	7
Cooch Behar	24,000	7
Purulia	16,000	8

Note: Road capacity is in equivalent tonnes of traffic per day.

In this analysis we observe that Calcutta scored the highest weight carrying capacity having a road degree of 6. Durgapur and Kharagpur come next to Calcutta both having the same weight carrying capacity.

4.1.7 *Road degree*

Local degree or road degree is the number of routes crossing or converging at a particular node. Usually the summation of rows and columns of the direct connectivity matrix yields the local degree of nodes.

The higher the local degree of an individual node the greater is its accessibility from the rest of the nodes.

It would be expected that the largest towns should both attract and generate the largest flows, and because they are large they should also have the highest degree of connectivity with the rest of the sub-system. Furthermore, the largest flows should be partially related to connectivity itself, for the higher the local degree the greater the amount of traffic that can be carried.

The average population figures are much higher for the nodes with the highest local degree and the traffic flow incidents upon these nodes are also considerably greater. Calcutta scored 6 in road degree followed by Durgapur 5 and Berhampore 4.

4.1.8 *Aggregate travel distance*

In order to determine the accessibility of a place to the rest of the nodes in the system, the centrality in terms of the route distance between each dyad in the system is measured. The lesser the total distance involved in reaching a place from all other places, the greater is its centrality and the greater is its base for interaction with the rest of the nodes. Centrality of a town is an expression, which means its 'centralness' considering the entire road network.

Based on the aggregate travel distance nodes are graded into higher and lower order centres in Table 4.8.

From the following Table 4.8, it is apparent that Howrah is the most central to the entire network. Howrah could be reached by covering the minimum distance in the system, and therefore the most central.

Berhampore has ranked after Howrah followed by Calcutta and Santipur. These three centres (Berhampore, Calcutta and Santipur) are connected by National Highway No. 34.

Centralisation takes place in the urban hierarchy since improved access increases the competitive ability of higher order centres compared to the lower order centres.

TABLE 4.8: Centrality of Nodes in the Network

Nodes	Aggregate Travel Distance (in kms)	Ranking
Howrah	3706	1
Berhampore	3712	2
Santipur	3759	3
Calcutta	3771	4
Habra	3857	5
Krishnanagar	3951	6
Basirhat	4046	7
Burdwan	4056	8
Naihati	4296	9
Bongaon	4394	10
Asansol	4444	11
Englishbazar	4522	12
Durgapur	4673	13
Kharagpur	5243	14
Midnapore	5413	15
Purulia	5615	16
Siliguri	7295	17
Jalpaiguri	8341	18
Cooch Behar	9914	19

4.1.9 *Distance to nearest Class I town*

Network development and connectivity pattern is controlled by the location of higher order centres. If a small centre is located near a higher order centre, it would be in an advantageous position than the other located far off. The total connectivity of smaller centres is influenced by it's relative location with reference to highly connected centres.

For each of the nineteen nodes (based on 100,000 and above population) distance to the nearest Class I node have been computed which is an inverse indicator of transport facility. If the node itself is Class I, then it's distance to any other Class I town nearest to it is measured. The distance measurement is based on shortest actual route distance.

The values thus derived are interpreted by higher value indicating lesser transport facility for that node and vice-versa.

TABLE 4.9: Nearest Class I town distances

Centres	Distance to nearest Class I town (in kms)	Ranking
Midnapore	10	1
Calcutta	18	2
Howrah	18	2
Santipur	19	3
Naihati	46	4
Habra	49	5
Durgapur	50	6
Asansol	50	7
Burdwan	63	8
Basirhat	65	9
Purulia	74	10
Berhampore	76	11
Bongaon	79	12
Kharagpur	105	13
Krishnanagar	156	14
Englishbazar	194	15
Siliguri	370	16
Jalpaiguri	476	17
Cooch Behar	558	18

From the above Table 4.9, we find that Calcutta and Howrah, both Class I towns, have eighteen kilometres distance separating them, and in the case of Midnapore the distance is ten kms from Kharagpur. If we consider this indicator of distance to nearest Class I town, then we can say that Midnapore is in an advantageous position than the others in the system, because of its location nearest to a Class I town.

Calcutta and Howrah scored high in all the other indices too, and no doubt the most accessible cities.

After these centres, Santipur is only nineteen kilometres distant from Krishnanagar, and therefore we can also say that Santipur is occupying an advantageous position.

PART - II

4.2 Aggregate Measures of Transport Facilities (Network) of Nodes

This part deals with the position of each node in relation to all others in the system. The position is obtained by applying some measures of accessibility which has already been discussed in Part-I.

The aggregate accessibility of each node in relation to others in the system is measured statistically through Multivariate Analysis. Based on component score, (which is one of the Multivariate methods) hierarchy of nodes has been ascertained so that the aggregate accessibility of each node in relation to others could be derived.

'There is established reciprocal relationship between the towns and transportation, as the latter is a vital factor in evolution, growth and development of the former, being thereby decisive in determination of its rank and size'.[4]

The six different indicators of nodal transport facilities discussed in Part-I, are the tools for measurement of aggregate accessibility score for each node in relation to all other nodes in the system. In order to give an insight into the nature of relations between these six indicators with each other, an inter-correlation matrix between the six indicators has been worked out in Table 4.10.

TABLE 4.10: Matrix of Correlation Coefficients

1. Road degree	1.00000					
2. Road capacity	0.79472	1.00000				
3. Total connectivity	0.70297	0.69536	1.00000			
4. Tortuosity Ratio	0.33740	0.49320	0.48131	1.00000		
5. Aggregate Travel distance	0.21068	0.08573	0.51027	-0.08516	1.00000	
6. Distance to nearest Class I town	0.23646	0.12059	0.53608	-0.07863	0.93912	1.00000

Both logical relationships and statistical values showing direction of change in the six variables are positive with the exception of tortuosity ratio which showed negative relationship with the aggregate travel distance and distance to Class I town, which are the inverse indicators of network facilities available to nodes. While attempting to compute an aggregate measure, the three inverse indicators (tortuosity ratio, aggregate travel distance and distance to nearest Class I town) have been calculated in an inverse way, i.e., they have been inverted to make them positive indicators of network facilities. Tortuosity ratio showed a weak correlation with the others.

4.2.1 *Elimination of bias of scale*

The problem of compositing variables which indicate different aspects of a phenomenon has been dealt extensively both by Social Scientists and Mathematicians. The problem of compositing has two aspects, the elimination of bias of scale and weightage of different variables.

The variables chosen in a study vary in their unit of measurement. For example, direct connectivity ranges from 1 to 6 (dimensionless number) road capacity between 16,000 to 72,000 equivalent tonnes of traffic per day and distance to nearest Class I town from 10 to 300 kms., while tortuosity ratio from 1.07 to 1.25 (dimensionless number). The variables are not suitable for addition until they are made free of the scale of observation.

The bias of the scale effect may be removed by applying any of the several statistical methods available. One of them is 'Ranking Method' which is still one of the more popular methods of removing bias of scale because of its simplicity and easeness of computation. This method is applied here. All the variables have been standardised by obtaining the deviations from the means of each variables and by dividing the deviations by the standard deviations of the respective series of the original data.

The substraction of mean from each observation lead to a shift in the origin and it equalises the variance and length of all variables. Thus all the points assigned to the selected variables are then equidistant from the origin, the distances being unity.

After the variables have been standardised, principal components analysis has been applied to find out the aggregate transport accessibility score of each node in respect to others.

In principal components analysis correlation coefficient matrix is first calculated. This is obtained by transforming the data matrix X (a nXm matrix) into a matrix of standard scores Z (a nXm matrix) and from this is calculated the correlation coefficient matrix R (a mXm matrix).

$$R = (Z^{T}.\ Z/N) \qquad (4.6)$$

where Z^{T} (a mXn matrix) is the transform of
Z matrix, and
N (a 1X1 matrix) is number of observations.

The procedure used is the centroid method. The method is developed originally for factor analysis models as there are more simple procedures available for principal components analysis (Holzinger and Harman, 1941).

First, the total of the correlation coefficients for each row of the matrix S_i has been calculated.

$$S_i = \sum^{6} ij \tag{4.7}$$

where, $j = 1 \quad i = 1$ to 6.

These S_i values are in fact, measures of association between the variables and the first principal component, but in order to represent them as correlation coefficient indices varying between -1.0 and +1.0, they have to be modified. The modification is achieved by scaling them with respect to the square root of the sum of the S_i. Thus,

$$T = \sum_{i=1}^{6} S_i \tag{4.8}$$

Loading for each variable is given by,

$$a_i = \frac{S_i}{\sqrt{T}} \tag{4.9}$$

TABLE 4.11: First Principal Component Analysis

	Loading component I (ai)	Squared loading (ai^2)
a_1	0.7745	0.5999
a_2	0.7526	0.5664
a_3	0.9264	0.8582
a_4	0.5068	0.2568
a_5	0.6278	0.3941
a_6	0.6498	0.4222
	Total	3.0976

As these a_i values are interpreted as correlation coefficients they indicate that all the variables are positively associated with the first component. Variable a_3 is highly correlated, followed by variables a_1, a_2, a_6, a_5, and a_4.

The eigen value or the sum of the squared factor loadings, for the first component is 3.0976. The total variation is 6, so the first component explains 3.0976/6 X 100 = 51.63 per cent of the variation in the original data matrix, leaving 48.37 per cent unexplained.

The first component represents the average variable in this matrix and the percentage of variance of the six variables associated with this average was 51.63 per cent. The squares of these loadings indicated that variables a_1, a_2 and a_3 are very closely related to the average pattern as isolated by the principal component. The first component accounted for about 52 per cent of the variance in the set of six variables by the average pattern.

It is obvious that the variables most explained by the first component left little variation to be associated with a second component, but variables 4, 5 and 6 which have only 25 per cent, 39 per cent and 42 per cent of their respective variations associated with the first, may well form the nucleus of a second common component. The first component describes the largest common dimension of variation in the correlation coefficient matrix, whereas the second component describes the largest common dimension of variation remaining in the matrix.

The second component has been calculated from the residual coefficient matrix pertaining to the variables left after the variation described by the first component. The first residual coefficient matrix has been constructed from the loadings.

From the loadings the correlation coefficient matrix is constructed; this matrix would have existed had the first component completely exhausted all the variation in the original data matrix. If A (6X1 matrix) is the vector of loadings, then this matrix Q (6X6 matrix) is obtained by multiplying A with its transpose.

$$A.\ A^T = Q \tag{4.10}$$

The first factor residual matrix is then obtained by subtracting matrix Q from matrix R.

The resolution vector must be 'forced' in direction of the maximum possible explanation of the residual variance, and this is achieved in the centroid procedure by a reflection, or change in signs, of the variables (Holzinger and Harman, 1941, pp. 361-365) since the first factor residual matrix needs some readjustments.

From the reflected residual matrix, S_i and a_i values can be calculated in the same way as the first component as per equations

4.7 and 4.9.

The related loadings, squared loadings and communality values are given in Table 4.12.

Communality is the sum of the squared loadings for a variable.

$$hj^2 = \sum_{i=1}^{k} Lij^2 \tag{4.11}$$

where, hj^2 is the communality for variable j.
k is the number of components.
Lij is the loading for variable j on component i.

TABLE 4.12: Second Principal Component Analysis

Variable	Loading Component II	Squared Loading	Communality (h^2)
a_1	-.4254	0.1809	.7808
a_2	-.4487	0.2013	.7677
a_3	+.0114	0.0001	.8583
a_4	+.5248	0.2754	.5322
a_5	+.7410	0.5491	.9432
a_6	+.7253	0.5261	.9483
		Total : 1.7329	

By observing Table 4.11 and 4.12, we can conclude the following:

(1) *Groups of related variables:* The two components pick out two clear groups, one comprise of a_1, a_2 and a_3 while the other groups of a_5 and a_6 with a_4 unrelated to either group as has been found from the communality. But a_4 is not completely exclusive as it has a loading of 0.5 for the first component but influence of any one of the groups is not strong.

(2) *Reducing the number of variables for the study:* Two groups has been identified and one variable from each group can be selected in order to simplify the study. For the first group, a_3 would be the ideal choice since it has the largest loading on Component I. Similarly a_6 would be the ideal choice for the second group.

(3) *Rewriting the data set:* The six original variables among which there was substantial inter-correlation, have been replaced by

two, which are weighted combinations of the former and one independent of each other.

The two variables chosen are the total connectivity and the distance to Class-I town, the former being the positive indicator while the latter inverse indicator. Therefore, of all the variables, these two have the greatest bearing on determining the aggregate total accessibility score of each node.

The components are identified in terms of the original variables; the larger the loading, the more important is that variable in the interpretation of the component. In this analysis total connectivity has the highest loading, therefore, it is the most important among all the variables for determining the aggregate accessibility scores of each node in the system (Fig. 4.4).

If an observation has high values for the variables with large loadings on the component, then it should have a high value on the component. To analyse the components, the component score for observation i on component k is found out, by the formula:

$$Sik = \sum_{j=1}^{n} Dij\,Ljk \tag{4.12}$$

where, *Sik* is the score of observation on component k,
Dij is the standardised value for observation i on variable j, and
Ljk is the loading of variables on component k.

The full set of scores for each observation on each component indicates the value for every node on all of the new variables. The component scores are outlined in Table 4.13.

According to equation (4.12), component scores are weighted summed values for the observations over the variables, the weights being the component loadings. The larger the value which an observation has on the variables which have high loadings on a component, the larger the score.

In terms of the component I (the level of accessibility of each node in the system), Calcutta with a high positive score is above average in regard to total accessibility, while Bongaon with high negative value indicates the reverse. Negative scores on component I show below average total accessibility.

TABLE 4.13: Aggregate Accessibility of Nodes : Component Scores

Nodes	Component Scores	
	Component I	Component II
Purulia	- 1.75	+ 0.22
Asansol	- 1.70	- 0.13
Durgapur	+ 2.58	- 1.61
Burdwan	- 0.24	- 0.51
Howrah	+ 0.86	- 0.20
Calcutta	+ 6.29	- 3.29
Kharagpur	+ 1.73	- 0.49
Midnapore	- 1.22	+ 0.18
Naihati	- 0.83	+ 0.40
Basirhat	- 0.56	- 0.54
Habra	- 1.59	- 1.14
Bongaon	- 3.18	+ 0.43
Santipur	- 0.23	- 0.99
Krishnanagar	- 1.01	- 0.16
Berhampore	+ 1.04	- 0.33
Englishbazar	- 1.22	+ 0.25
Siliguri	+ 0.95	- 1.85
Jalpaiguri	- 0.32	+ 4.28
Cooch Behar	+ 0.40	+ 5.08

Calcutta also shows high negative score on the second component, since this component is an inverse indicator of accessibility. Therefore, Calcutta is highly accessible.

Calcutta is highly accessible followed by Durgapur, Kharagpur, Berhampore, Siliguri and Howrah. Burdwan, Basirhat and Santipur has the potentiality of becoming highly accessible nodes.

Purulia, Midnapore, Naihati, Bongaon, Englishbazar and Jalpaiguri are the nodes with very poor score value indicating these nodes are indeed the poorly accessible nodes.

Asansol and Krishnanagar are the exceptions, though very poorly scoring, yet these cities could not be termed in the above categories.

From this component analysis, we can say that the general accessibility and the growth of transport network facilities have indirect effect for the need of enhancing connection of some of the urban centres, although the components themselves are not directly affected by such additional network facilities. An emphasis on

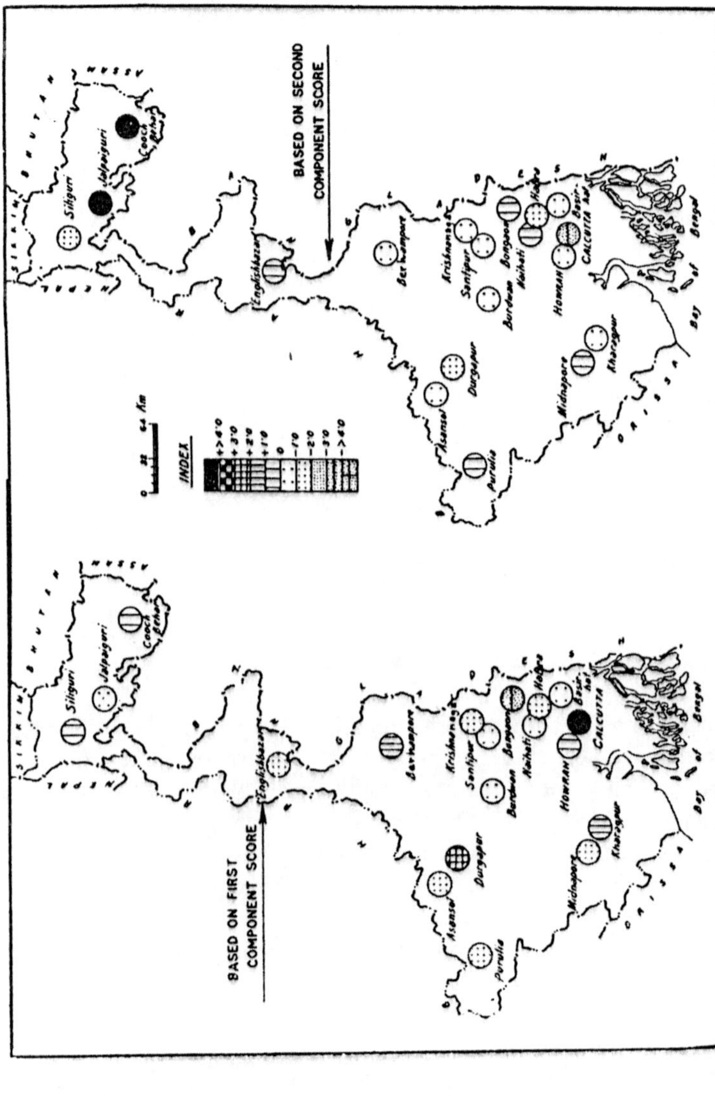

FIG. 4.4: Inter-urban Aggregate Accessibility Index (1974).

providing alternate shorter routes between already connected nodes is also felt. The physical constraints on the development of network is further established, in this analysis.

If we consider the positive indicators, i.e., direct connectivity, local degree or road degree, road capacity and total accessibility, Asansol ranked very poor. This is obvious because of the topologically extreme location of Asansol. Fundamentally, the transport system of the region is designed to meet the demand of the coal mining areas and the centres of traditional industries like iron, steel and refractories. Though Asansol functions as the inter-regional traffic corridor for eastern India yet in the system it reflected a poor accessibility. It is only the intra-state facilities, not the inter-state ones that are reflected in the measures.

Calcutta is a city of commerce and manufacture, the focal point of huge regional network of transportation and communication. This city exerts a powerful economic influence on the total Indian economy. The existing pattern of urbanisation in this region of eastern India is related very close to the geographical distribution of natural resources, and to the associated networks of transportation facilities.

Because of the concentration of industrial cities in its hinterland, Calcutta acts as the main producer and distributor of goods and services, as the source of finance for countless public and private enterprises, as the headquarters of a wide variety of companies and organisations, as the centre for advanced learning and specialised medical services and above all as the generator of changing ideas and attitudes fundamental to progress.[5] It could be said that the high accessibility is one of the most vital measurement of Calcutta's growing economy. Since Calcutta is favoured regarding the accessibility very much, which in fact is a factor for its increasing economic importance.

The Calcutta Metropolitan District (CMD) is formed around the cities and towns which have grown together in one linear pattern of urban development along both banks of the river Hooghly, it provided the best means of transportation to and from the deep water port to the hinterland. Calcutta's unique importance lies in the fact that a vast hinterland is closely bound to it by strong economic ties and looks to it for a host of essential urban services. This again is closely interlinked with the transportation facilities, i.e., accessibility.

In a word, Calcutta's supremacy is no doubt interrelated with accessibility. Followed by Calcutta is the urban complex of Durgapur scoring high accessibility value. Though we speak of Asansol-Durgapur complex, yet in the system Durgapur reflected high accessibility score than Asansol. The reason has already been explained earlier. The Asansol-Durgapur region accommodates a major industrial complex of eastern India.

All the indices chosen for measuring aggregate accessibility of each node in relation to other nodes in the system reflected poor response in Asansol while the case was completely reverse in case of Durgapur. The accessibility established in the system does provide a basic framework that can be improved and modified.

The Durgapur complex covers an area of roughly 77.7 sq.kms. stretching east to west on the Grand Trunk Road. This trunk road and the railway main line (Eastern Railway main line) are the two transportation features which have given Durgapur perhaps a linear shape.

Durgapur is the most rapidly industrialising and urbanising centre today, next only to the Greater Calcutta area. It has been observed by the Planning Organisation in 1966 that "on present indications the major centres of growth in West Bengal over the next twenty years will be the Calcutta Metropolitan District, the Asansol-Durgapur region, Haldia and greater Siliguri".[6]

In view of the strong industrial base established, Durgapur is the fastest growing centre in the whole of the Asansol Sub-division. During the period 1966-1971, in particular, maximum stress and attention had been given for achieving a sufficiently rapid rate of growth in this major centre.

Almost all important urban centres in the system are linked by the existing network system. Therefore, inadequacy of communication linkages or the difficulties of providing adequate linkages are no longer the factors, only the problem is largely one of improving the standards and conditions of the considerable existing linkages and promoting the easy, and economic flow of inter-regional traffic units, through and out of these urban centres.

Kharagpur has also ranked as highly accessible node, followed by Durgapur. It has been found from the analysis that all the centres which are highly accessible, are also centre of urban agglomeration.

As has been pointed out by Planners that urban agglomeration would take place in the following region:

(i) Asansol-Durgapur region,
(ii) Kharagpur-Haldia region,
(iii) Greater Siliguri.

And transportation played the major role in accelerating this agglomeration in the above-mentioned nodes. Though Kharagpur is located in southern West Bengal, it's dominance over the other nodes is due to its accessibility. This region, when integrated with Haldia, will be forming another important growth centre.

Berhampore located on National Highway No. 34, is also categorised as highly accessible. Being located in the central position of the system, it enjoyed connectivity from all parts of West Bengal.

Siliguri is a major centre in the transport lines between south Bengal, north Bihar, Assam, Sikkim and Bhutan. In other words, Siliguri acts as a focal point in the transport system of North-Eastern India. Hence, the centre is reflected with high accessibility value. Siliguri is today the most important traffic and transportation junction in North Bengal.

Purulia, Midnapore, Naihati, Bongaon, Englishbazar and Jalpaiguri are nodes with poor accessibility. Purulia is the most backward and neglected centre, and is surrounded by a number of developed and developing urban industrial complexes and therefore full advantage of its location could be taken if accessibility improves. A large commercial and transport centre may be developed here for which infrastructural development, e.g., building of roads, bridges, etc., is called for.

The Planning Commission have declared Purulia, Midnapore and Darjeeling districts of West Bengal as backward districts which deserve special attention for development of road communications. The connectivity of these centres are low, as found in this analysis.

Since the places are defined partly on urban size criteria and partly on their topological position, Midnapore being located at the end of the topology scored a low value. And all such remaining nodes scored poor accessibility not only due to their extreme topological position but also due to road capacity, road degree, aggregate travel distances, route factor and distance to nearest Class-I town. Only total connectivity is related very closely to the topological transformation of network.

It has been found from the study that centralisation takes place in the urban hierarchy because improved access increases the competitive ability of higher-order centres vis-a-vis lower order centres. A reciprocal relationship exists between interaction and structure and changes in one give rise to changes in the other. The characteristics of a place is influenced to a large extent by the type of links it has with other places.

Transportation makes cities possible, cities are not self-sufficient; they exist only because of the specialised functions they perform for their surrounding areas or hinterland. All these functions depend upon transportation network, which enable cities to fulfil their contributory or service areas. The economic base of a city conditions and in its turn conditioned by the transport network.

It has been evidenced in the study that many of the larger urban centres have shown higher growth in inter-nodal connectivity. On the other hand, many small centres which do not record high absolute growth in some distances indicate more than expected rate of growth if each indices are dealt separately. Following points of general references emerged from the analysis:

(1) Accessibility is a function not so much of centrality but of location of major trunk lines.
(2) Network accessibility is less representative than connectivity in evaluating the transportation facilities of a node.
(3) The total connectivity of smaller centres is influenced by their relative location with reference to highly connected centres.
(4) The location of higher order centres controls the network development and connectivity pattern.

NOTES

1. Vincent Tidswell, *Pattern and Process in Human Geography*, p.262.
2. The distance matrix (route distance and straight line distance) are shown at the end in the Appendix-V.
3. Alan Hay. *Transport for the Space Economy: A Geographical Study*, 1973.
4. Some Aspects of Transportation in Dhanbad *(National Geographical Journal of India*, Vol. 8. 1972). S.L. Kayastha and D.N. Singh, p.64.
5. Basic Development Plan, C.M.D.A., 1966-1986, p.2.
6. Interim Plan (Asansol), p.16.

5

GROWTH OF AUTOMOBILE TRANSPORT IN WEST BENGAL

Pre- and Post-Independence Period

During the beginning of the First Five Year Plan, the need of an adequate system of inland transport began to make itself felt, as the majority of the villages suffered from extreme isolation. An adequate internal linkage system at once brings out the relative importance of automobile transport, as there is a rise in the demand for facilitating movement of goods, raw materials and people.[1] With the increasing economic activity in the region, good roads as well as transport facilities register a demand of high priority. Increase in road linkages leads to increase in transport activity, and higher transport activity demands still more increase of road linkages, and this circle continues. Since accessibility and mobility are involved in almost everything that developing states seek to achieve, automobile transport has assumed a special significance in the country's economic development.

After the First World War, mechanised road transportation began to be introduced on somewhat larger scale in the country's economy. Today, the motor truck is rapidly replacing the bullock cart as the main form of conveyance for all types of goods movement by road. Motor cars and buses have almost entirely replaced the horse drawn vehicles for passenger transport. Some of the cities and towns have now well-organised but services. Long distance road transport services carrying passengers and goods between important towns and cities have been established on the regular basis, firmly and extensively. People in the countryside also, are now becoming conscious about the need of smooth and efficient system of passengers and goods transport by buses and trucks.

The useful role of road transport was amply demonstrated during the Indo-Pakistan conflict in 1965. In the words of Shri Raj Bahadur, the then Union Minister of Transport, "Road transport operators, played a magnificent role. They most willingly offered their vehicles at short notices for the carriage of defence personnel and material to the front and for the movement of essential supplies within the country. Their drivers and cleaners and, in many cases, the owners themselves showed a unique sense of patriotism and drove the vehicles in the forward areas without caring for their personal safety".

Automobile transport is a major factor in the economic growth of a country and it plays a significant role in the country's development and it's defence.

5.1 Genesis of Automobile Transport in West Bengal

There were only a few thousand vehicles before the commencement of the First World War, consisting largely of motor cars and taxis, in British Bengal. During the war, a large number of vehicles were imported, mostly motor cars. Sizeable imports of commercial vehicles, i.e. buses and vans started only from the early twenties.

With the end of the First World War, the introduction and development of automobile transport increased in dimension, and it demanded better roads capable of withstanding the centuries old bullock cart traffic as well as the new form of transport. The existing roads at that time could not survive the combined disintegrating action of such mixed traffic.

Table 5.1 shows the development of automobile transport in Bengal from 1913 to 1947. The proper index of development of motor transport is the number of motor vehicles operating in the State in the particular year.

Average value of imports of motor cars, motor cycles and spare parts thereof for the five years from 1909-10 to 1913-14 was Rs. 32,94,344 as against Rs. 38,95,236 for 1914-15 to 1918-19. In the subsequent three years of 1919-20, 1920-21 and 1921-22, these figures were Rs. 14,178,362, Rs. 49,068,555 and Rs. 9,133,633. In 1934-35 the value of imports of motor cars into Calcutta was Rs. 76,37,867 and in 1935-36 Rs. 77,30,598.

Prior to 1914, the operation of motor vehicles in the provinces of Bengal were regulated by various provincial acts. Indian Motor Vehicles Act, 1914, was the first all India enactment for controlling of motor vehicles. It did not make any distinction between different types of motor vehicles nor any attempt was made to restrict their free movement.

TABLE 5.1: Motor Vehicles Registered in Bengal and in use in Bengal (1913-1947)

	Selected Years											
	1913	1914	1923	1924	1925	1926	1938	1939	1940	1941	1942	1943
(a) Private Cars	3,199	3,937	10,300	12,385	14,560	17,369	17,042	15,876	19,322	16,202	13,477	13,746
(b) Motor buses	—	—	15	35	280	448	1,952	1,974	2,205	2,337	1,413	2,537
(c) Taxis	136	322		1,430	949	956	2,087	2,245	2,132	3,090	1,611	4,111
(d) Commercial goods vehicles	—	—	867	1,032	818	760	2,829	3,055	4,681	3,360	2,829	4,812
(e) Motor cycles	723	966	2,443	2,863	3,141	3,482	375	417	1,003	506	854	917

Source: Indian Road Development Committee, 1927-28.

Note: The figures shown (except motor buses, taxis and commercial goods vehicles) for the years 1925 and 1926 represent the total number of such vehicles registered upto the end of the year and not the number of vehicles in use. The figures of motor buses, taxis and commercial goods vehicles for the years 1925 and 1926 represent the total number of vehicles registered and re-registered (renewal of registration) during these years. The figures shown do not include vehicles which are running in Bengal but are registered in other Provinces. During and immediately after the Second World War there was a rapid expansion of goods vehicles in the country. The number of motor vehicles of all kinds imported into India was only 4,419 in 1913-14 but has risen to 25,950 in 1927-28.

In comparison to the growth of motor vehicles, growth of bullock carts which was then the most important form of road transport, would be understood from the following Table 5.2:

TABLE 5.2: Number of Bullock Carts in Bengal

	Years				
	1919-20	1924-25	1930-31	1935-36	1940-41
Number of bullock carts	7367	8546	8499	8599	8219

On a resolution passed by both chambers of the Indian Central Legislature in 1927, a Committee was appointed with M.R. Jayakar as Chairman to examine and report on the development of roads in India. The Committee observed that the lack of bridges and crossing was a serious obstacle to traffic of all kinds. As for motor transport regular services would not be satisfactorily established on an unbridged road. The deterioration of the road surfaces was also being aggravated by the operation of motor transport.

The Committee concluded that the development of the road system was desirable, especially so, as it would make economic, social and political advancement of the rural population on which the future of the nation depends.

The most important recommendation made by the Committee affecting road development was that, an additional duty of 2 annas per gallon (12 paise per 4.5 litre) should be levied by the Centre on motor spirit for the specific purpose of road development and that the proceeds should be credited to a separate Road Development Fund. This recommendation was accepted by the Government and the Central Road Fund came into existence on March 1, 1924.

The increasing diversion of traffic from railways to the road and the consequent financial losses to the railways, particularly against the background of steeply declining revenues with the onset of the World-wide depression, drew attention to the importance and urgency of developing a sound policy for regulating road-rail competition.

The Indian Railways Enquiry Committee (1937), better known as the Wedgewood Committee after the name of its Chairman, discussed the question of rail-road competition. As a result of these, the Transport Advisory Council was set-up as a policy making body at the Centre, with the Central Minister (then called Member) dealing with motor transport and the State Ministers of Transport as Members. Motor Vehicles Act was passed in 1939 and in accordance with this Act, rules were framed by the State (Provincial) Governments. The Act provided for the creation of Regional and Provincial Transport Authorities with full powers to grant permits to operate "stage carriers" (buses) "Public carriers" (Public goods vehicle owners) and "Private Carriers" (owners of goods vehicles carrying their own goods) etc. and to lay down conditions (routes, timings, specifications of vehicles, standards of maintenance, etc.) under which the permit holders must operate.

The Act laid down an elaborate procedure and prescribed certain conditions which should be taken into account while considering the issue of permits. Passenger buses which had often been free to move from place to place before the passing of this Act, were now confined to specific routes, under provincial rules which were framed under the Act. Bus stands were also notified and time tables specified. Thus for the first time, passenger transport was provided with a certain amount of regularity.

With the onset of economic depression in 1930, competition between Railway and Road Transport was intensified and in 1932, Government appointed two officers, K.G. Mitchell, Road Engineer and L.H. Kirkness, Railway Officer to enquire into this competition and the possibility of future co-ordination and development. According to their report, the competition between Rail and Road Transport was mainly confined in the field of passenger traffic and that also existed within the zone of 1 to 50 miles. In the report of K.G. Mitchell and L.H. Kirkness, the importance of motorable roads to supplement Railways was felt.

Moreover bus services at that time were mainly for short distances. The following competitive bus services were being run on the G.T. Road and were mostly to cater short distances (1931).

In addition to the bus services on the G.T. Road there were a few services over other roads as given in Table 5.5.

It was observed that competition was acute in short distances than in long distances. As the Report of Mitchell and Kirkness visualised that sharper competition existed between the two forms resulting from improvements of motor vehicles and better organisation of motor transport. As a solution it was suggested that railways themselves should operate automobile transport on routes running parallel to them. Moreover, the number of buses on any route might be restricted and the issue of time tables publication of schedules of fares and compulsory insurance for them, might be instituted.

TABLE 5.3: Railway and Road Mileage (1932)

	Rail-way (all gauges)	Metalled Roads	Improved or Motor-able Unmetalled Roads	Total Motor-able Roads	Metalled roads which have Railways parallel & within 10 miles to it	Percentage of	
						Metalled road para-llel to Railways	Railway parallel to Metal-led roads
	Miles	Miles	Miles	Miles	Miles		
Bengal	3450	3500	—	3500	1,234	35	36

Source: Report on the present State of Road and Railway Competition by Mitchel & Kirkness.

TABLE 5.4: Short Route Bus and Railway Services (1931)

Section	Mileage		No. of buses	Fares	
	Railway	Road		Railway Rs. a. p.	Road Rs. a. p.
Howrah-Ballykhal	6	6	24	0 1 5	0 2 3
Ballykhal-Serampore	7	8	32	0 2 0	0 2 6
Serampore-Chinsura Court	11	13	28	0 3 3	0 5 0
Chinsura Court-Tribeni	8	9	9	0 2 3	0 4 6
Burdwan-Memari (On route Kalna Court)	16	17	2	0 5 0	0 5 0
Burdwan-Masagram (via Memari) on route to Chakdighi	15	21	1	0 4 0	0 4 0
Burdwan-Kankar	23	25	2	0 7 0	0 10 0
Asansol-Gopalpur-Panagarh	35	37	2	0 10 3 (a)	0 13 0 (b)
Raniganj-Asansol	12	7	9	0 5 0	0 4 0
Raniganj-Barakar	22	25	6	0 10 0	0 8 0
Asansol-Barakar	11	12	10	0 5 0	0 4 0

(a) Return journey (b) Single journey.
Source: Report of East Indian Railway.
Note: Bus Services in G.T. Road.

TABLE 5.5: Short Route Bus and Railway Services (1931)

Section	Mileage		No. of buses	Fares	
	Railway	Road		Railway Rs. a. p.	Road Rs. a. p.
Sheoraphuli-Singur	7	8	2	0 2 0	0 2 0
Sainthia-Suri	12	13	8	0 4 0	0 6 0
Suri-Dubrajpur	12	7	3	0 3 6	0 6 0
Ondal-Ukhra	8	7½	1	0 2 6	0 5 0
Pandeveswar-Asansol	29	24	2	0 8 0	0 6 0
Asansol-Rupnarayanpur	13	12	1	0 3 9	0 8 0

Source: Report of the East Indian Railway.
Note: Bus Services in roads other than G.T. Road.

The Road Transport Reorganisation (Masani) Committee, 1958 on the other hand, was of the opinion that owing to inherent superiority of road transport, being cheaper to construct, giving higher dividend on capital invested and convenience to the user, there should be free competition between the two (Rail and Road) and no restrictions should be imposed on motor transport. But it is considered necessary to co-ordinate the two types of transport systems in the national interest, to avoid duplication and prevent a rate war. For this reason the Motor Vehicles Act 1939 introduced the permit system and set-up Regional and State Transport Authorities.

The Government promulgated a rail-road co-ordination scheme which aimed at unified control of transport and its development. It was intended to prevent unregulated competition, stop rate wars and duplication of services.

The problem of rail-road co-ordination was recorded during Second World War when the entire transport system of the country was subjected to heavy strain. However, in fear of the situation that might develop after the War, Government of India, Department of War Transport, set-up a Technical Sub-Committee on Transport in 1943, to consider the future of the road transport and road-rail relation in the country.

Their recommendations were:

(1) Goods transport on National Highways should be controlled by the Centre.
(2) The short distance goods traffic by road should be controlled by the Centre.
(3) As regards long distance goods transport by road, competition

between road and rail should be prevented by a system of regulation, combining an expert judgement on the merits of each case on the basis of social and economic needs with scientific zoning.

(4) As regards passenger transport the principle of maximum amalgamation of passenger service operators to form substantial concerns on main routes, and of controlled monopolies on light traffic routes, should be the basis of policy.

(5) Minimum fares both for railways and road transport should be established by agreement.

(6) Railways should develop closer co-operation with road passenger transport and ultimately acquire a commanding interest.

(7) Within the general framework of the constitution adjustment should be made so as to give the Province an interest in Railways and Centre an adequate voice in road transport.

J. White in his article entitled "The Future of Co-ordination between Rail and Road" makes the following comment, "Road improvement will doubtless be carried out at a faster pace, new motor roads widenings, by-pass, wider passes, via ducts and so on. Road capacity will be increased, but the additional capacity is likely to be absorbed faster than it can be created especially in the cities. . .".[2]

Under the Act, State Governments were empowered to prohibit or restrict conditionally by notification in the State Gazette, the conveying of long distance goods traffic by road or of specific classes of goods by private or public carriers with the object of promoting co-ordination between road and rail transport. The regulatory restrictions under the Motor Vehicles Act were later to be embodied in the "Code of Principles and Practices in the Regulation of Motor Transport" and circulated to State Governments for adoption in 1950.

The Motor Vehicles Act, 1939 as amended in 1956, provided the legal framework for the regulation of road transport in the country. It is a Central Act administered by the State Governments through the Regional Transport Authorities (RTA) and the State Transport Authorities, which control the operation of commercial motor vehicles by a system of permits. For inter-state movement the competent authority to grant or countersign permits is the Inter-State Transport Commission.

Road construction was inescapable because roads were the only means of linking the remotest parts of the country. But it would not pay if the roads were only built and the development of road transport lagged behind.

The Government of India therefore appointed in 1958 the Road Transport Reorganisation Committee under the Chairmanship of Shri M.R. Masani to conduct a comprehensive enquiry regarding the existing machinery for the administration of road transport and to make recommendations for the States and other cognate matters.[3]

5.2 Progress under Plans

The progress of road transport under the stimulus of planned programme of development has indeed been striking. In 1951 about 50,561 motor vehicles were plying in West Bengal, which increased by about 40 times, i.e., 2,04,180 in 1976.

Prior to plan periods motor vehicles on road in 1948 was 42,052 which increased to 42,758 in 1949 to 43,397 in 1950 of which private cars were more in number than stage carriers and goods vehicles, the total of such private cars at the end of 1948 was 21,734, which amounted to 21,890 in 1949 and to 22,103 in 1950. Buses were only 2029 in 1948, 2270 in 1949 and 2281 in 1950. Goods vehicles numbered more than buses, total of which were 10,231, 10,490 and 10,580 in those three years.

A true picture of the growth of motor vehicles would emerge if the resigtered motor vehicles in West Bengal were considered. Table 5.6 is constructed by taking the number of registered vehicles in 1967 as base, by studying this table it will be possible to get an insight into the growth of motor vehicles (Fig. 5.1).

TABLE 5.6: Growth of Registered Vehicles in West Bengal (1967-1974)

Year	Goods vehicles	Motor Cycles	Public Service vehicles	Other vehicles	Motor Cars
1967	100	100	100	100	100
1968	143	206	118	84	88
1969	149	286	113	111	99
1970	151	302	117	73	108
1971	184	323	117	85	110
1972	159	348	127	90	117
1973	173	447	139	152	123
1974	176	475	145	140	130

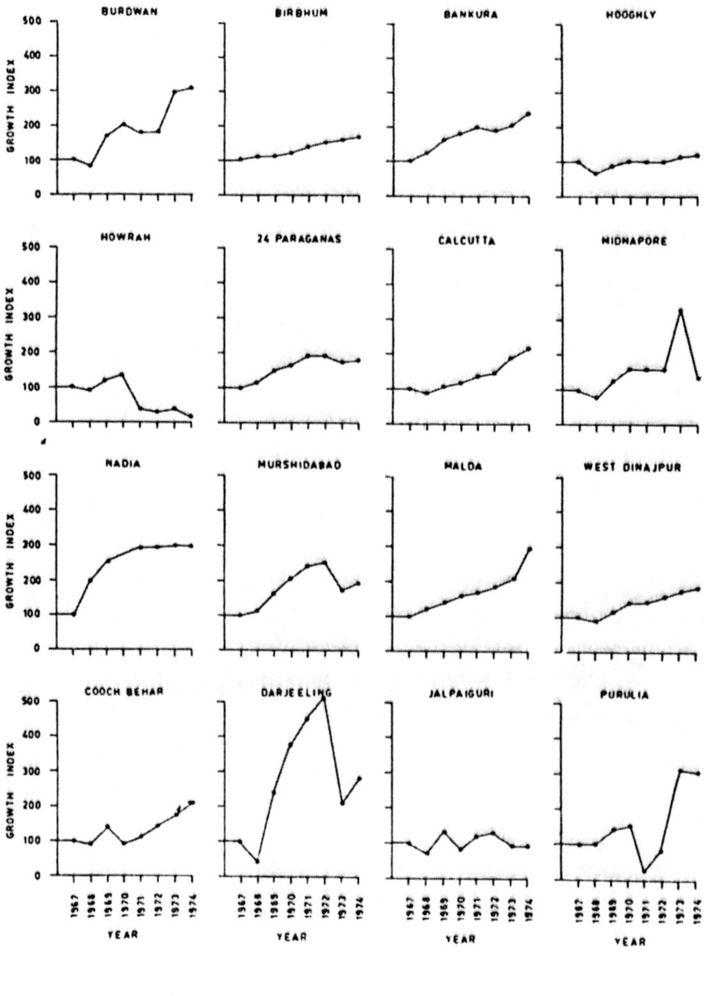

FIG. 5.1: Growth Index of Registered Motor Cycles in Districts of West Bengal.

Growth of motor cycles[4] are high in comparison to all other vehicles, in the period considered. Total motor cycles in West Bengal at the end of 1974 were 35,359 from 7,436 in 1967, representing an increase of 375 per cent, most of these were concentrated in Calcutta. District-wise growth index of registered vehicles focuses some light on the development of motor vehicles in West Bengal. The actual number of registered motor vehicles in each district are tabulated later in Appendix-VII. Growth of Goods vehicles was high in Purulia, Burdwan, Birbhum, Hooghly, Calcutta and Malda. Goods vehicles showed increasing trend in Purulia, there were only 463 goods vehicles in 1967 which increased to 1836 in 1974. Industrialised district like Calcutta and Burdwan depend more on goods vehicles, the total goods vehicles has increased by 22 per cent in Calcutta and 30 per cent in Burdwan, 24-Parganas also showed 17 per cent increase, from 1967 to 1974. West Bengal showed an increasing tendency of goods vehicles, 43 per cent increase in 1968 and 76 per cent increase in 1974, from 1967 (Fig. 5.2).

Public Service Vehicles which includes taxis, stage carriages (State and Private), contract carriages, mention should be made for the growth in this regard of Howrah, Birbhum, Midnapore, 24-Parganas, Purulia, Burdwan and Calcutta in southern West Bengal while Malda, Jalpaiguri, Cooch Behar in the north. The number of such vehicles in Calcutta have increased by 13 per cent, Burdwan by 15 per cent, 24-Parganas by 12 per cent and Midnapore by 13 per cent from 1967 to 1974.

State buses are registered only in the districts of Calcutta and Burdwan in the south and Cooch Behar in the north; and in West Dinajpore, 30 State buses were registered in 1974. During 1974, Cooch Behar issued the largest number of registered State buses amounting to 315. All the other districts possessed only taxis and private buses.

The State buses are concentrated in those three districts because these districts are the headquarters of State Transport Corporations. Calcutta State Transport Corporation having its headquarter in Calcutta, North Bengal State Transport Corporation in Cooch Behar and Durgapur State Transport Corporation in Durgapur.[5]

Public service vehicles were, however, less in number than the goods vehicles in these districts, i.e., Calcutta, Burdwan and Cooch Behar. At the end of 1974, there were only 12,252 public service vehicles in Calcutta, 1,270 in Burdwan and 509 in Cooch Behar, whereas goods vehicles were 18,639 in Calcutta, 4,023 in

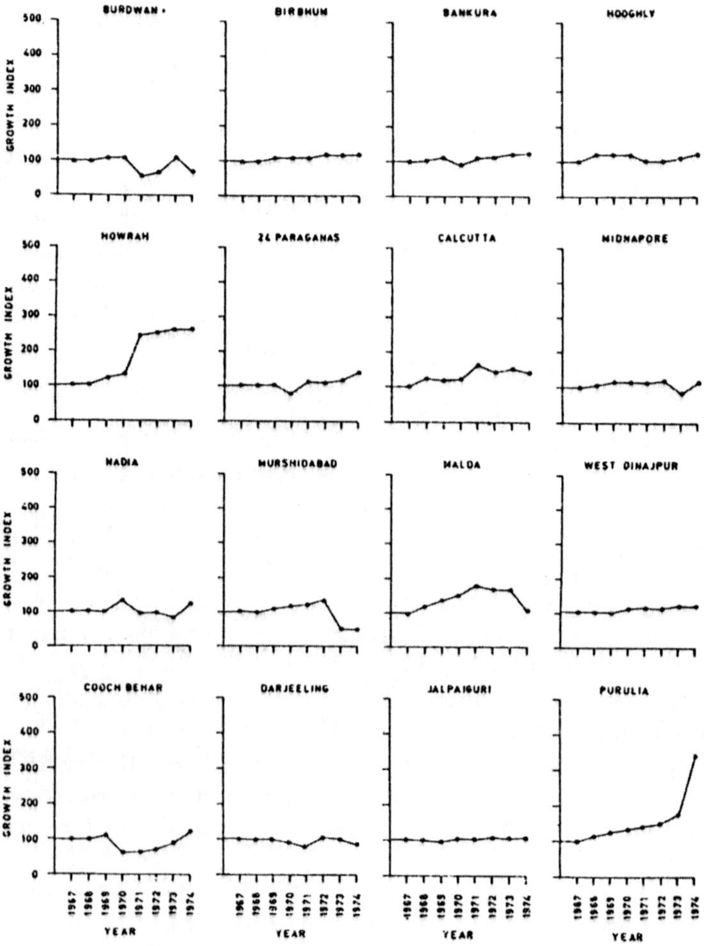

FIG. 5.2: Growth Index of Registered Goods Vehicles in District of West Bengal.

Burdwan and 579 in Cooch Behar. Public service vehicles in West Bengal increased by 18 per cent from 1967 to 1968, and by 45 per cent from 1967 to 1974 (Figs. 5.3 & 5.4).

Motor cars or private cars are the direct indicator of growth of economy in any State. Total number of motor cars in Calcutta was 64,847 in 1974 from 45,163 in 1967, Burdwan has 3,897, 24-Parganas 8,534, Howrah 2,243, Darjeeling 3,584 and Jalpaiguri 1,948 in 1974. West Bengal, however, has recorded a very fluctuating growth of motor cars, it increased by 40 per cent from 1967 to 1974. The number of goods vehicles on the road had increased more than three times during this period, also the number of minor vehicles in the State increased five times since 1950 (Fig. 5.5).

The State had only 43,397 motor vehicles on road as on March 31st, 1950 to 1,90,279 in 1974 to 2,04,180 in 1976. District possessing more registered vehicles are also marked with more motor vehicles on road. As Calcutta's figures are not available (motor vehicles on road) comparison is not possible.

5.3 Road Growth/Motor Vehicles Growth

Since 1951-52 the first year of the First Five Year Plan, road kilometerage has increased from 3.4 thousand kilometres to 5.6 thousand kilometres in 1973-74, the last year of the Fourth Five Year Plan, representing an increase of about 65 per cent.

On the basis of figures of road length for 1973-74, West Bengal has on an average 64 kms. of road length per 100 sq. km. of geographical area of the State as against 36 kms. in the country as a whole. Road transport, however, has increased from 6.4 thousand vehicles in 1953 to 19.0 thousands vehicles on road during 1974, an increase of nearly 195 per cent.[6]

High positive correlation exists between development of roads and development of total vehicles on road in Bankura, Hooghly, Burdwan, Jalpaiguri, Cooch Behar and Birbhum districts. While Howrah, 24-Parganas, Murshidabad, Malda are the districts where both these developments are positively correlated (Fig. 5.6).

Midnapore, West Dinajpore, Darjeeling and Purulia on the other hand show negative correlation between the total length of roads and total motor vehicles on road indicating that development of roads was not proportional to the volume of the vehicular traffic. It could be said that Burdwan, Hooghly, Bankura, Birbhum, Jalpaiguri and Cooch Behar are the districts with well developed road network which facilitated good number of motor vehicles (Fig. 5.7).

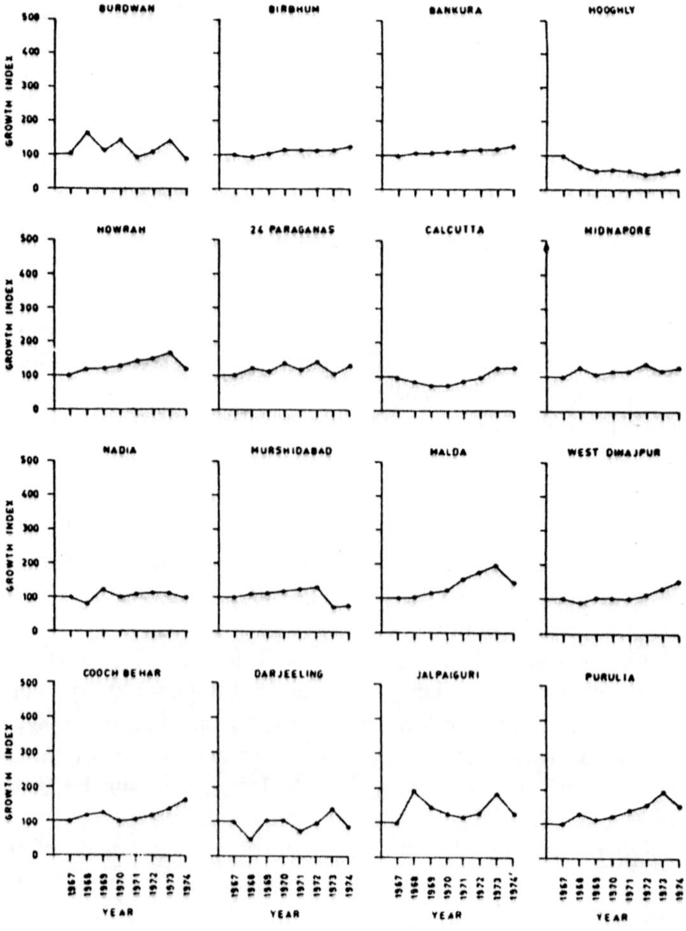

FIG. 5.3: Growth Index of Registered Public Service Vehicles in Districts of West Bengal.

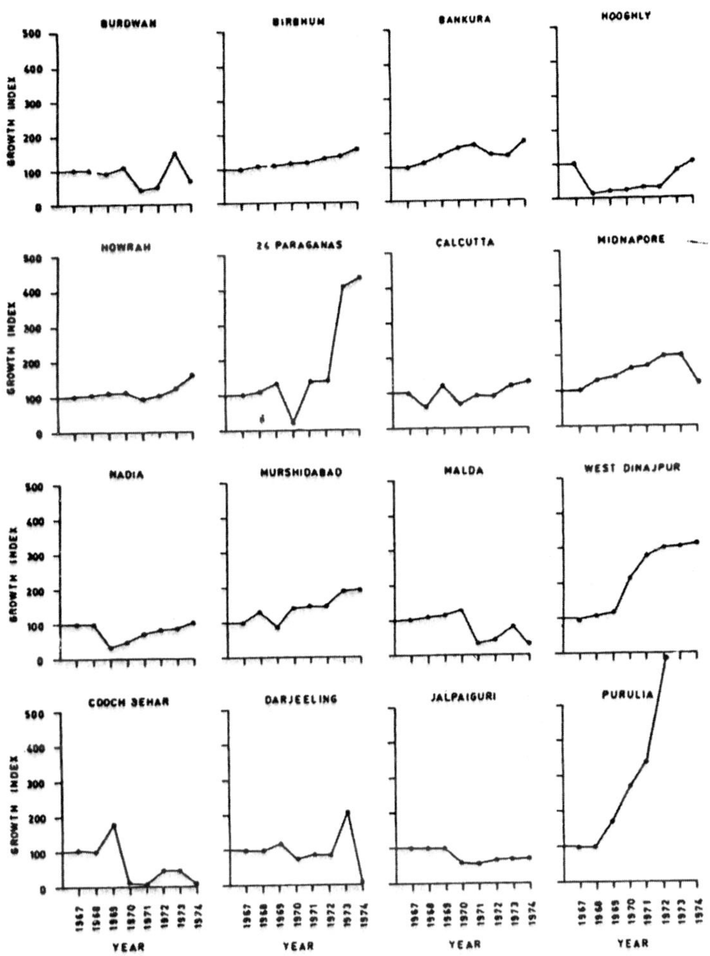

FIG. 5.4: Growth Index of Registered other Vehicles in Districts of West Bengal.

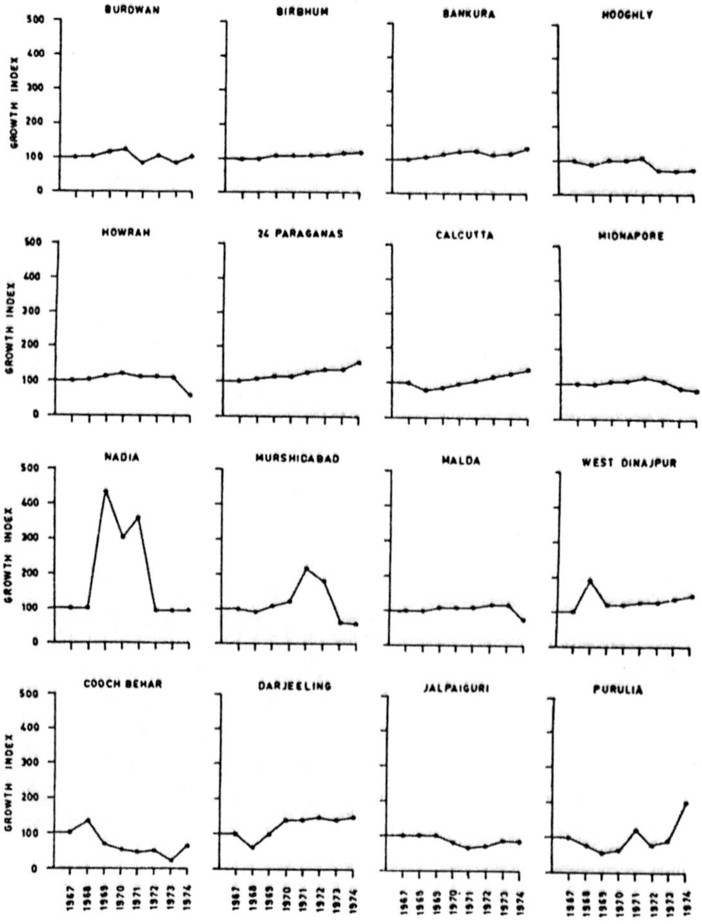

FIG. 5.5: Growth Index of Registered Private Car and Jeep in Districts of West Bengal.

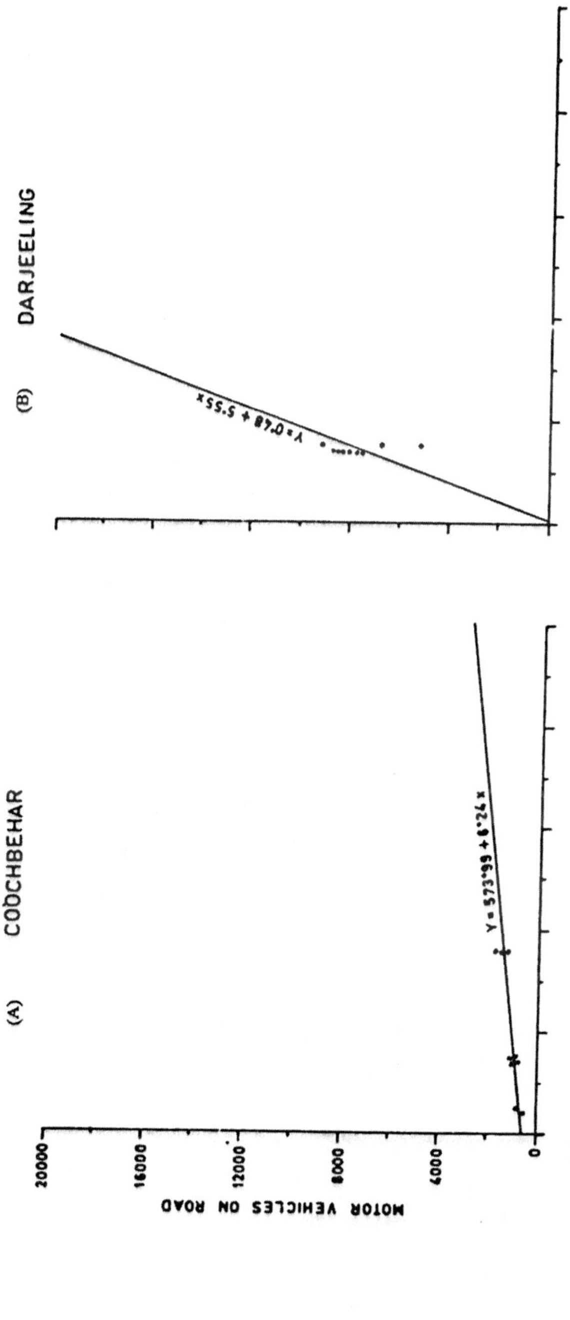

FIG. 5.6: (A, B) Scatter Diagram Showing Relation between Total Road Lengths in kms and Total Motor Vehicles on Road (1966-1974).

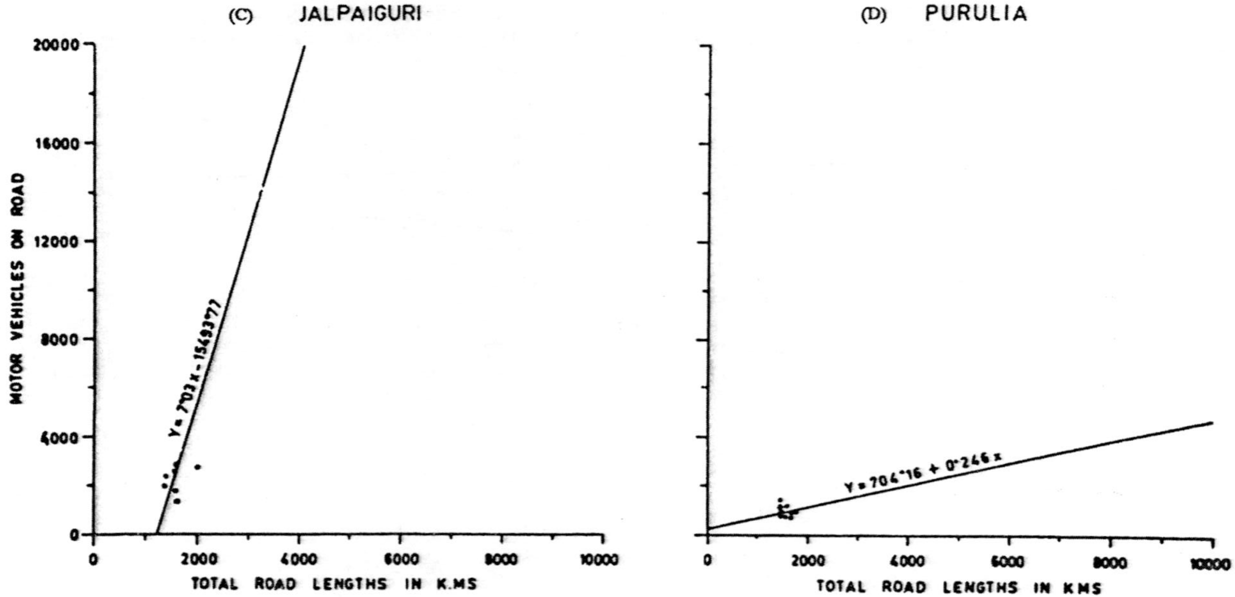

FIG. 5.6: (C, D) Scatter Diagram Showing Relation between Total Road Lengths in kms and Total Motor Vehicles on Road (1966-1974).

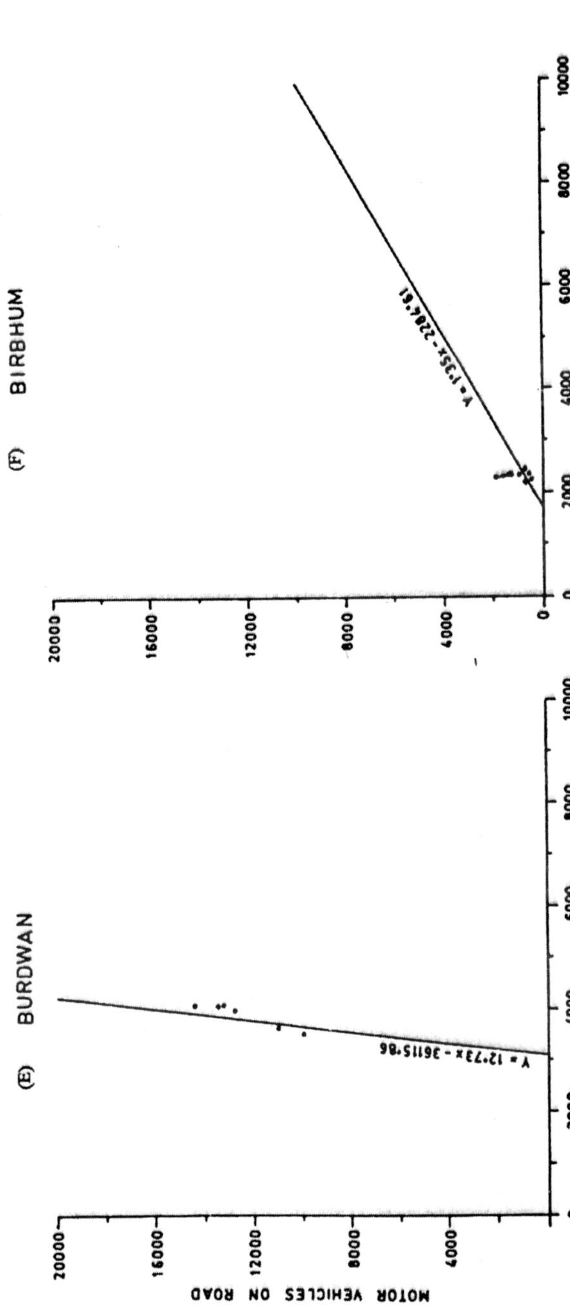

FIG. 5.6: (E, F) Scatter Diagram Showing Relation between Total Road Lengths in kms and Total Motor Vehicles on Road (1966-1974).

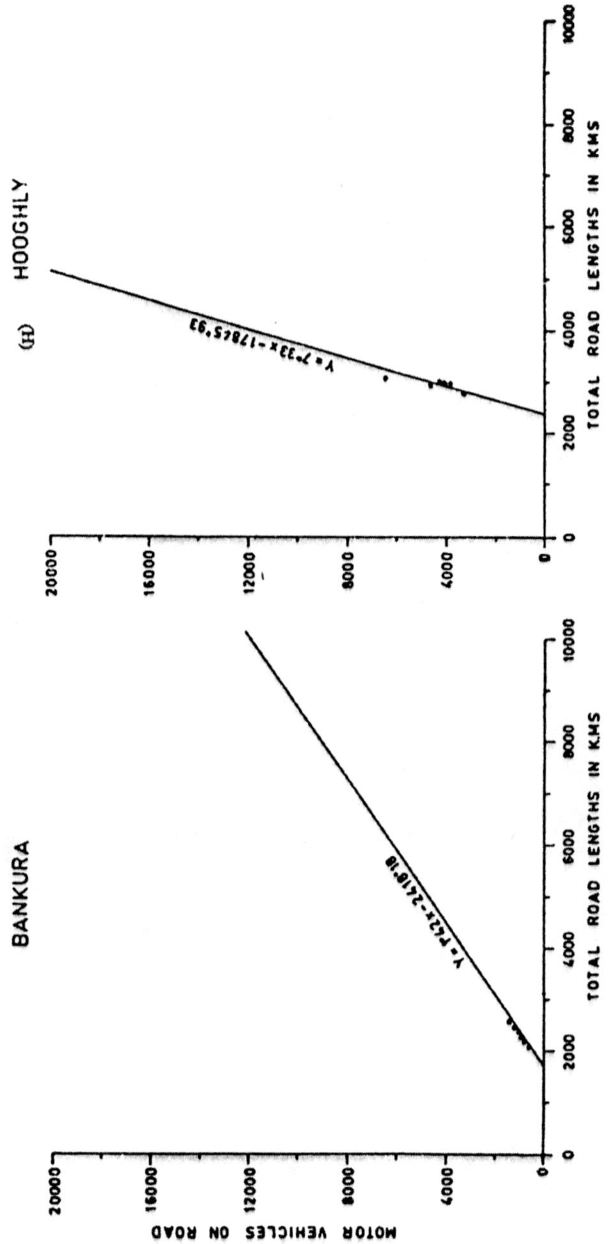

FIG. 5.6: (G, H) Scatter Diagram Showing Relation between Total Road Lengths in kms and Total Motor Vehicles on Road (1966-1974).

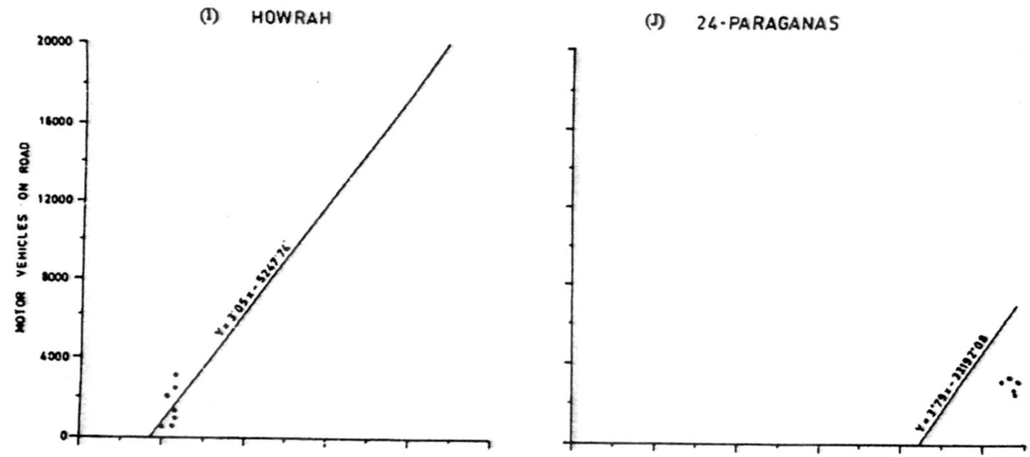

FIG. 5.6: (I, J) Scatter Diagram Showing Relation between Total Road Lengths in kms and Total Motor Vehicles on Road (1966-1974).

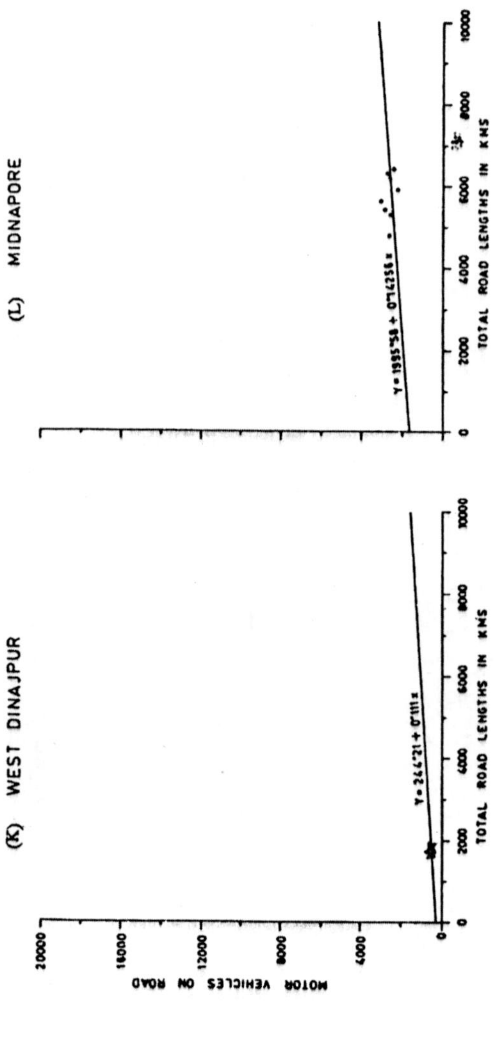

FIG. 5.6: (K, L) Scatter Diagram Showing Relation between Total Road Lengths in kms and Total Motor Vehicles on Road (1966-1974).

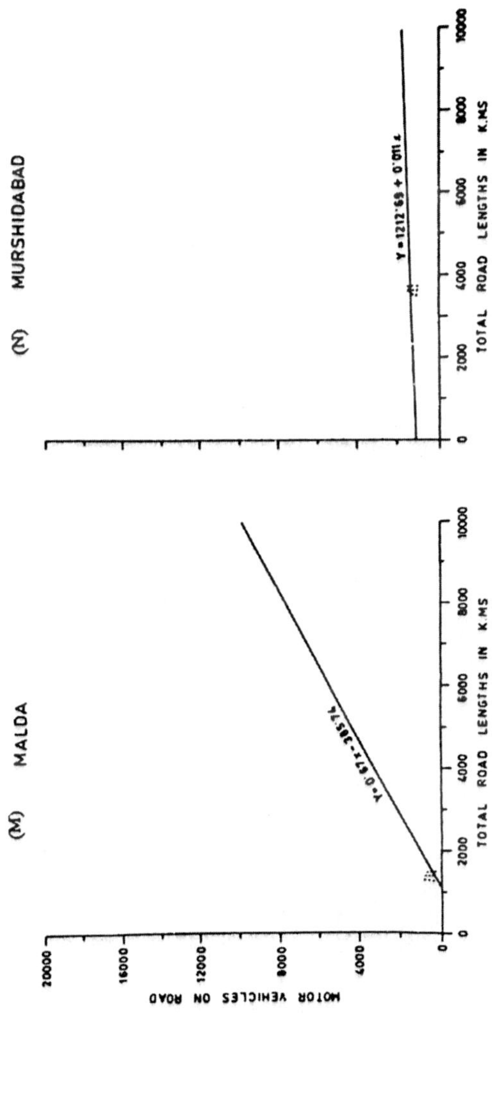

FIG. 5.6: (M, N) Scatter Diagram Showing Relation between Total Road Lengths in kms and Total Motor Vehicles on Road (1966-1974).

In Howrah and 24-Parganas only after 1970 expansion of road transport was significant, these two districts, however, are favoured with extensive road network. Murshidabad and Malda, Purulia and Midnapore do possess extensive road system but motor vehicles on road are not large in number. Darjeeling is the only district where motor cars on road are high as compared to total road kilometerage. The reasons may be for its importance as a tourist centre, and also for defence requirements.

TABLE 5.7: Number of Vehicles in West Bengal in Relation to Area and Population as on 31st March

	Road length per per 100 sq.km. of area	Road length per lakh of population	No. of motor vehicles	
			Per 100 sq.km. of area	Per lakh of population
1960	95.4	94.9	307	306
1961	119	115	339	329
1963			147	350
1966	59	129	162	352
1969			194	390
1972	60.7	120	217	430

Source: Road Facts India 1969 and Basic Road Statistics 1971-72.

It is apparent from the above Table 5.7, motor vehicles per lakh of population and per 100 sq. km. of area, scored highest in 1972, a very fast development in road transport so far.

5.4 Nationalised Road Transport

With the growth of the economic activities in the State, the pressure on the road transport also increased. The State Government nationalised the motor transport services in Calcutta, North Bengal and Durgapur with the objective of providing assured minimum facilities to the public. These nationalised road transport services are now known as:

(1) Calcutta State Transport Corporation (CSTC) operating in Calcutta;
(2) North Bengal State Transport Corporation (NBSTC) operating in Cooch Behar;

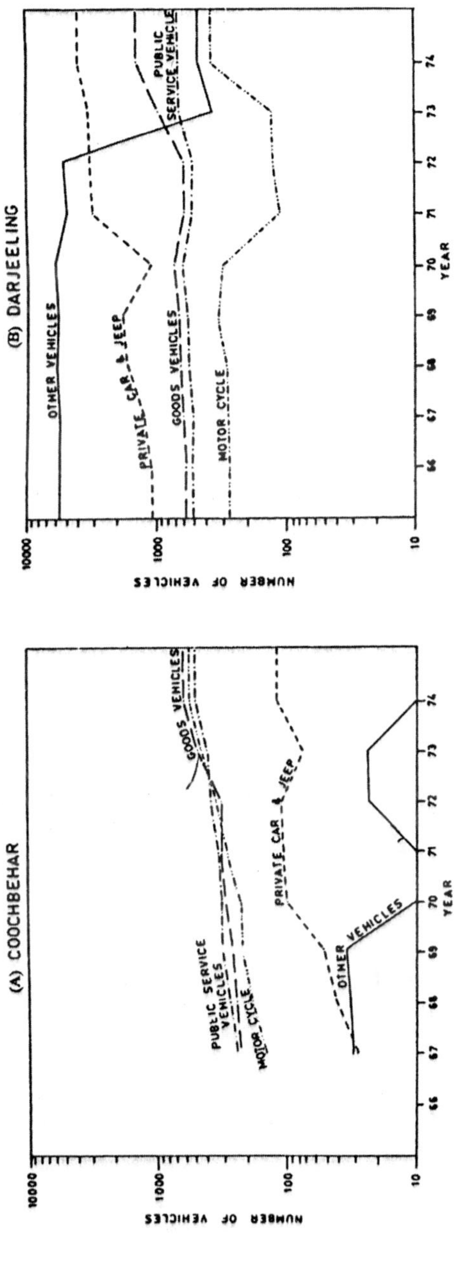

FIG. 5.7: (A, B) Motor Vehicles on Roads in Districts of West Bengal.

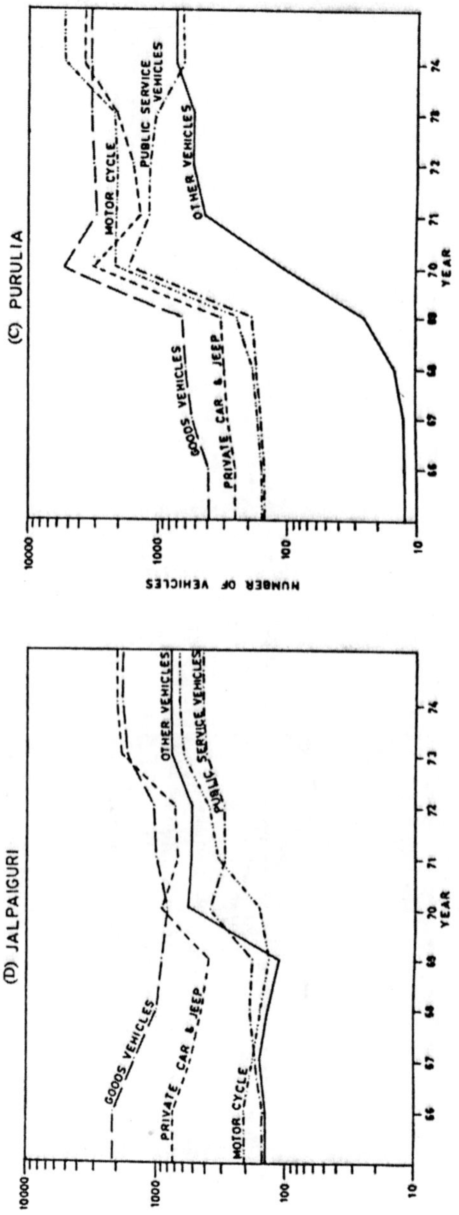

FIG. 5.7: (C, D) Motor Vehicles on Roads in Districts of West Bengal.

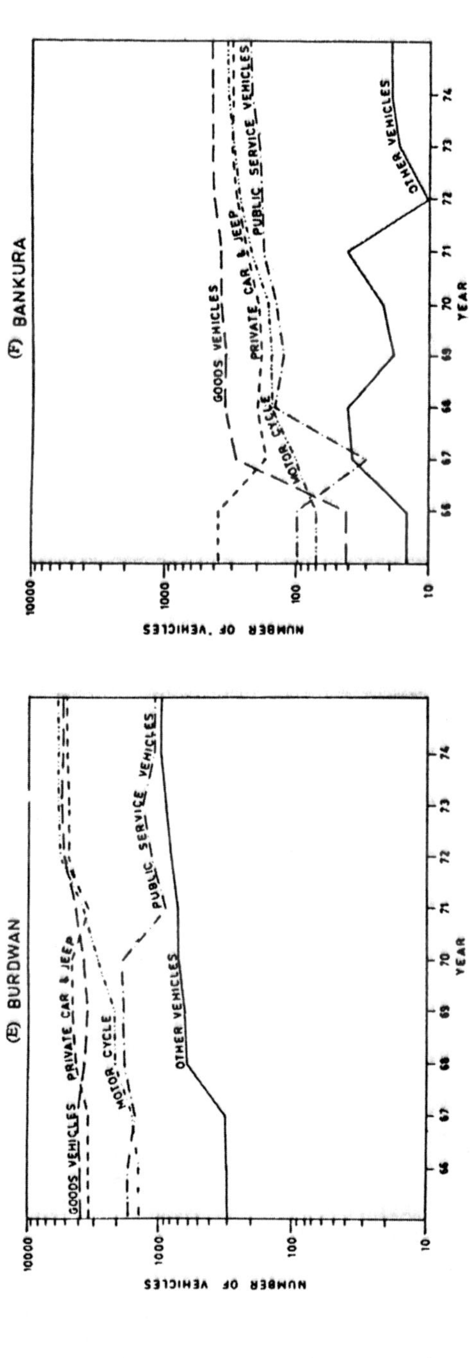

FIG. 5.7: (E, F) Motor Vehicles on Roads in Districts of West Bengal.

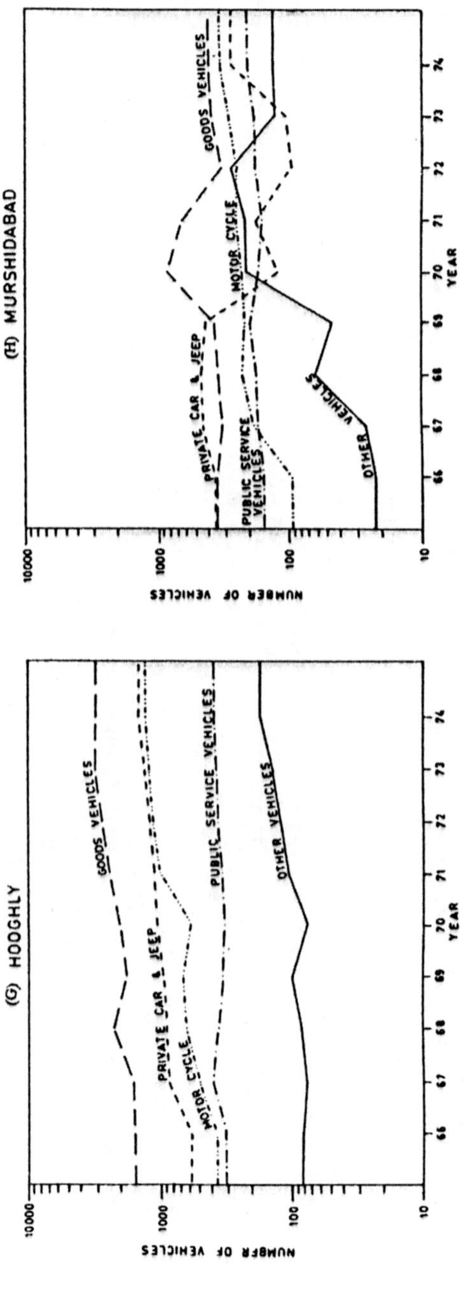

FIG. 5.7: (G, H) Motor Vehicles on Roads in Districts of West Bengal.

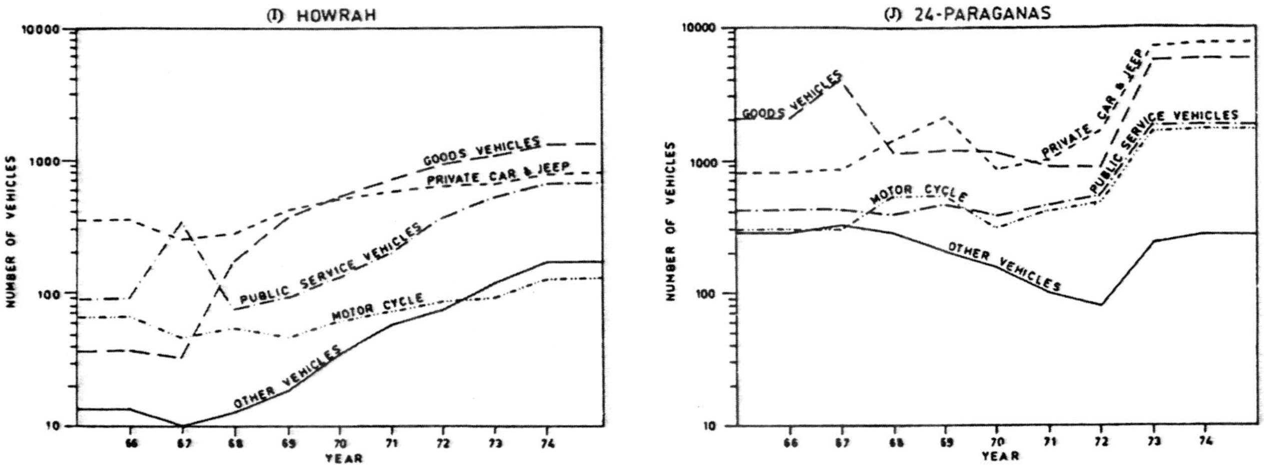

FIG. 5.7: (I, J) Motor Vehicles on Roads in Districts of West Bengal.

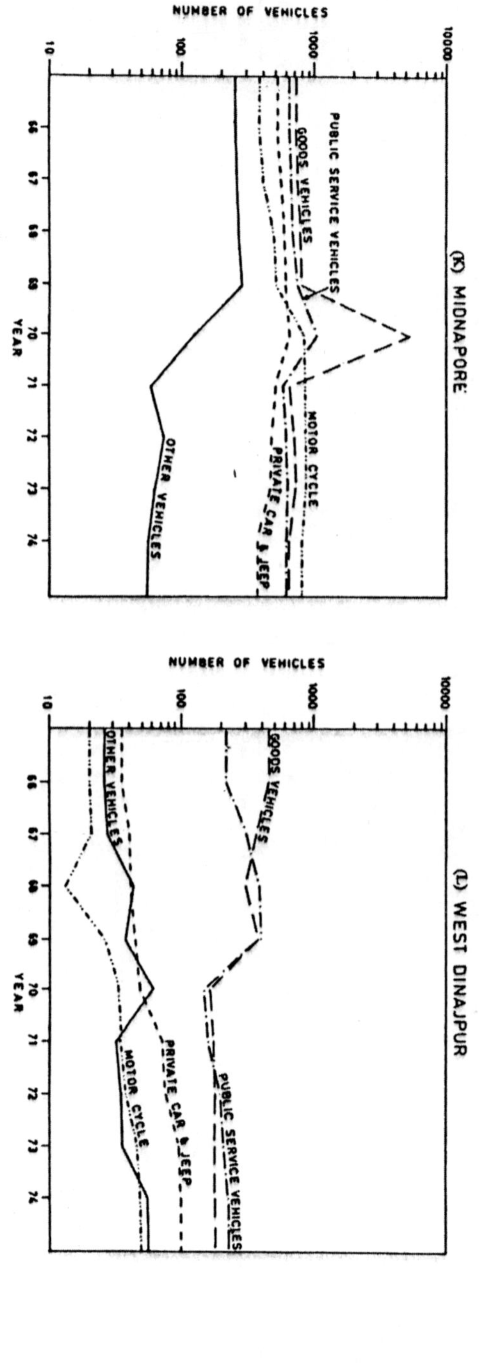

FIG. 5.7: (K, L) Motor Vehicles on Roads in Districts of West Bengal.

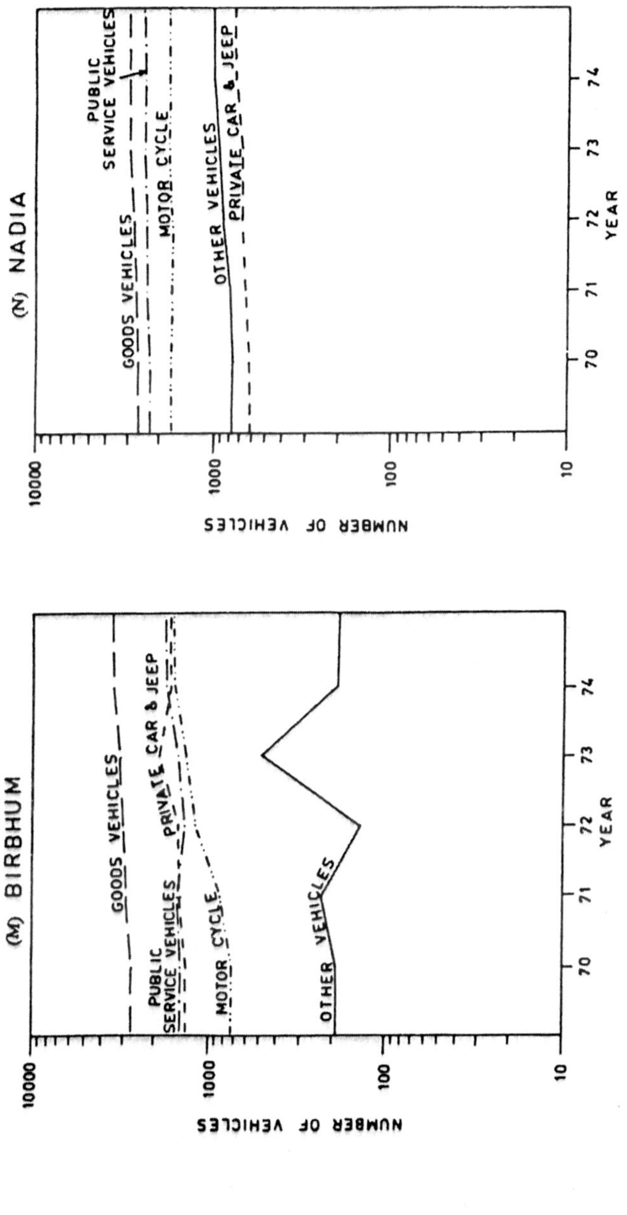

FIG. 5.7: (M, N) Motor Vehicles on Roads in Districts of West Bengal.

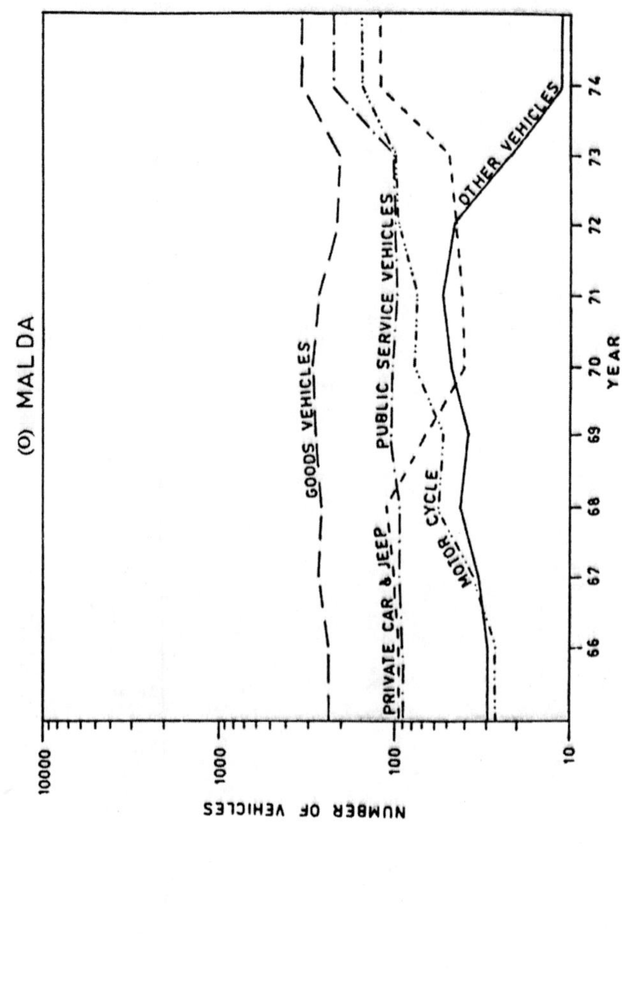

FIG. 5.7: (O) Motor Vehicles on Roads in Districts of West Bengal.

(3) Durgapur State Transport Corporation (DSTC) operating in Durgapur;
(4) Calcutta Tramways Company Ltd. (CTC) operating in Culcutta.

The first three organisations owned by State Government play a very important role in the inter and intra State Transport. Calcutta Tramways and C.S.T.C. also play a very important role in mass transit in the city of Calcutta.

With a fleet of only twentyfive petrol buses, the State Transport Services in Calcutta was inaugurated by the Government of West Bengal on 31st July, 1948. Diesel buses appeared in the streets of Calcutta in 1952. The next step in the development of State passenger transport was a decision to nationalise the private bus services in Calcutta in accordance with a phased programme implemented during 1955-56.

The Calcutta State Transport Corporation was established in April, 1960, by the State Government under the Road Transport Corporation Act, 1950. The Corporation runs passenger buses within the city of Calcutta and its surrounding areas and also on certain specified long distance routes. The North Bengal State Transport Corporation which has its headquarter in Cooch Behar serves not only this district but also entire Jalpaiguri division as well.

The Cooch Behar State Government started a transportation service in Cooch Behar in the month of April, 1945, with a fleet of 3 buses and 3 trucks under the last war reconstruction scheme, promulgated by the said government for giving road transport facilities to the general public, specially to those living in the interior places where there were no railway communications. After the merger of Cooch Behar with the State of West Bengal from 1st January, 1950, the Government of West Bengal took over control of this undertaking under the Home Transport Department. The operation of the transport was extended to the districts of West Dinajpore and Malda in the year of 1956 and thereby covering all the five districts of North Bengal excepting hill section of the Darjeeling district.

Function

Calcutta State Transport Corporation (CSTC)

(i) To promote development of the road transport in the areas comprising Calcutta and the districts of 24-Parganas, Howrah and Hooghly in West Bengal,

(ii) To co-ordinate the road transport with railway transport in the said areas, and

(iii) To extend and improve facilities for road transport in the said areas and provide an efficient and economical system of road transport services therein.

North Bengal State Transport Corporation (NBSTC)

(i) To develop road transport in the districts of Cooch Behar, Jalpaiguri, Darjeeling, West Dinajpore and Malda for the advantages of public, trade and industry,

(ii) To establish co-ordination between the road transport and railway transport facilities, and

(iii) Expansion and improvement of road transport to provide an efficient and economic system of road transport in the aforesaid districts.

5.5 Growth of State Transport

The Calcutta State Transport Corporation was established in 1960, but the services in Calcutta was started in 1951. From then, the total kilometerage ran by C.S.T.C. has increased by 3.07 times from 1951 to 1976. N.B.S.T.C. has increased from 8.9 lakhs kms. to 160.75 lakhs kms. from 1951 to 1976, that is eighteen times increase in more than two decades of service. D.S.T.C. route kilometerage increased from 1.1 lakh kms. in 1963-64 to 46.04 lakhs kms. in 1975-76 (Fig. 5.8).[7]

The State sector operates primarily in the large urban areas dealing with the commuters. Only the North Bengal State Transport Corporation has a fleet of trucks for the movement goods.

5.5.1 *Calcutta State Transport Corporation (CSTC)*

As has been stated earlier the State Transport Service began as a departmentally run undertaking with only 25 petrol buses.

Between 1948 and 1955, the fleet was enlarged to 481 buses consisting of 200 petrol and 281 diesel driven imported buses. The 200 petrol buses were gradually abandoned as uneconomical and more diesel buses were procured from abroad. Gradually the fleet strength further rose and by 1960 the State Transport Organisation had 670 buses in service (Fleet strength for the period 1961-62 to 1975-76 is shown in the Fig. 5.9).

Although the nominal fleet strength showed numerical growth, the average number of buses on road, average number of passengers carried, did not show corresponding increase as it would be revealed from Fig. 5.10. With the growth of the fleet, the State Transport Organisation also faced competition from private operators and this proved uneconomical operation for the State Transport. In order to eliminate the private operators from certain routes for preventing competition, the State of West Bengal decided in 1954, on progressive nationalisation of routes. This became a definite and phased programme in 1955-56, when the Planning Commission recommended gradual nationalisation of transport services all over the country. In spite of this, the number of routes, however, increased from 31 in 1961 to only 38 in 1976.

C.S.T.C. introduced long distance services since 1968 (Fig. 5.11) by opening Calcutta-Digha route. Calcutta to Digha, distance is 252 kilometres and could be reached by six hours at a fare of Rs 12.50. Since then many new routes were opened of which the longest distance route being 415 kms. i.e., Calcutta to Ranchi via Kharagpur, Ghatsilla and Tatanagar. Journey time of this route is 9 hrs. and the fare is Rs. 28.40 which has opened since 8-10-1976.

Calcutta-Bishnupur (via Dankuni), Calcutta-Dattafulia, Calcutta-Hasnabad, Calcutta-Diamond Harbour, Calcutta-Garbeta and Calcutta-Purulia (via Burdwan) routes were opened in 1977. The total long distance services has increased to 47 routes in 1977 from only one in 1968.

The total earnings of C.S.T.C. was raised by 119 per cent i.e. Rs. 574.89 lakhs in 1976 from 1951.

5.5.2 *North Bengal State Transport Corporation (NBSTC)*

North Bengal State Transport Corporation has expanded to a great extent than what it had been in 1951. Though the Corporation is established in 1960, yet it started its service with only 3 buses in 1945. At present the total fleet strength of the Corporation is 353 in passenger transport, 97 in goods transport, in the year 1975-76 (Table 5.8). North Bengal State Transport Corporation is the only concern which handles goods movement inter- and intra-district.

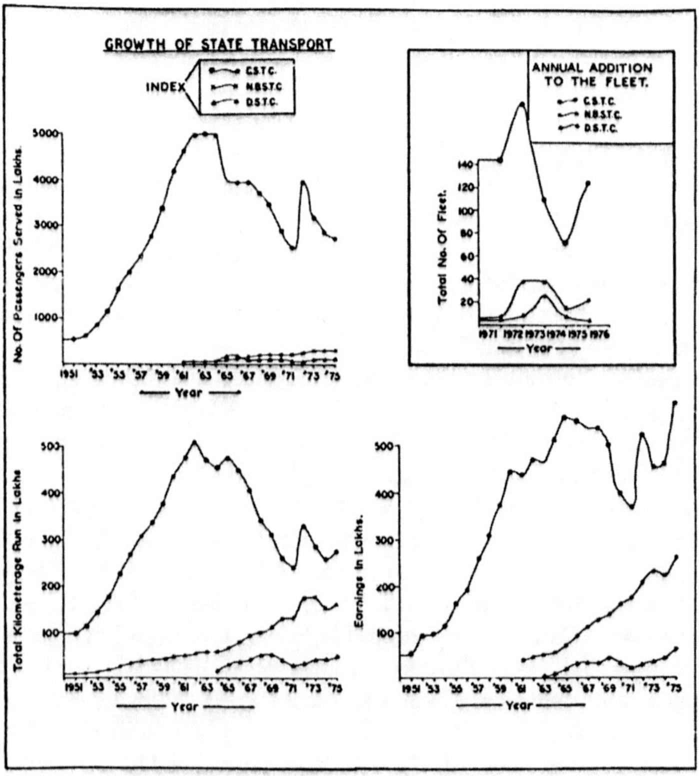

FIG. 5.8: Growth of State Transport.

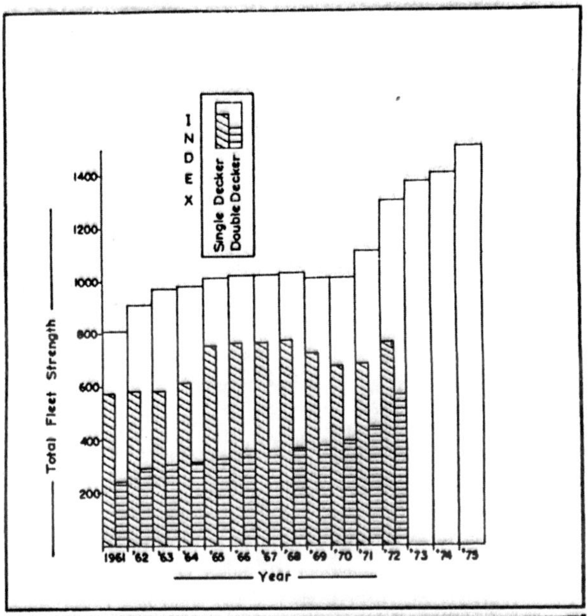

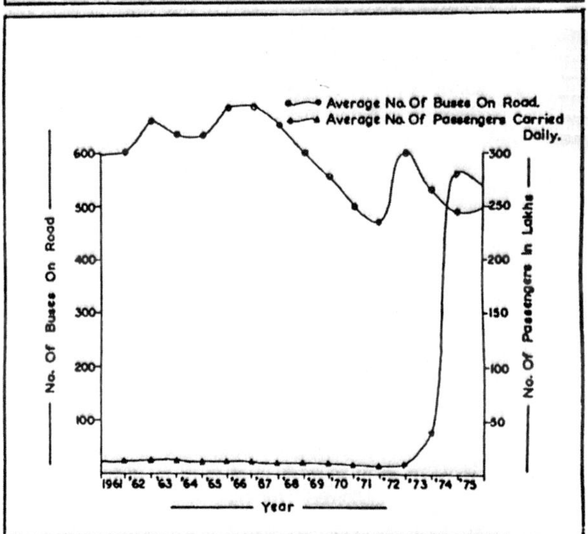

FIG. 5.9: Calcutta State Transport Corporation (Fleet Strength, 1961-75).

FIG 5.10: Diagram Showing Average number of Buses on Road and Average number of Passengers carried daily by C.S.T.C. (1961-75).

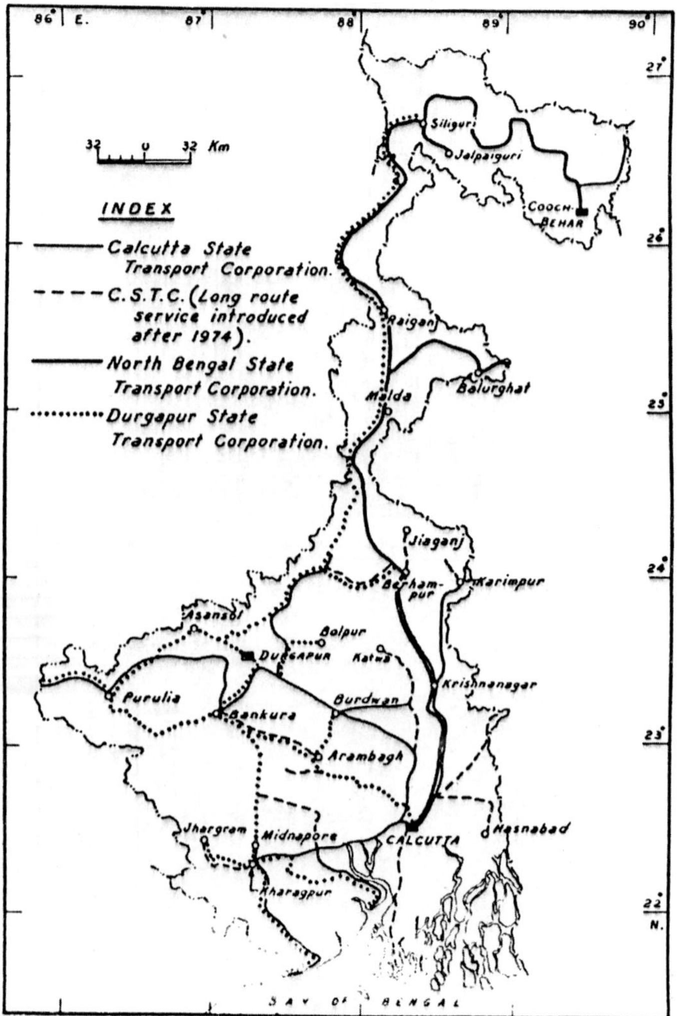

Fig.30.

FIG. 5.11: Long Distance Bus Route Map (S.T.C.) 1974.

TABLE 5.8: Growth of North Bengal State Transport Corporation

Route year	Length of operation (Kms.)	Av. No. of vehicles put on road daily	Av. No. of persons employed per day	Total effective Kms.	Goods Transport Survey			
					Fleet strength	Total No. of vehicles put on road	Goods served in (tonnes & sq.ft.)	Earnings in lakhs of rupees
1961-62	5,050	110	750					
1962-63	5,921	114	860					
1963-64	5,958	110	953					
1964-65	6,621	119	992					
1965-66	7,840	135	1,028	58070	19	19		3.59
1966-67	8,446	138	1,078	806372	25	23		8.22
1967-68	9,382	152	1,415	1028745	33	30	10178 tons.	10.34
1968-69	9,969	179	1,826	1160934	34	33	12909 tons. 3686 sq.ft.	13.44
1969-70	11,333	185	1,948	1306312	36	35	14370 tons. 6766 sq.ft.	14.61
1970-71	11,925	190	2,072	1344008	39	35	14421 tons 6169 sq.ft.	16.00
1971-72	14,057	193	2,210	1441105	40	35	14417 tons 8938 sq.ft.	19.23
1972-73	18,552	231	4,024	2128198	68	52	18582 tons 9826 sq.ft.	19.08
1973-74	18,552	193	4,443	1492860	68	40	18345 tons. 9327 sq. ft.	17.55
1974-75	16,680	160	4,432	1398092	94	37	18848 tons. 7086 sq. ft.	18.30
1975-76	19,114	190	4,127	1508426	97	51	23150 tons. 9588 sq. ft.	24.33

Source: Economic Review, 1961-62 to 1975-76.

Long route service is first resumed in 1968 when Siliguri to Calcutta route was opened up. The Corporation introduced Ranigunje-Jalpaiguri long route service on 23-3-1970 and Siliguri-Gauhati long route service on 25-2-1970.

Total kilometerage run by N.B.S.T.C. has increased eighteen times from 1951 to 1976. The total earnings of the Corporation has increased 48 times from 5.40 lakhs in 1951 to 259.21 lakhs in 1976.

Number of passengers served by the Corporation on the other hand increased 4.81 times since 1961 (Data before that period are not available). Goods transport expanded from 5.8 lakhs kms. served in 1965-66 to 15.1 lakh kms. served in 1976, while the total number of trucks stood at 97 in 1976 from 19 in 1965-66. Total goods handled increased from 10,178 tonnes in 1967-68 to 23,150 tonnes in 1975-76 and total earnings from 3.59 lakhs in 1965-66 to 24.33 lakhs in 1975-76, in respect of goods transport (Fig. 5.12).

Development Scheme for the Year 1976-77

North Bengal State Transport Corporation undertook a development scheme for the people of the hill areas for the year 1976-77 which includes launching of 6 micro buses, 4 mini buses, one mini wracker and 4 mini trucks at a cost of Rs 16.50 lakhs. Besides Rs. 33.50 lakhs will be spent for construction of bodies of 16 standard lorries, improvement of workshops, extending workshop facilities to different depots, as well as improving passenger amenities.

5.5.3 *Durgapur State Transport Corporation*

This Corporation is now servicing North Bengal as well as South Bengal from Siliguri to Haldia. Durgapur being the headquarter of D.S.T.C. not only enjoys the city service but long distance service too, as would be apparent from the map (Fig. 5.11). Total kilometerage run by D.S.T.C. increased from 1.1 lakhs kms. in 1963-64 to 46.04 lakhs kms. in 1975-76. i.e., a 41.8 times increase.

Total passengers served by the Corporation also increased from 18.45 lakhs in 1961-62 to 110.90 lakhs in 1975-76, i.e., it increased by 49 times while the earning of the Corporation was raised from Rs 5.6 lakhs in 1963-64 to Rs 64.53 lakhs in 1975-76.

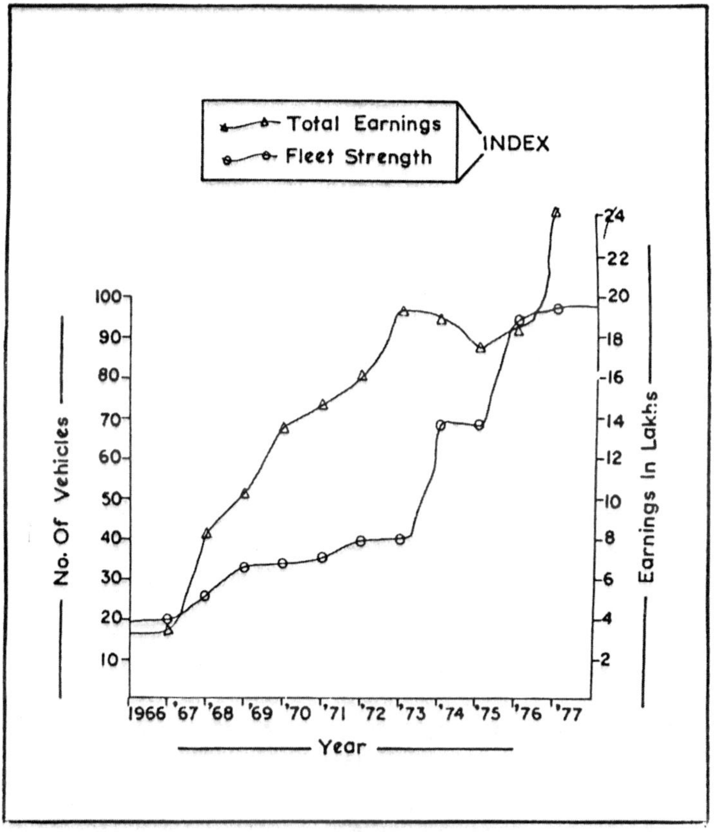

FIG. 5.12: North Bengal State Transport Corporation (Goods Transport Survey).

Importance of C.S.T.C. over other State Transport Corporation is revealed from the following Table 5.9.

City services were improved remarkably in 1969 while District and Hill services showed steady improvement since 1960-61 to 1968-69, as indicated by total kilometerage run per bus per day.

5.6 Performance of Private Companies

Road transport services are managed by both Public and Private sectors, both of which play a dominant role in the country's economy

TABLE 5.9: Showing Annual Addition to the Fleet

Year	Annual addition to the fleet of		
	Calcutta State Transport Corporation	North Bengal State Transport Corporation	Durgapur State Transport Corporation
1971-72	145	7	5
1972-73	192	38	8
1973-74	110	38	27
1974-75	73	17	7
1975-76	124	23	4

Source : Economic Review, 1977-78.

by moving goods and people. As expected, the scale of operation in the public sector is quite large, however, the bulk of road transport is handled by private agencies of various sizes. For the private sector transport organisations, survival is akin with making financial gain in their operations in the face of such constraints as various labour laws, labour unrest, shortage of spares, unauthorised use of facilities, shortage in the supply of vehicles etc. Nationalisation of this sector of the economy is not desirable, because it may not be possible for the State sector to operate on such a large scale efficiently and to make a huge investment. The State sector has so far been a financially loosing sector and atleast, for the time being both the sectors should be permitted to function in such a manner, so as to avoid competition and to help to foster growth (Table 5.10).

All the private bus operators in Calcutta Metropolitan District are organised into bus syndicate or route committees. On an average, private buses cover approximately 31,800,00 kms. a year, and is on road for 25–26 days in a month to earn sufficient revenue to maintain the service. In the memorandum submitted by the Federation of Bus Syndicate it was stated that almost all the private bus operators in Calcutta, Howrah and 24-Parganas own only one vehicle and depend upon it for their livelihood. According to the memorandum, effective life of a vehicle is generally about 6-8 years and there is a high percentage of old vehicles, i.e. more than 8 years old running on the road, which may be attributable due to the incapacity of the owner to replace it by a new one because of high capital investment required, and the fact that after six to eight years the service has ceased to be viable. It has been ascertained that there are 430 private buses running on 20 routes in Howrah. It also appears from the statement that there are 1,516 private buses plying in Calcutta and its suburbs on 85 routes comprising 29 city routes and 56 suburban routes. Also 398 suburban buses are allowed to ply in Calcutta city and a few more are called to meet temporary needs. The routes are of varying lengths from 6.7 kms. to 82 kms.

TABLE 5.10: Performance and Input Utilisation of Undertakings for Different Services (1960-61 to 1968-69)

	1960-61	1965-66	1966-67	1967-68	1968-69
A. *City Services*:					
(1) No. of kms. run per bus per day	150	151	150	153	163
(2) Litres of fuel consumed per 100 sq.kms.	25.27	28.99	29.37	28.14	28.00
B. *District Services*:					
(1) No. of kms. run per bus per day	139	160	163	166	174
(2) Litres of fuel consumed per 100 sq.kms.	21.00	22.68	23.32	22.80	23.28
C. *Hill Services*:					
(1) No. of kms. run per bus per day	67	81	75	80	88
(2) Litres of fuel consumed per 100 sq.kms.	22.90	27.03	30.18	28.16	28.16
D. *All Services*:					
(1) No. of kms. run per bus per day	139	156	157	160	168
(2) Litres of fuel consumed per bus per 100 kms.	22.51	24.25	25.84	24.13	24.47

Source: Basic Road Statistics, 1968-69.

On certain bus routes in Calcutta region, which had once been nationalised and reserved for buses of Calcutta State Transport Corporation only, now have a large number of private buses operating, because State buses alone cannot meet the needs of the travelling public. These buses should have the same fare structure as State buses, for the simple reason that State and private buses rendering the same class of service, must not charge different fares in the same route. An unfair competition will result in such a case, which will only injure the stage carriage transportation service in the city.

It can be said that unlike buses of C.S.T.C. private buses do not operate in Calcutta, Howrah and 24-Parganas as organised units. Buses are owned by individual route permit holders and a great deal of individualism prevails amongst them.

In Calcutta region which includes 24-Parganas, about 1,000 buses (State & Private) run on different routes on an average, the buses have capacity to carry 70 passengers.

(a) Seated - 35 and
(b) Standing - 35.

In peak hours, the number of passengers carried by the buses are quiet high, as the buses are inadequate this becomes necessary. Usually a bus makes 1 to 5 trips a day. The number of trips depends on the route length. A bus is kept 5 to 10 hrs. on the run. In 1940 when R.T.A. was constituted under the Motor Vehicles Act of 1939, only 550 private stage carriages owned by 322 private operators used to run on 24 routes.

The routes operated by the private buses are shown in Appendix-XII. All the districts of West Bengal have the benefit of long distance transport services and local services are also available (analysis based on detailed enumeration of routes have been shown in Fig. 5.13). The frequency or number of buses are not more, still the districts are advantaged by both long distance service of the State bus and the local service carried out by private buses. The routes and the markets served by these buses are shown in Appendix-XIII. In Calcutta, there is a marked increase in rates of use of both public and private transportation brought about by population growth and the effect of improved personal income levels which motivated desires for personal mobility. The inadequacy of the streets and highways system is further complicated by poor standards of maintenance, unsatisfactory traffic control, rash and reckless driving habits, insufficiency in road span, and a traffic consisting of automobiles, trucks, pedestrians, handicrafts, rickshaws, bicycles, bullock carts and a miscellany of animals. The total congestion resulting from the growth in road traffic without corresponding roadway improvement and development programmes, affects all movements and causes a serious slow down of public transportation, the capacity and effectiveness of which are thereby considerably reduced.

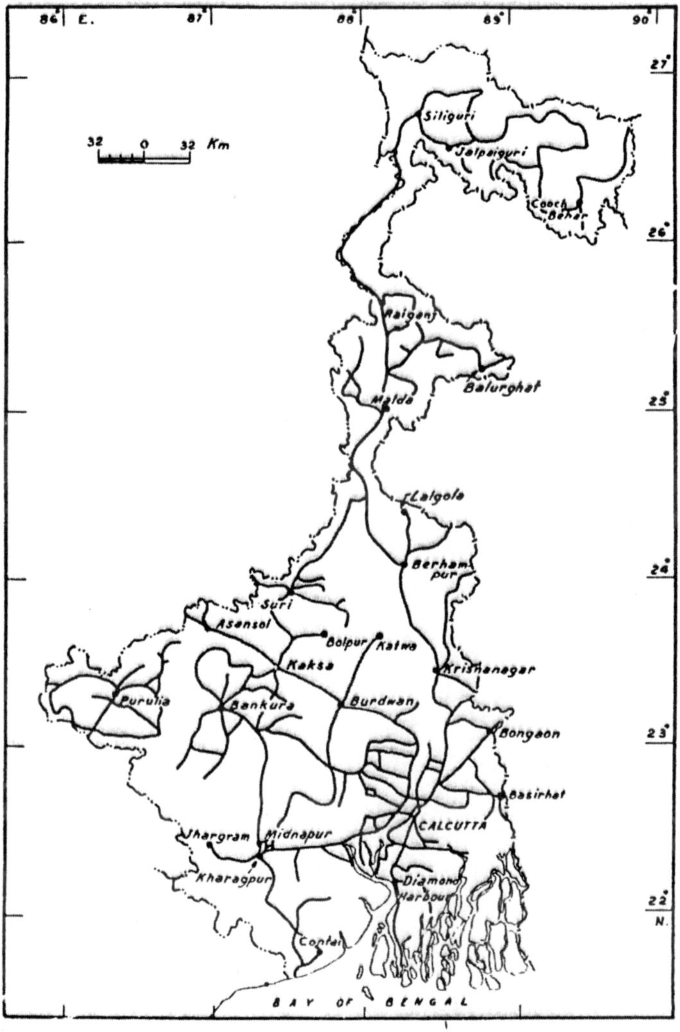

FIG. 5.13: West Bengal Bus Route Map (local) 1974.

5.7 Recent Improvement in Calcutta's Traffic and Transportation Made by Calcutta Metropolitan Development Authority

A big project for improvement of traffic operation was undertaken by C.M.D.A. in the Howrah Station area where the traffic jam had become a regular feature. One of the important features under the said project is the Howrah subway meant for the pedestrians which opened on 31st January, 1975. Another important feature is the flyover approaching the Howrah bridge from Brabourne Road opened to traffic in 1977.

Out of 60 city roads taken up for improvement by C.M.D.A., 43 are completed and out of 25 schemes taken up for widening of existing roads, 10 schemes have been completed. The Chetla Bridge, Aurobindo Setu, Kalighat Bridge and Bijan Setu – the railway overbridge near Ballygunge Station, are all completed by 1978. The work of elevated carriageway at Sealdah has commenced in 1980 (completed). To ease congestion in the Calcutta roads, C.M.D.A. has certainly started their work in a planned manner, and improvement can now be noticed, but considerable and judicious investment in traffic and transportation is still required in order to overcome the existing deficiencies.

5.8 Financial Outlays

TABLE 5.11: Outlays and Eexpenditure Under the Plans

(Rs. in lakhs)

Transportation & Communication	Outlay	Expenditure	Percentage
First Five Year Plan:			
(i) Transport & Communication	1553.59	1510.26	97.2
(ii) Roads	1383.16	1337.07	96.7
(iii) Road Transport	170.43	172.59	101.3
Second Five Year Plan:			
(i) Transport and Communication	1946.88	1695.30	87.1
(ii) Roads	1747.69	1459.91	83.5
(iii) Road Transport	199.19	223.10	112.0
Third Five Year Plan:			
(i) Transport & Communication	2650.00	1619.91	98.9
(ii) Roads	2500.00	2260.53	90.4
(iii) Road Transport	100.00	273.47	273.5

Contd.

TABLE 5.11 *Contd.*

1	2	3	4
Fourth Five Year Plan:			
(i) Transport & Communication	1567.36	1367.36	87.2
(ii) Roads	1453.00	1238.21	85.2
(iii) Road Transport	35.82	83.97	234.4

Source: Statistical Handbook 1976-77, West Bengal.

NOTES

1. The author concerns exclusively with the road transport service in this paper. A outline of historical development of roads has been discussed in Chapter 1 and specific development of roads during the Plan Period has been outlined in Chapter 2.
2. This paragraph has been already mentioned in Chapter 1.
3. Road Facts India 1961, Govt. of India, Ministry of Transport and Communications, Dept. of Transport (Roads Wing), p.6.
4. Scooter and auto rickshaws are included in motor cycles.
5. The progress of the State Transport Corporations has been dealt later in para 5.4.
6. Table of road growth/motor vehicles growth is shown in the Appendix-IX.
7. Growth of State Transport, C.S.T.C., N.B.S.T.C. and D.S.T.C. has been shown in Appendix-X.

6

MEASUREMENT OF TRANSPORTATION EFFICIENCY

6.1 Measurement of Transportation Efficiency

Based on the index of transportation efficiency, an attempt has been made to determine regional hierarchies. The regional hierarchies are initially connected with the levels and patterns of network development for transportation and communication.

Measurement of transportation efficiency index is based on the analysis of space potential. Space potential can be interpreted as a measure of the relative efficiency of various nodes in a transportation system for assembling all of the masses in a region.[1] It is the relative efficiency of the nodes for movement of men and materials in a region. The values of the space potential model signify the "aggregate accessibility" of all masses in a region to a given point.

Transport system happens to be a pace setter for a growing economy. It, therefore, forms the base study of growth potential. Transportation is a measure of the relation between areas and, therefore, essentially geographical. It is one of the ingredients in the concept of spatial interaction and following from that of areal differentiation. Modern economic systems are characterised by area specialisation of functions, and interaction among specialist areas form a highly independent system.

A simple space potential model is used in the case study, to derive transportation efficiency index, for analysing the development problem of West Bengal (Fig. 6.1).

There are two iimiting factors which determine the strength of interaction between two places. These two factors are distance and population. Distance is the crude factor, when the distance increases between two places or areas of a given size, the interaction between these places also increases and vice-versa. Spatial differentiation cannot develop without movement or circulation and distance is fundamental to movement, since all movement involves a cost which in turn is related to distance.

Population is used to represent the mass factor in the space potential model because it is a relatively universal factor for dealing with the problems of human activity. By this factor, the relative attraction between two places can be measured. Greater the population between two centres, greater is the interaction and vice-versa.

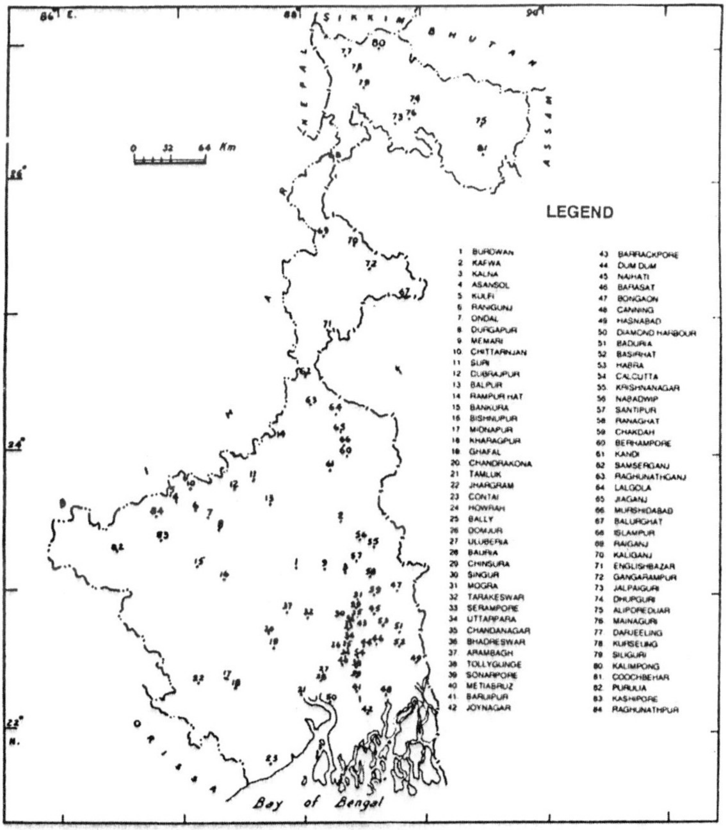

FIG. 6.1: Location of Towns.

6.2 Analysis of the Transportation System in West Bengal

In this analysis of the transportation system of West Bengal, two population space potentials are compared, by the formula:

$$Vi = Pi + \sum_{j=1}^{n} \frac{Pj}{dij} \tag{6.1}$$

where, Vi is the total population space potential at town i,
Pi is the total population at town i,
Pj is the total population at town j,
dij is the route distance between town i and town j,
j is from 1 to n.

Straight line distance in kilometres between the nodes is taken as the distance factor in the first calculation, while actual route distance is taken as the distance factor in the second space potential model. The latter distance obviously is longer than the distance calculated by straight line method and the resultant space potential model reflects less values as compared with straight line distance.

The difference between the two space potential values is used as a measure of the transportation efficiency and also the locational advantage at the node. In this analysis, population size of 10,000 and above is taken as the criteria for selection of the nodes. The difference between the two population space potential values indicating the transportation efficiency of each node for assembling population, has been calculated. The percentage changes in the space potential values are shown in Table 6.1. High score indicates less connections of that node with all other nodes in the system, i.e. larger the percentage deviation, the less efficiently the node is served by the existing transportation system.

The resultant transportation efficiency values are categorised into five relative efficiency groups:

(1) Very inefficient
(2) Inefficient
(3) Average
(4) Efficient
(5) Very efficient

The nodes based on these categories are depicted in the transportation efficiency map (Fig. 6.2) and in Table 6.1. Percentage increase in potential of the nodes are shown in Table 6.1, which are given by,

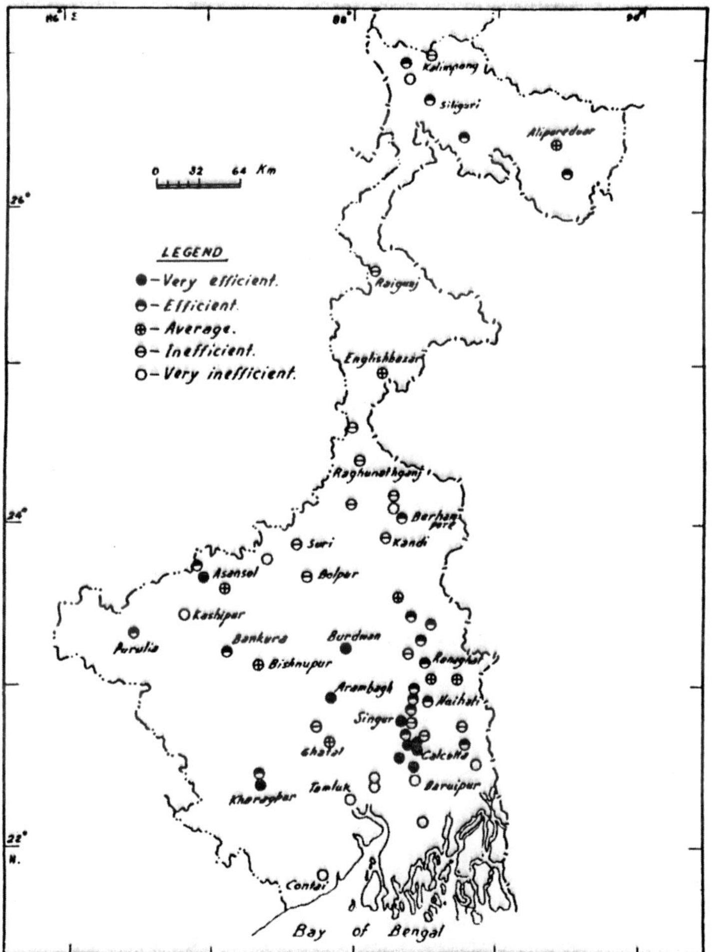

FIG. 6.2: Transportation Efficiency (1956).

$$\text{Percentage increase in potential} = \frac{\begin{pmatrix}\text{Actual road}\\\text{distance}\\\text{potential}\end{pmatrix} - \begin{pmatrix}\text{Straight line}\\\text{distance}\\\text{potential}\end{pmatrix}}{\text{Straight line distance potential}} \times 100 \quad (6.2)$$

The transportation efficiency of the nodes are computed for three years 1956, 1966 and 1974 and the nodes are selected on the basis of census population of 1951, 1961 and 1971 respectively.

TABLE 6.1: Transportation Efficiency of the Nodes

Sl. No.	Nodes/Centres	Percentage increase in potential		
		1956	1966	1974
1	2	3	4	5
Very Inefficient:				
1.	Tamluk	48.6	–	–
2.	Contai	51.3	–	–
3.	Uluberia	51.8	–	–
4.	Bowrea	50.5	41.7	51.5
5.	Sonarpur	55.8	–	–
6.	Joynagar	49.3	–	–
7.	Hasnabad	50.0	–	–
8.	Murshidabad	58.7	–	–
9.	Kurseong	54.8	42.2	–
10.	Kashipur	59.5	42.7	–
11.	Dubrajpur	53.1	42.6	–
12.	Lalgola	–	50.8	42.0
13.	Dhupguri	–.	51.8	–
14.	Raghunathpur	–	51.1	43.9
15.	Canning	–	44.5	–
16.	Domjur	–	–	50.5
17.	Tarakeswar	–	–	47.0
18.	Diamond Harbour	–	–	42.9
Inefficient:				
1.	Kalna	39.6	–	–
2.	Suri	38.1	–	–
3.	Bolpur	45.3	–	–
4.	Rampurhat	44.4	–	–

Contd.

TABLE 6.1 *Contd.*

1	2	3	4	5
5.	Chandrakona	39.3	–	–
6.	Barasat	42.4	–	–
7.	Barrackpore	42.0	34.8	–
8.	Baduria	41.6	–	–
9.	Tamluk	–	33.0	–
10.	Uluberia	–	32.2	–
11.	Arambagh	–	35.4	–
12.	Joynagar	–	40.3	38.8
13.	Hasnabad	–	33.7	–
14.	Samserganj	42.6	34.2	–
15.	Murshidabad	–	34.6	34.4
16.	Dubrajpur	–	–	37.6
17.	Singur	–	–	38.6
18.	Canning	–	–	32.0
19.	Islampore	–	–	37.0
20.	Gangarampore	–	–	38.8
21.	Dhupguri	–	–	35.0
22.	Kandi	44.2	–	–
23.	Raghunathganj	37.9	–	–
24.	Jiaganj	43.6	–	–
25.	Balurghat	38.1	–	–
26.	Raiganj	43.6	–	–
27.	Kalimpong	40.9	–	–
28.	Jhargram	–	40.8	31.9
29.	Kurseong	–	–	35.6
30.	Kashipur	–	–	31.8
Average:				
1.	Katwa	30.1	29.3	22.4
2.	Raniganj	27.8	21.7	–
3.	Bishnupur	29.8	–	–
4.	Ghatal	22.3	23.1	23.0
5.	Bongaon	30.5	–	–
6.	Chakdah	26.0	–	–
7.	Alipurduar	28.8	–	–
8.	Kandi	–	30.4	23.8
9.	Kalna	–	27.0	22.5
10.	Suri	–	27.8	21.8
11.	Bolpur	–	26.7	21.8
12.	Rampurhat	–	30.2	26.6
13.	Chandrakona	–	29.1	23.5
14.	Contai	–	27.6	–
15.	Chittranjan	–	21.6	–

Contd.

TABLE 6.1 *Contd.*

1	2	3	4	5
16.	Sonarpur	–	24.9	–
17.	Metiabruz	–	24.6	–
18.	Barasat	–	21.4	–
19.	Baduria	–	26.0	–
20.	Habra	–	23.5	–
21.	Raghunathganj	–	25.4	21.2
22.	Balurghat	–	23.0	–
23.	Raiganj	–	22.4	–
24.	Alipurduar	–	21.6	–
25.	Mainaguri	–	30.1	26.2
26.	Kalimpong	–	24.6	26.3
27.	Samserganj	–	–	27.7
28.	Ondal	–	–	28.6
29.	Tamluk	–	–	27.9
30.	Uluberia	–	–	30.7
31.	Arambagh	–	–	24.9
32.	Baruipur	–	–	30.2
33.	Hasnabad	–	–	29.0
34.	Jiaganj	–	–	23.6
35.	Kaliaganj	–	–	28.7
Efficient:				
1.	Kulti	12.4	19.3	15.1
2.	Chittranjan	–	–	16.3
3.	Purulia	18.0	13.5	11.5
4.	Bankura	15.3	–	–
5.	Midnapur	16.5	–	–
6.	Chinsura	13.4	–	–
7.	Chandannagar	15.1	–	–
8.	Mogra	23.9	14.2	–
9.	Bhadreswar	–	17.9	14.7
10.	Bally	12.1	–	17.0
11.	Uttarpara	14.7	–	–
12.	Naihati	13.7	11.2	–
13.	Basirhat	21.2	12.1	–
14.	Krishnanagar	15.1	–	–
15.	Nabadwip	13.5	–	–
16.	Santipur	17.6	12.7	–
17.	Ranaghat	23.0	11.8	–
18.	Berhampore	13.6	–	–
19.	Englishbazar	23.9	14.1	–
20.	Jalpaiguri	18.1	13.3	12.1
21.	Darjeeling	21.9	15.8	15.2

Contd.

TABLE 6.1 *Contd.*

1	2	3	4	5
22.	Siliguri	22.6	—	—
23.	Cooch Behar	22.1	15.3	12.3
24.	Durgapur	—	16.0	—
25.	Bishnupur	—	20.3	17.3
26.	Sonarpur	—	—	19.1
27.	Metiabruz	—	—	11.8
28.	Barasat	—	—	15.6
29.	Bongaon	—	—	14.6
30.	Habra	—	—	12.8
31.	Chakdah	—	—	14.1
32.	Raniganj	—	—	15.1
33.	Alipurduar	—	—	17.6
Very Efficient:				
1.	Burdwan	10.1	6.1	4.8
2.	Asansol	10.	6.4	4.5
3.	Durgapur	—	—	3.4
4.	Kharagpur	5.9	4.5	4.3
5.	Howrah	1.7	1.2	0.9
6.	Serampur	6.1	7.2	6.8
7.	Tollygunge (Jadavpur in 1974)	5.1	1.04	0.30
8.	Metiabruz	7.0	—	—
9.	Dum Dum	8.8	3.8	2.2
10.	Calcutta	0.20	0.12	0.11
11.	Arambagh	11.2	—	—
12.	Midnapore	—	11.0	9.6
13.	Bankura	—	10.4	8.7
14.	Bally	—	6.6	—
15.	Chinsurah	—	7.2	6.5
16.	Uttarpara	—	7.3	5.6
17.	Chandannagar	—	9.8	9.1
18.	Krishnagar	—	9.9	7.8
19.	Nabadwip	—	9.0	7.8
20.	Berhampore	—	10.5	9.2
21.	Siliguri	—	10.0	6.9
22.	Barrackpore	—	—	7.1
23.	Basirhat	—	—	10.4
24.	Santipur	—	—	10.9
25.	Ranaghat	—	—	9.4
26.	Balurghat	—	—	10.0
27.	Englishbazar	—	—	10.9

The economic development of an area requires adequate and effective transportation system. The transportation is a precondition or prerequisite for economic growth. A vital question is programming the spatial incidence of economic growth is the regional impact of transportation investment. As a result, certain centres are advantaged by their increased transportation efficiency.

Theoretically, the improvements should help to create conditions that increase the attractions of the regional centres as foci for capital investment, given the permissive role of transportation in the process of economic development. However, it is apparent that economic growth as occurring in a matrix of location points which are the building blocks around which economic space is constructed, evolve in the direction of even greater spatial integration (Friedmann generalized location points as cities and towns which serve as basic decision points in the growth process).[3] Because of their valuable urbanisation and localisation economics, they are attractive as centres of growth.

Transportation makes cities possible, cities are not self-sufficient; they exist only because of the specialised functions they perform for their surrounding areas or hinterlands. All these functions depend upon transportation, which enables cities to become the foci of their contributory service areas. The hierarchical system of cities as found in this study indicates the economic status of the cities.

Much of the literature of transport economics and of the transport geography of the less developed countries reveal a widespread belief in the importance of transport and its efficiency in accelerating the development progress. Transport automatically promotes development and constitutes an important element in a varied infrastructure necessary for economic growth.

It is found from the analysis that Calcutta continues to be the most efficient among all the nodes in the system. Calcutta is economically the most developed part of the State, its per capita income, percentage of work force, literacy, banking, road density, post office, population density indicate the existence of the greatest degree of economic opportunity. Calcutta scored 0.20 per cent increase in potential in 1956, 0.12 per cent in 1966 to 0.11 per cent in 1974, signifying the most developed node in the system, which agree with the real world picture. High accessibility of Calcutta leads to its position of primacy in the urban centres (Fig. 6.3).

The space potential technique does in fact provide meaningful insight into the problem of transportation efficiency. Cities, the principal seat of population, have long been intimately related to transportation, and having recognised their dependence on it, have sought to improve their connections.

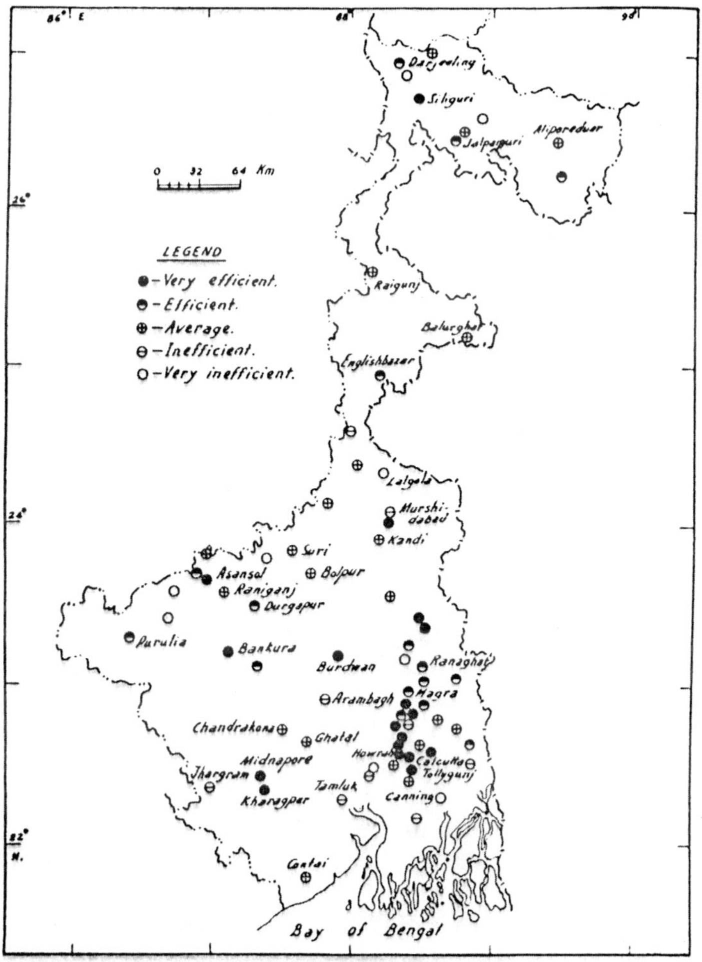

Fig.34.ii.

FIG. 6.3: Transportation Efficiency (1966).

Transportation efficiency of each node in West Bengal can be evaluated both according to its ability to assemble the population of the area and to it's connectivity to other centres in the system.

It can be concluded from the analysis that the preponderance of towns and cities with very efficient transportation are mostly located in the southern part of West Bengal. The important factors which make the southern region studded with cities with efficient transportation, are:

(i) that is region being located with the most populous cities,
(ii) there is a fairly dense construction of large cities in the region,
(iii) large population naturally command the best transportation facilities within a region.

Of the total 84 nodes selected in the space potential model, 25 nodes or about 29 per cent of the total are classified as very efficient in the system in 1974. The corresponding figures for 1956 and 1966 are 10 and 18 only. The number of nodes which are efficient are 17 in 1974, 21 in 1956 and 14 in 1966.

Some of the nodes which are categorised as efficient in 1956, has been transformed into very efficient in 1974, e.g., Chinsurah, Chandernagar, Uttarpara, Basirhat, Krishnanagar, Nabadwip, Berhampore, Santipur, Ranaghat, Englishbazar, Siliguri, Durgapur. Twelve nodes are newly evolved as very efficient in transportation in 1974 (Fig. 6.4).

Tollygunge and Howrah ranked next to Calcutta as very efficient in transportation. Since Howrah is centrally located, its growth is closely related with that of Calcutta. Transportation efficiency score for Howrah was 1.7 per cent increase in potential in 1956, 1.2 per cent in 1966 to 0.9 per cent in 1974. Efficiency however increased together with the increase in population.

Tollygunge in 1966 ranked next to Calcutta scoring 1.04 per cent increase in potential in 1966 to 0.30 per cent in 1974. (Tollygunge P.S. was named in Jadavpur in 1971 census which included the population of Tollygunge).

Mention should be made of Durgapur, a comparatively new town, as very efficient in 1974. Durgapur stands on the fringe of Raniganj coalfields. Due to the advantageous location and the availability of water, raw materials and power, Durgapur has become a major industrial complex.

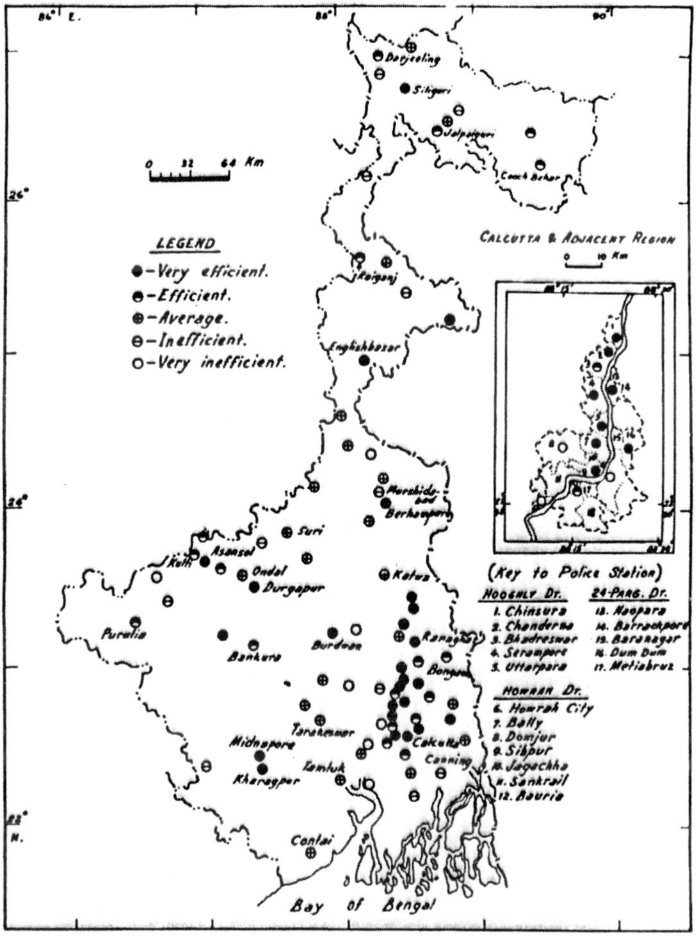

FIG. 6.4: Transportation Efficiency (1974).

In the north, Siliguri, Alipurduar, Jalpaiguri, Darjeeling and Cooch Behar have been categorised as efficient transportation nodes. These are the major transport nodes in the north. Siliguri is the nerve centre of the north-eastern zone of the State in regard to road transportation. Darjeeling being a tourist centre with tea plantations assumed nodality and exhibited efficiency in transportation, defence needs also increased the efficiency. Cooch Behar is about 176 kms. away from Siliguri, it is not only the administrative headquarters of the district but also the largest urban and trading centre, next only to Siliguri in North Bengal.

Out of the 84 towns, 20 towns, i.e. about 24 per cent of the total were in the average efficiency level in 1974. It appears from the analysis that sixty two towns out of the total 84 towns, do not apparently have any acute road network problems. In other words, about 74 per cent of the total towns of over 10,000 population do have fair transportation efficiency.

6.3 Regional Characteristics of Transportation Efficiency

In this section, the State has been demarcated with different transportation efficiencies. Four efficiency regions have been identified and a map has been drawn to locate these regions (Fig. 6.5).

The existing disparities in transportation efficiency in different regions and the realisation of growth potential of regions have been specified.

The efficiency regions based on transportation efficiency are shown in Table 6.2. Since transportation efficiency is related with resultant space potential values, therefore, the regions depend on these values.

TABLE 6.2: Efficiency Regions

	Efficiency Regions	Transportation Efficiency
(i)	High	Very efficient and efficient
(ii)	Medium	Average
(iii)	Low	Inefficient
(iv)	Very low	Very inefficient

Eastern India as a whole and West Bengal in particular, is highly diversified in industrial activity. Substantial industrial development took place in West Bengal both in public and private sectors during the last three Five Year Plan Perioos (2nd, 3rd and 4th Plans). The rapid economic development achieved in the region is related closely with commensurate increase in efficiency in the transportation system, during this period.

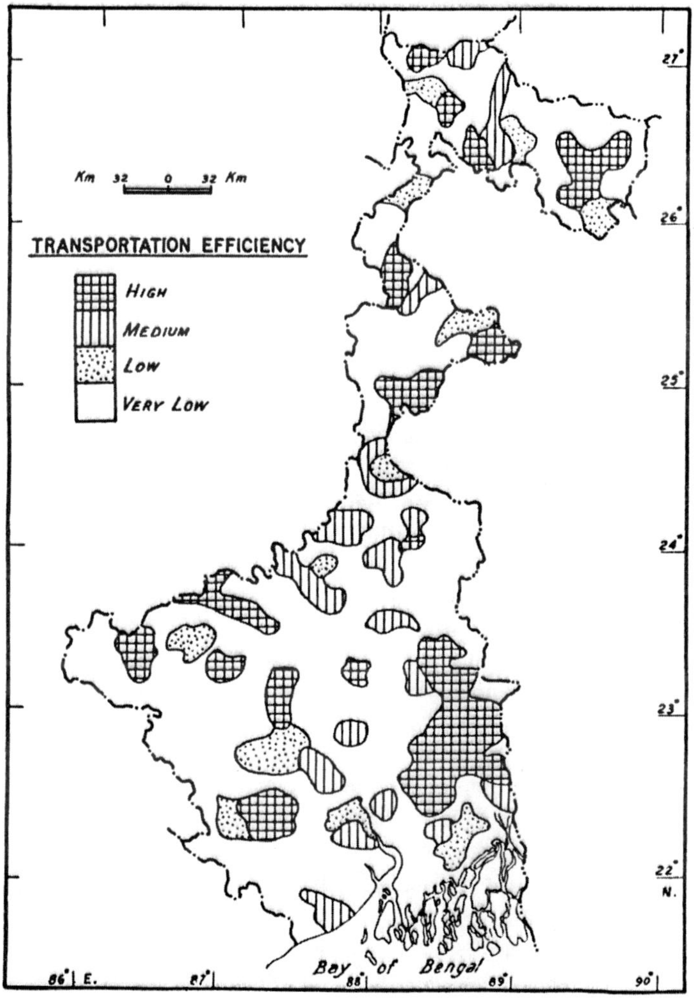

FIG. 6.5: Regional Characteristics of Transportation Efficiency (1974).

6.3.1 *High Efficiency Region*

South of West Bengal: The southern part of West Bengal have developed into the most efficient transportation system. The southern part can be identified with three distinct regions, which are:

(1) Calcutta Industrial Region,
(2) Durgapur-Asansol Region,
(3) Midnapore-Kharagpur Region.

6.3.2 *Calcutta Industrial Region*

High transportation efficiency is found in the region, in and around Calcutta, more precisely the Calcutta Metropolitan District and around Howrah city. The Hooghly-Howrah sub-region on the western side of the Hooghly river covers 388.5 sq.kms., while Barrackpore-Calcutta- Budge Budge sub-region on the eastern bank of the river has about twice that area. Engineering, jute textiles, cotton textiles, chemicals, rubber, food processing and miscellaneous light industries constitute this highly efficient region.

In general, it can be said that large urban centres reflect high efficiency in transportation, which may be due to their dynamic and important position in the economy. These hierarchies may be strictly interpreted as rank structures of the level of centrality of place, where centrality itself refers to the relative business or marketing importance of places, to the areas that surround them.

Transportation efficiency as confronted in West Bengal today consists of extremely sharp regional disparities, particularly between Calcutta Metropolitan District Agglomerate and the rest of West Bengal. The agglomerate includes Calcutta and its surroundings, Metiabruz, Howrah, Dum Dum, Barrackpore, Naihati, Basirhat, Serampore, Uttarpara, Magra, Chandannagar, Chinsurah, Bally, Bhadreswar, Sonarpore, Chakdah, Ranaghat, Santipur, Krishnagar, Bongaon and Habra.

Basic to this study is the notion that there exists a high degree of interdependence between the development of a transportation system and the geographical pattern of urban economic growth. Calcutta is the regional capital of Eastern India. This contiguous region owes its origin to the Metropolitan city which exerts its specific functional dominance over urban systems where transportation system has a leading role. It is said that Calcutta is a great metropolitan city of unequalled importance in the economy of the nation as a whole, and of the region which it serves. The state is inseparably linked with Calcutta and the economic development of the entire region depends on Calcutta's capacity to perform its metropolitan functions efficiently.

The urban and industrial centres in Calcutta's hinterland must be linked efficiently along with development in transport. A partial explanation of the need of this efficient region may be that the central cities, namely, Calcutta and Howrah, are beginning to reach a saturation point in their capacity to absorb further growth. Both are surrounded by established municipalities or physical barriers that restrict territorial expansion, and both are suffering at present with techno-economic constraints, limiting their capacity to intensify development within their jurisdictional area. Most of the metropolitan growth is, therefore, beginning to take place in areas outside the central city complex, dominated by Calcutta Metropolitan District, the most crucial urban growth pole.

6.3.3 *Durgapur-Asansol Region*

This region is the second most important industrial region and next in importance regarding transportation efficiency to Calcutta industrial region. The region includes Asansol-Chittaranjan-Kulti-Durgapur-Raniganj. The Durgapur-Asansol region accommodates a major industrial complex of Eastern India and is an integral part of the Damodar Valley Resource Region that stradles inter-state boundaries. The Five Year Plans created the new industrial areas of Durgapur and Chittaranjan, adding to the hierarchy of urban centres of Asansol, Kulti and Raniganj region. The industries in this region are iron and steel, machinery, coke, coal, paper, glass, drugs, ceramics, fire bricks, oil mills, aluminium, bicycles, locomotives, electrical wires, rice, mills, etc.

The locomotive factory at Chittaranjan and the industrial township of Durgapur turned the Asansol sub-division into a major industrial centre of the State. Comparatively high level of accessibility to the National Highway have also assisted in the proliferation of urban growth over the area. The role of the Durgapur-Asansol region as an important growth node next to Calcutta Metropolitan District is further highlighted by the paucity of well developed urban centres all over Eastern India.

6.3.4 *Midnapore-Kharagpur Region*

This region serves agriculturally rich Midnapore district, and as per space potential analysis, this region is highly efficient next only to Durgapur-Asansol region. Local industries include, food processing, railway workshop, machinery building, etc. With the growth of Haldia, this region will have potentiality of extending southwards and eastwards.

Only 12.8 kms. apart from one another, Kharagpur-Midnapore, for all practical purposes, constitute one functional urban unit. Midnapore is the administrative headquarter and Kharagpur is the largest industrial centre in Midnapore district.

Midnapore-Kharagpur commands a strategic location in the transport network of the district. National Highway No. 6 links these towns directly with Calcutta and they are served by the Calcutta-Bombay and Calcutta-Madras National Highways. A major State highway runs north to south linking Midnapore-Kharagpur with Orissa on the one hand and Asansol-Chittaranjan-Durgapur area on the other. Thus, this town is very easily accessible from the highly industrialised areas of Tatanagar, Ranchi, Asansol-Durgapur and Calcutta Metropolitan District. This region when integrated with Haldia, will be forming another important urban growth pole.

Other efficient regions of importance in southern West Bengal are Purulia, Bankura-Bishnupur, Burdwan and Berhampore. Purulia is the potential nodal centre in the backward district of Purulia. The backwardness can be principally attributed to the lack of direction in development. Because the district was formerly in Bihar, the pattern of transport is now being reoriented, though the progress has not yet been picked up. Bankura and Bishnupur in Bankura district are also identified as efficient regions.

6.3.5 *North of West Bengal*

In the North, Englishbazar, Balurghat, Raiganj, Darjeeling, Siliguri, Jalpaiguri, Cooch Behar-Alipurduar are the efficient regions. Due to the problems created by the partition of India, Siliguri slowly grew to be a major focus in the transport and commerce lines between South Bengal, North Bihar, Assam, Sikkim and Bhutan. The role of Siliguri assumed vital strategic importance during the national emergency declared in 1972. As a result of the convergence of transportation routes in a single node, Siliguri has become the most important trading and commercial centre of the entire northern region. Siliguri is the nerve centre of the north-eastern zone of the country, in respect of road transportation.

Darjeeling is one of the densely populated mountainous regions of West Bengal, and it assumed nodality in the Darjeeling District, probably due to the mixed character of varied economy of agriculture, plantation, handicrafts, defence and tourism.

Cooch Behar, about 176 kms. away from Siliguri, is another efficient region. Cooch Behar is the administrative headquarter of the district and at the same time, the largest urban and trading centre next only to Siliguri in North Bengal. It is the headquarter of North Bengal State Transport Corporation which maintains goods and passenger services connecting Calcutta, Assam and Bhutan.

Alipurduar in Jalpaiguri district is an important commercial and trading centre in North Bengal. Because of its strategic location near Bhutan, the service areas of Alipurduar extend beyond the border of the district making this node highly efficient in transportation.

Berhampore is the administrative headquarter and the largest urban and commercial centre in Murshidabad district. It is served by National Highway No. 34, which is a major transport corridor linking this town with Calcutta Metropolitan District and North Bengal towns. This node is also classified as highly efficient in transportation.

Of all the nodes in the north, Siliguri appeared to be the only region according to Planning Commission, as the crucial urban growth centre.

6.3.6 *Medium Efficiency Region*

Average efficiency in transportation prevails in many areas of West Bengal. In the south, Contai, Tamluk, Uluberia, Arambagh, Baduria, Baruipur, Hasnabad, Chandrakona, Katwa, Kandi, Raghunathpur, Bolpur, Kalna, Ghatal, Ondal, Suri, Jiaganj and Samserganj have average efficiency in transportation. In Midnapore district, along the Rupnarayan river and Haldi and Hijli tidal canals where Tamluk and Contai are situated, there is only an average efficiency in transportation, though there is high density of population in these areas.

Closer hinterland of Calcutta Metropolitan District, namely, Hasnabad, Baruipur, Baduria, Arambagh, are favoured with average transportation efficiency. Ghatal, which is a centre of brass and bell metal industries along with agriculture, Suri, Rampurhat in Birbhum district, Kandi, Katwa and Kalna in Burdwan district, which are centres of agro-based industries; all of them have the advantage of average efficiency in transportation. Bolpur, situated in the south-central part of Birbhum is the largest municipal urban centre in the District and is served by a road network which makes it accessible from the large agricultural catchment areas lying in Burdwan and Birbhum districts. The present locational advantage of Bolpur over other neighbouring towns can be attributed partially to its proximity to commercial centres and the industrial township of Asansol and Durgapur and the University town of Viswa-Bharati.

In the north, Kaliaganj, Mainaguri and Kalimpong are facilitated with average transportation efficiency. It can be said that these regions are not suffering from any major transport problem in so far this analysis is concerned, but if proper attention is given to these regions, it may help to improve the efficiency in transportation.

6.3.7 *Low and Very Low Efficiency Region*

Few of the regions could be grouped in low efficiency which are Jhargram in Midnapore district, Singur in Hooghly district, Joynagar, Canning in 24-Parganas district, Gangarampur, Islampur in West Dinajpur district, Kurseong in Darjeeling district, Dhupguri in Jalpaiguri district, Kashipur in Purulia district. Twenty-two nodes out of eightfour nodes are found inefficient.

Excepting Murshidabad, Dhupguri and Kurseong, others are mainly rural economy based, smaller in population and poorly served by road links which ultimately lead to a very poor transportation efficiency. Murshidabad and Dhupguri require attention for improvement in transportation. And rest of the areas in West Bengal categorised as very inefficient in transportation, and these constitute the very low efficiency region.

Very low efficiency region exists mainly due to the rural character and low population of the towns. Transport networks catering to the need of agricultural products, have not developed much. Because of economy is poor, these areas do not attract flows of population, which could have put an impetus to the growth of transportation.

6.4 Summary

As evidenced from this analysis, a region advantaged by high degree of accessibility induces a high degree of industrialisation. However, despite the existence of efficient transportation, many of the nodes have not developed in their true sense.

Growth potentialities of these nodes have been evaluated on the basis of analysis of the transportation network existing on these nodes. Transportation is one of the most important infrastructural facilities of a growing region. By studying the transportation efficiency of West Bengal, it can be said that growth of a region occurs mainly by:

(1) Increase in population of the existing urban areas,
(2) Addition of new units to the urban scene.

In West Bengal, from the view point of growth of transportation efficiency, there are four growing nodal regions which are Calcutta Industrial Region, Durgapur-Asansol region, Midnapore-Kharagpur region, and greater Siliguri region.

Urbanisation and transportation efficiencies are two positive indicators of growth potential of a centre. Growth of urbanisation points to general economic growth of an area. In this study, positive weakness of districts of Birbhum, Bankura and Midnapore can be identified; where urban centres are few and urban population is very low compared to the total population of the respective districts.

To develop transportation, both inter- and intra-district linkages are to be given more attention, with the general improvement of the existing roads. Non-metalled roads are mostly narrow and restrict free flow of traffic, these roads are to be widened and metalled. Efforts should be made to establish all weather roads for strengthening our economic base.

Since country's distribution system depends mostly on the road network, a planned approach to be made for establishment of roads, and bridges with alternative routes available to connect the production centres with the consumers, for all round economic growth.

NOTES

1. A Space Potential Derived Measure of Transportation Efficiency — Robert J. Tata, Symposium on Quantitative Methods in Geography, *21st International*

Geographical Congress 1968, p. 50.

2. The word circulation used by French Geographer has no exact English equivalent, but it represents very well concern with all spatial interaction and connections whether may be flows of goods, people, money, credit, ideas and innovations, (Transportation and Social Framework — Michael Eliot Hurst, *Economic Geography*, Vol. 49, No. 1-4, 1973, p. 163).
3. Howard L., Gauthier, *Geography, Transportation and Regional Development*, p. 618.

7

CONCLUDING OBSERVATIONS

This chapter is devoted to general observations on issues which emerge from the discussion of the earlier chapters.

Road transport development is a positive indicator of growth and growth potential of a centre and a geographical area. West Bengal with an area of 87853 sq.kms. (of which rural belts command 85,903.1 sq.kms. or 97 per cent of the total geographical area where about 75 per cent of population lives) has 1,38,165 kms. of roads ranking next to Uttar Pradesh in so far as total road length is concerned. Surfaced roads account for 22 per cent of the total kilometerage of the State and the remaining 78 per cent are unsurfaced.

Today, West Bengal ranks seventh among the states in India with regard to surfaced roads. Close examination of the road network of West Bengal affords a deeper insight into the factors which affected the spatial diffusion of roads at a time when inter-connection is a prominent motive for transport development.

Road linkages between the districts of West Bengal, intra-district road linkages and general development of roads leave much to be desired. Non-metalled roads accounting for 78 per cent of the total road length, await widening and surfacing for better use and for strengthening the linkage pattern of the region. Large rural tracts await proper linkage with urban centres. For easy, smooth and fast communication facilities, most of the roads await structural improvement. Majority of these roads are unusable during rains. Bankura, Midnapore, Birbhum and Purulia show a particularly low road kilometerage which can possibly be explained by the level of low industrial development of this region.

Lack of adequate length of all weather roads is acting as a serious constraint on the economic development of the region. It is obvious, therefore, that a rational approach is necessary to make the linkage system viable by construction of approach roads, concrete bridges.

The districts of West Bengal could therefore be subdivided, based on degrees of accessibility, into five divisions. The following classification is based on 5 kms. distance from a surfaced road computed from 1974 road map:

TABLE 7.1: Degree of Accessibility of Districts

Sl. No.	Percentage of area within 5 kms. of road	Degree of accessibility	Name of the districts
1.	70%	Very Poor	Purulia
2.	71% – 75%	Poor	Midnapore and 24-Parganas
3.	76% – 80%	Fair	Bankura, West Dinajpore, Jalpaiguri, Malda, Cooch Behar and Darjeeling
4.	81% – 85%	Good	Birbhum
5.	86% – 90%	Very Good	Howrah, Hooghly, Murshidabad, Nadia, Burdwan and Calcutta

Source: P.W.D. Road Map.

This table indicates that in density of roads Calcutta has a definite lead over all other districts. She is followed by Hooghly, Howrah and Nadia which clearly exemplifies the influence of Calcutta on its immediate neighbourhood.

In the north, Jalpaiguri, Malda and West Dinajpur show below average growth of roads. Interior rural areas here still remain largely inaccessible. Total length of municipal roads in these districts is insignificant. Though the total road length has gone up considerably since the partition, yet the situation leaves much to be desired. Most of the roads need improvement excepting the P.W.D roads. Roads maintained by local bodies are largely unsurfaced and therefore unusable during rains. These have to be metalled. The tea plantation region has a serious paucity of good metalled all weather roads. The economy of this region demands the development of a well-knit network system if it is to be diversified by relieving its total dependence on tea. There is lack of feeder roads here which have to be developed.

Purulia lags behind all other districts and its backwardness can principally be attributed to the lack of direction in its total economic development. Burdwan and Murshidabad, together with Calcutta, Howrah, Hooghly and Nadia, have the highest ranking. This is because of mining and industrial development in case of Burdwan and because of the locational advantage enjoyed by Murshidabad as a link area between north and south West Bengal. Murshidabad was a focal point of commerce till the early days of British rule. This helped to create a base whose effects are felt even today. High accessibility has not only strengthened the metropolitan economy but has led to the quick development of suburbanisation along the river Hooghly. However, it should be noted that this has taken place in an unplanned manner leading to sharp deterioration of the physical environment and to creation of a serious problems of metropolitan transport system.

Chapter four has focussed attention on the spatial structure of transportation network pointing towards the existence of unplanned highway system which do not provide alternate routes to connect cities within the State. However, the network has progressively expanded reflecting a slow but higher degree of development. The position of nodes in relation to the total system has been analysed in regard to their aggregate accessibility, the indicators being connectivity, route factor, road capacity, distance to Class I town and aggregate travel distance. The following points of general reference have emerged from this analysis:

(1) Accessibility is not so much a function of centrality but location of major trunk lines.
(2) Network accessibility is less represented than connectivity in evaluating the transportation facilities of a node.
(3) The total connectivity of smaller centres is influenced by relative location with reference to highly connected centres.
(4) The location of higher order centres controls the network development and connectivity pattern.

Calcutta is highly accessible followed by Durgapur, Kharagpur, Howrah, Burdwan, Berhampore and Siliguri. All of the above-mentioned nodes except Siliguri are located in highly accessible districts. Siliguri in the north located in a corridor of movement between north and north-eastern India, has developed into a very significant transport node of northern Bengal.

In order to visualise an ideal situation of road transport development, an attempt has been made to workout an index of transportation efficiency based on the analysis of space potential model.

Based on this model the transportation efficiency values are categorised into five relative efficiency groups and likewise the nodes have been ranked hierarchically.

TABLE 7.2: Relative Efficiency of Nodes

Relative Efficiency Group	Name of the Nodes
Very efficient	Calcutta, Howrah, Burdwan, Asansol, Durgapur, Kharagpur, Serampore, Tollygunge, Dum Dum, Arambagh, Midnapur, Bankura, Bally, Chinsura, Uttarpara, Chandernagar, Krishnanagar, Nabadwip, Berhampore, Siliguri, Barrackpore, Santipur, Ranaghat, Balurghat, Englishbazar.
Efficient	Kulti, Chittaranjan, Purulia, Bhadreswar, Jalpaiguri, Darjeeling, Cooch Behar, Bishnupur, Sonarpur, Metiabruz, Barasat, Bongaon, Habra, Chakdah, Ranigange, Alipurduar.
Average	Katwa, Ghatal, Kandi, Kalna, Suri, Bolpur, Rampurhat, Chandrakona, Raghunathganj, Mainaguri, Kalimpong, Samserganj, Ondal, Tamluk, Uluberia, Arambagh, Baruipur, Hasnabad, Jiaganj, Kaliaganj.
Inefficient	Joynagar, Murshidabad, Dubrajpur, Singur, Canning, Islampur, Sangrampur, Dhupguri, Jhargram, Kurseong, Kashipur.
Very inefficient	Bowrea, Lalgola, Raghunathpur, Domjur, Tarakeswar, Diamond Harbour.

This analysis reveals that Calcutta is the most efficient node in the system. Calcutta region is economically the most developed part of the State in regard to per capita income, percentage of working force, literacy, banking, post office, population density, etc., indicating the existence of wide economic opportunity. All these phenomena have obviously been influenced by the efficiency of the road system. As a result, Calcutta has developed into a primate city in a system of urban centres. It's transportation efficiency reflects this primacy.

The southern nodes of West Bengal enjoy efficient transportation primarily due to the fact that there is a fairly dense concentration of large cities in the region. Large population concentrations naturally led to the development of the best transportation facilities within the region which in turn attracted more people. This has been on in a cyclical manner for a long time.

The transportation efficiency of each node in West Bengal can be evaluated according to the degree of mobility it affords to the population of the area and to the resultant connectivity with other centres in the system. From this point of view the study has revealed the existence of extremely sharp regional disparities, particularly between the Calcutta Metropolitan Agglomeration and the rest of West Bengal.

In southern West Bengal three industrial complexes spread over corridors have developed efficient transportation system, viz.,

(i) Calcutta Industrial region,
(ii) Durgapur Asansol complex, and
(iii) Kharagpur-Midnapore region.

North Bengal has been able to develop only one such complex in the form of greater Siliguri region. The study reveals the position of weakness of the districts of Birbhum, Bankura and Midnapore where the urban centres are but a few and urban population also is very low compared to the total population of the respective districts.

Finally, from the point of view of accessibility and efficiency of transportation the districts of West Bengal are grouped into the following regions:

(i) Developed region,
(ii) Developing region,
(iii) Less developed region, and
(iv) Problematic region.

(i) Developed Region

Calcutta, Howrah, Hooghly and Nadia.

General Characteristics

These regions support very large industrial and urban population. Metropolis of Calcutta has been exerting a tremendous pull on the developmental forces for a very long time. The metropolitan economy has resulted in rapid suburbanisation along the river Hooghly.

Development Approaches

To cope with this rapid urbanisation the roads need widening as to accommodate more lanes.

National Highways in West Bengal do not have two lane width as in Gujarat, Maharashtra and Tamilnadu. In addition, these roads are not well maintained and most of them need constant repairing.

Moreover, there are no bus stations in the long route services as are found in Bihar, Gujarat and Tamilnadu.

C.M.D.A. has taken up the work of widening the city roads and completion of the M.T.P. rapid transit work would reduce the traffic problem to some extent within the city in near future.

(ii) **Developing Region**

Burdwan, Birbhum.

General Characteristics

These districts have immense resource potential and have developed the coal-steel belt with a fairly well developed road network.

Development Approaches

These fast growing industrial districts however demand bigger kilometerage of surfaced roads. Durgapur Expressway (not yet completed) has reduced the total route length from Burdwan to Calcutta and also the time.

(iii) **Less Developed Region**

Bankura, Midnapore, 24-Parganas, Malda, West Dinajpore and Murshidabad.

General Characteristics

This region has shown development in agricultural activities but lack of industrial development (except within the C.M.D.) or adequate mineral exploitation have kept it at a lower level of economy. This is reflected in the poorly developed transport network. This region has facilities of highways but lack in surfaced feeders. During rains these feeders become unusable making the National Highways largely ineffective. Rural roads are very poorly developed over the entire region.

Development Approaches

There has been some road expansion in parts of North Bengal and coastal districts of West Bengal. These regions are mainly agricultural and as a result extension of these roadways would help agricultural extension work.

(iv) **Problematic Region**

Darjeeling, Jalpaiguri, Cooch Behar and Purulia.

General Characteristics

This region has been identified as the frontier region. It is characterised by more difficult geologic and physiographic environment. Agricultural productivity is low. No-agricultural resource utilisation has also been of a very low order. The tea economy did not help growth of infrastructure needed for non-tea agro-economy. Purulia has always been a marginal area away from developmental initiatives.

Development Approaches

Commercial exploitation of resources like tea plantations in North Bengal and limestone and bauxite mining in Purulia did not bring adequate benefit to the areas concerned. Though during the Fourth Plan roads have been expanded in Cooch Behar, yet these areas still lag far behind other districts of West Bengal. Absence of motorable roads restricts bus services, hinders mobility of people and affects the total economy.

The problems of road transport in West Bengal may be summed up as follows:

(i) *Inaccessibility* — As is clear from Chapter three that hill stations in the north have poor accessibility. This area has immense defence importance and requires extensive development of roads in view of the difficulty in railway construction in the hills.

(ii) *Lack of bridges and poor surface condition of roads* — Lack of bridges is an acute problem for the easy movement of passengers and goods. The road width considered suitable some 50 years back, before the advent of automobiles, is still prevalent with the result that most roads are unable to cope with the requirements of the present day motor transport system.

(iii) *Type and grade mix of traffic* — It is a common feature of the roads of this country. Due to lack of specified division of roads for different modes of transport, fast movement of traffic over many stretches faces serious handicaps.

(iv) *Organisational problems* — Various agencies of road transport viz., Public Works Department looking after the construction and maintenance of roads and bridges, private and public operators running the vehicles. Regional Transport Authorities issuing license, are quite detached and no co-ordinated organisation looks after the integrated development of road transport.

(v) *Legal restrictions* — The free operation of vehicles is much restricted from one region to another and from one state to another due to different policies followed by different States. It is well reflected in the differences of taxes charged by various States.

Some suggestions could be made regarding the development of road transport in West Bengal. The roads linking the four growth centres and other urban places in the State must be developed to become major arteries and new major routes must be constructed to form an integrated road network that will serve the internal needs of the State and link it effectively with outside areas. The importance of agricultural activity in West Bengal also imposes on the transportation system a demand for a widespread network of roads capable of serving the kind of dispersed activity that is characteristic of agriculture.

Among the current proposals the ones that are of greatest importance for the development of the four urban complexes are the following:

Projects already under Construction

National Highway No. 2 Bypass (Calcutta-Adi Saptagram).
Durgapur Expressway (Calcutta-Durgapur).
Road link between Haldia and National Highway No. 6.

Proposals

Eastern Metropolitan Bypass and Barrackpur-Kalyani Expressway.
New bridges across the Hooghly river.
North-south Regional Highway proposed in the Asansol-Durgapur Interim Development Plan.
Extension of Durgapur Expressway to Asansol, parallel to the Grand Trunk Road.

Position Today

The West Bengal road network is one of the largest in India. The total road length comprising National Highways, State Highways and other P.W.D. state roads was 18,385 km. in 1985.

Since by 1981, more than 90 per cent of the average All India target was being fulfilled considering the combined achievement of the various states. While the All India picture regarding expansion of road network actually during 1961–1981 is somewhat bright, this is not sc for West Bengal and West Bengal can easily be bracketed with the few underdeveloped states on this account.

The Planning Commission treated for the first time in the Fifth-Five Year Plan the Rural Roads (i.e. Village Roads and other District Roads) as a part of the Minimum Needs Programme (MNP). The revised aim of the MNP in the Sixth Plan is to link all villages with a population of 1500 and above and 50 per cent of the villages with a population of 1,000 — 1,500 by 1990. Because of the imperative need of developing the economic condition of Rural Bengal, the preparation of the 20 Years Road Plan, West Bengal has been made with the following aims in view (20 Year Road Development Plan (1981-2001) for W.B.).

1. To develop the National Highway System as per modified Grid & Star Formula.
2. To widen and strengthen the existing State Highways to a moderate crust width of 5.5m.
3. To widen and strengthen the Major District Roads and other District Roads which have larger volume of traffic.
4. To strengthen all deficient MDRs and ODRs constructed upto the Third Five Year Plan.
5. To replace the existing temporary/week bridges and culverts.

6. To construct bridges to link up unbridged gaps of MDRs and ODRs.
7. To construct new roads which are mostly Rural Roads in order to connect all villages having population of 1,000 and above in plains and villages of population 500 and above in hills.

As already observed the Road Development Programme through successive Five Year Plans and Annual Plans since Third Five Year Plan suffered immensely because of the fact that roads tax so far failed to find place in the priority sector in the plan programmes.

A substantial part of the 1981-2001 Road Development Plan is the Construction of Rural Roads. The linking is but towns and administration centres by roads is but the beginning of development. To carry development into the interior, to bring each village into swift communication with market, to carry fertilisers and implements and other good facilities into every village, so as to develop an integrated road system and road transport services.

So far as the Growth of State Transport is concerned, it has showed an increasing trend, the fleet strength has extended to 1,244 in 1987-88 from 670 in 1961. Likewise the number of routes has increased to 128 in 1988 from 31 in 1961. In comparison to this the private buses has extended the number of routes to 148 in 1988 from 3 routes in 1966. It is noted that during the plan period, the CTC and the CSTC received considerable assistance under the CMDA programme for stabilisation of the fleets and other connected improvements. However, in the absence of clear policy regarding the future role of these public transit system, it has not been possible for either unit to evolve a long term programme of fleet stabilisation augmentation, renovation of depot and workshop facilities etc. which alone would enable optimum utilisation of personal overheads. The CSTC should be regarded as the predominant mode of bus transport in the city and should gradually replace again the private bus operations.

Roads are like areteries in a human body maintaining the economic health of a country through proper and efficient exchange of men and materials. The patterns of development of roads at in West Bengal has not led to their most efficient utilisation.

APPENDICES

APPENDIX-I

Statement Showing the Length of Road Communication Maintained by the Public Authorities in Bengal during the year 1900-1901

(This statement does not include roads and streets within Municipalities' limits and maintained from Municipal Funds)

(length in miles)

Name of Division	Name of District	Length of metalled roads maintained by the P.W.D.	Length of unmetalled roads maintained by the P.W.D.	Length of metalled roads maintained by Local Authorities	Lenght of unmetalled roads maintain ed by Local Authorities	Total of metalled roads	Total of unmetalled roads
1	2	3	4	5	6	7	8
Burdwan	Burdwan	4	–	271 3/4	255	275 3/4	255
	Bankura	–	–	224 1/4	395 1/4	224 1/4	395 1/4
	Birbhum	–	–	128 5/8	378 1/2	128 5/8	378 1/2
	Midnapore	113	1 1/2	404 7/8	304	517 7/8	305 1/2
	Hooghly	45	–	79 3/8	312 1/8	124 3/8	312 1/8
	Howrah	24 2/3	–	14 1/8	68	38 19/24	68
Presidency	24-Parganas Proper	–	–	238 3/8	1,327 3/4	238 1/8	1,327 3/4
	Calcutta	–	–	–	–	14 5/12	–
	Nadia	14 5/12	–	106 7/8	688 7/8	106 7/8	688 7/8
	Jessore	–	–	142 5/8	936 7/8	142 5/8	936 7/8
	Khulna	–	–	8 3/8	1,043	8 3/8	1,043
	Murshidabad	–	–	23 7/8	519 1/4	23 7/8	519 1/4
Rajshahi	Dinajpur	–	–	20 1/2	1,026 3/8	20 1/2	1,026 3/8
	Rajshahi	–	–	63 3/4	473 1/2	63 3/4	473 1/2
	Rangpur	–	28	16 1/4	1,373 7/8	16 1/4	1,401 7/8
	Bogra	–	–	–	338 3/4	–	338 3/4
	Pabna	–	–	5 1/4	579	5 1/4	579
	Darjeeling	143	194	–	351 3/8	143	545 3/8
	Jalpaiguri	8 1/2	–	27 3/8	660 7/8	35 7/8	660 7/8
Dacca	Dacca	–	–	6 7/8	264	6 7/8	264
	Faridpur	–	–	9	147 3/4	9	147
	Bachegonge	–	–	15 7/8	231 1/4	15 7/8	231 1/4
	Mymensingh	–	–	28 1/2	752 3/8	28 1/2	752 3/8

Contd.

APPENDIX I (Contd.)

1	2	3	4	5	6	7	8
Chittagong	Chittagong	–	–	–	612	–	612
	Noakhali	–	–	6 7/8	363 1/4	6 7/8	363 1/4
	Tippera	–	–	8 1/2	386	8 1/2	386
	Chittagong Hill Tracks	–	–	–	–	–	–
Patna	Patna	10 1/8	–	104 1/4	1,120 1/2	114 2/3	1,120 1/2
	Gaya	67	–	213 3/8	1,261	280 3/8	1,261
	Shabadad	58	–	180 3/8	1,677 1/2	238 3/8	1,677 1/2
	Muzaffarpur	–	–	48 1/4	1,037	48 1/4	1,616 5/8
	Darbhanga	–	–	89 5/8	2,266 1/2	89 5/8	1,037
	Saran	–	–	428 3/4	1,288 1/8	428 3/4	2,266 1/2
	Champaran	1 1/8	–	15 7/8	1,320	17	1,288 1/8
Bhagalpur	Monghyr	–	–	88 1/4	1,716 1/4	88 1/4	1,320
	Bhagalpur	–	–	63 3/4	2,036 1/4	63 3/4	1,716 1/4
	Purnea	–	–	118 7/8	536 1/4	118 7/8	2,036 1/4
	Malda	–	–	7 1/2	785 1/4	7 1/2	536 1/4
	Santal Parganas	–	–	2 3/8	452 1/2	2 3/8	785 1/4
Orissa	Cuttack	66 3/4	20	26 1/4	452 1/2	93	472 1/2
	Tributary Maluts	–	204	–	–	–	204
	Balasore	95 1/2	–	37 1/2	428 1/2	133	428 1/2
	Puri	113	–	81 3/8	155 1/2	194 3/8	155 1/2
Chota-nagpur	Hazaribagh	195 1/2	12 3/4	43 3/8	518	238 7/8	530 3/4
	Ranchi	101	–	1 1/8	906 1/2	102 1/8	906 1/2
	Palamau	–	–	–	376 3/8	–	376 3/8
	Singhbhum	48	–	–	448 5/8	48	448 5/8
	Manbhum	82	8 1/4	13 1/8	575 7/8	95 1/8	584 1/8
	Total	1,190 5/8	468 1/2	3,415 3/4	34,312 1/8	4,606 1/8	34,780 5/8

APPENDIX-II

Road Development in Bengal 1913-1947

(Length in miles)

Year	Roads maintained by Public Authority		Roads maintained by Local Bodies		Total length of all roads	
	Metalled	Unmetalled	Metalled	Unmetalled	Metalled	Unmetalled
1913-14					50,075	
1923-24					53,421	
1924-25					53,629	
1925-26					54,864	
1926-27	26,850	20,920	32,260	119,110	59,110	140,030
1927-28	23,398	23,677	37,540	120,374	60,938	144,051
1928-29	24,353	24,355	43,071	154,117	67,424	178,472
1929-30	24,767	23,772	45,954	159,634	70,721	183,406
1930-31	27,339	21,294	46,709	157,795	74,048	179,089
1931-32	27,634	21,044	46,907	168,927	74,541	189,971
1932-33	27,680	20,369	47,629	170,165	75,309	190,534
1933-34	27,936	20,201	48,146	172,594	76,082	192,795
1934-35	28,327	20,099	48,783	178,751	47,110	
1935-36	30,718	17,508	51,558	206,877	82,276	224,385
1936-37	30,293	16,534	52,006	215,348	82,299	23,188
1937-38	24,236	15,158	39,470	205,327	63,706	220,455
1942-43	29,901	18,214	37,829	140,149	67,730	158,363
1943-44	31,349	17,920	38,627	139,367	69,976	15,728

APPENDIX-III

Achievements in Road Development during the different Plan Periods

(A) Roads maintained by P.W.D. in different districts of West Bengal (1951-74)

(Length in kms.)

Districts	1951	1956	1961	1966	1969	1974
1	2	3	4	5	6	7
National Highway:						
Burdwan	158	158	158	158	154	154
Bankura	—	—	—	—	—	—
Birbhum	—	—	—	—	—	—
Howrah	21	21	42	42	71	71
Hooghly	72	72	72	72	110	110
Midnapore	122	112	112	112	106	106
24-Parganas	98	98	98	98	111	111
Calcutta	—	—	—	—	—	—
Nadia	66	118	118	118	108	108
Murshidabad	—	62	115	122	138	138
Darjeeling	83	99	99	99	102	102
Jalpaiguri	139	139	139	139	207	207
Malda	—	58	58	58	76	76
West Dinajpore	—	45	141	141	165	165
Cooch Behar	—	—	—	55	61	61
Purulia	66	66	66	66	67	67
Total	814	1048	1273	1280	1476	1476
State Highways:						
Burdwan	32	32	62	62	28	28
Bankura	85	149	203	203	211	211
Birbhum	—	64	88	174	168	168
Howrah	19	19	24	24	142	142
Hooghly	10	51	93	96	127	127
Midnapore	120	120	120	120	132	132
24-Parganas	218	262	277	277	565	565
Calcutta	—	—	—	22	22	22
Nadia	—	—	—	—	28	28
Murshidabad	—	112	112	112	89	89
Darjeeling	80	80	80	80	264	264
Jalpaiguri	80	69	86	86	67	67
Malda	—	—	18	18	130	150
West Dinajpore	—	—	128	122	128	128
Cooch Behar	—	—	—	5	43	43
Purulia	106	106	106	106	187	187
Total	750	1064	1402	1491	2331	2351

Contd.

APPENDIX III (Contd.)

1	2	3	4	5	6	7
Major District Roads:						
Burdwan	–	54	320	354	709	709
Bankura	–	138	138	138	191	191
Birbhum	–	43	107	162	277	277
Howrah	–	32	102	102	99	99
Hooghly	13	50	162	210	185	265
Midnapore	–	310	378	40	630	630
24-Parganas	–	182	301	363	597	597
Calcutta	–	–	–	–	–	–
Nadia	–	195	237	269	309	331
Murshidabad	–	69	104	165	263	264
Darjeeling	–	14	37	37	19	19
Jalpaiguri	–	18	64	64	156	156
Malda	–	56	149	149	34	34
West Dinajpore	–	–	13	13	59	59
Cooch Behar	–	–	–	107	161	161
Purulia	–	–	–	78	111	111
Total	13	1161	2219	2651	3800	3903
Other District Roads:						
Burdwan	53	69	91	195	195	211
Bankura	48	48	154	254	193	336
Birbhum	24	24	110	213	104	186
Howrah	3	3	29	51	51	165
Hooghly	–	–	45	176	204	204
Midnapore	37	66	213	298	254	314
24-Parganas	112	66	213	298	254	314
Calcutta	–	–	–	–	–	–
Nadia	15	21	58	142	94	182
Murshidabad	–	–	93	197	200	235
Darjeeling	368	368	389	514	345	345
Jalpaiguri	155	155	280	384	300	480
Malda	–	2	24	122	150	184
West Dinajpore	50	50	83	187	257	257
Cooch Behar	–	–	–	226	167	256
Purulia	66	66	82	132	35	115
Total	931	938	1984	3624	2829	4007

Contd.

APPENDIX III (Contd.)

1	2	3	4	5	6	7
Village Roads:						
Burdwan	—	26	27	54	62	95
Bankura	—	—	21	48	48	61
Birbhum	—	—	—	82	82	82
Howrah	—	—	—	21	24	30
Hooghly	—	40	70	173	173	173
Midnapore	—	22	56	123	123	133
24-Parganas	—	62	115	194	194	194
Calcutta	—	—	—	—	—	—
Nadia	—	30	98	98	98	—
Murshidabad	—	21	61	109	124	131
Darjeeling	—	—	—	—	—	—
Jalpaiguri	—	—	—	29	29	29
Malda	—	—	2	24	44	66
West Dinajpore	—	—	35	101	114	167
Cooch Behar	—	—	—	—	—	33
Purulia	—	—	—	—	—	—
Total	—	201	417	1056	1115	1315

Source: Chief Engineer, P.W.D.

(A) Extra Municipal Road length under P.W.D. in different districts of West Bengal as on 31st March:

(*Length in kms.*)

Districts	1975	1976	1977
Burdwan	1394	1394	1408
Birbhum	868	893	893
Bankura	969	1018	1023
Midnapore	1691	1691	1700
Howrah	547	547	556
Hooghly	1065	1066	1066
24-Parganas	2112	2336	2392
Calcutta	22	22	22
Nadia	822	833	851
Murshidabad	911	939	939
Darjeeling	844	864	843
Jalpaiguri	1061	1061	1068
Malda	546	572	572
West Dinajpore	846	853	853
Cooch Behar	1385	1383	1385
Purulia	609	656	662

Source: Economic Review 1977-'78 & 1978-'79.

Contd.

APPENDIX III (Contd.)

(B) Roads Maintained by District Boards in West Bengal (1956-1974):

(Length in kms.)

Districts	1956		1961		1966*		1969*		1974*		Total
	Metalled	Unmetalled	Metalled	Unmetalled	Metalled	Unmetalled	Metalled	Unmetalled	Metalled	Unmetalled	
Burdwan	484	2258	417	2268	291	2192	432	2282	—	—	4142
Bankura	634	866	640	832	506	867	506	867	—	—	1469
Birbhum	134	1139	92	1160	291	1184	238	1150	—	—	1306
Howrah	82	1508	58	1489	45	1476	31	1417	—	—	1426
Hooghly	79	1738	53	1540	50	1518	51	1519	—	—	1427
Midnapore	496	2541	446	2393	445	2960	446	3206	—	—	4095
24-Parganas	143	8312	114	6297	84	6618	108	6654	—	—	6631
Calcutta	—	—	—	—	—	—	—	—	—	—	—
Nadia	42	1530	35	1503	42	1415	1255	38	—	—	1319
Murshidabad	51	2538	45	2507	45	2446	19	2470	—	—	2476
Darjeeling	23	504	5	483	—	481	3	481	—	—	416
Jalpaiguri	253	473	182	531	126	497	139	495	—	—	774
Malda	27	739	14	734	6	817	11	812	—	—	816
West Dinajpore	—	—	5	1297	3	1089	3	1024	—	—	762
Cooch Behar	—	—	—	—	—	—	—	—	—	—	—
Purulia	—	—	212	903	106	824	66	753	—	—	1008
Total:	2448	24146	2319	23937	1868	24384	3308	23168	—	—	28067

* Zilla Parishad

Source: Directorate of Panchayat, West Bengal.

Note: Length of Metalled and Unmetalled roads separately are not available.

Contd.

APPENDIX III (Contd.)

(C) Roads Maintained by Muncipalities in West Bengal (1956-1974):

(*Length in kms.*)

Districts	1956		1961		1966*		1969*		1974*	
	Metalled	Unmetalled	Metalled	Unmetalled	Metalled	Unmetalled	Metalled	Unmetalled	Metalled	Unmetalled
Burdwan	167	80	171	80	186	93	208	108	230	100
Bankura	63	47	76	58	76	57	75	60	117	99
Birbhum	77	31	76	31	64	41	63	39	65	49
Howrah	216	64	227	58	276	47	286	36	287	21
Hooghly	187	135	362	203	335	216	355	211	455	194
Midnapore	137	138	138	180	156	197	172	256	250	348
24-Parganas	814	518	846	538	948	548	1129	711	1321	880
Calcutta	702	35	763	43	765	43	765	44	786	34
Nadia	101	189	204	290	228	209	332	189	399	208
Murshidabad	153	150	167	148	189	130	204	116	231	124
Darjeeling	72	111	101	87	107	95	134	131	135	74
Jalpaiguri	14	13	21	23	27	80	36	69	61	112
Malda	32	35	40	32	43	24	61	26	62	25
West Dinajpur	11	60	32	37	12	14	15	67	24	88
Cooch Behar	26	21	27	21	50	18	52	17	52	17
Purulia	—	—	23	35	24	34	28	21	33	29
Total:	2773	1620	3274	1858	3486	1846	3915	2101	4509	2401

* Zilla Parishad.

Source: (1) Muncipalities.
(2) *Calcutta Corporation Year Book.*

APPENDIX-III-A

Achievements up to 31.3.1981 (P.W.D. Surfaced Road)

Districts	Category of Road				
	National Highway	State Highway	Major District Road	Other District Road	Village Road
Burdwan	189.27	246.79	562.0	266.0	357.0
Bankura	—	333.48	191.0	460.0	220.0
Birbhum	—	248.23	136.0	98.0	300.0
Howrah	61.50	21.00	206.0	55.0	150.0
Hoogly	67.70	153.00	274.0	199.0	347.0
Midnapore	161.00	505.50	202.0	482.0	548.0
24-Parganas	93.00	359.00	466.0	445.0	778.0
Calcutta					
Nadia	117.00	159.0	225.0	126.0	273.0
Murshidabad	134.00	222.80	108.0	360.0	264.0
Darjeeling	133.30	224.60	34.0	341.0	81.0
Jalpaiguri	293.40	222.01	165:0	367.0	169.0
Malda	68.50	49.00	98.0	168.0	192.0
West Dinajpur	168.00	152.20	89.0	140.0	374.0
Cooch Behar	55.50	93.26	123.0	218.0	96.0
Purulia	63.49	159.00	164.0	237.0	16.0

Source: 20 Year Road Development Plan (1981-2001) for West Bengal, Govt. of W.B.

APPENDIX-IV

Total Connectivity Matrix — 'C' Matrix

	1	2	3	4	5	6	7	8	9	10	11	12	13	14	15	16	17	18	19	Total
1.	502	501	889	717	474	497	390	477	191	164	170	46	282	299	778	255	127	29	29	6817
2.	501	502	889	717	474	497	390	477	191	164	170	46	282	299	778	255	127	29	29	6817
3.	889	889	2086	1424	1130	1174	1058	802	588	503	537	124	705	761	1382	650	186	98	98	15084
4.	717	717	1424	1260	965	1431	920	785	584	521	546	184	684	659	1119	486	154	74	74	13304
5.	474	474	1130	965	1456	2012	1329	727	1039	1018	1111	307	1234	579	1016	273	138	22	22	15335
6.	497	497	1174	1431	2012	3802	1963	1062	1648	1616	1714	624	1797	997	1034	375	87	34	34	22398
7.	390	390	1058	920	1329	1963	1321	612	1014	986	1077	303	1149	594	794	293	76	30	30	14329
8.	477	477	802	785	727	1062	612	590	425	406	427	146	540	367	815	222	128	20	20	9048
9.	191	191	588	584	1039	1648	1014	425	854	832	910	266	950	435	488	162	42	15	15	10649
10.	164	164	503	521	1018	1616	986	406	832	834	904	272	942	381	456	117	40	6	6	10168
11.	170	170	537	546	1111	1714	1077	427	910	904	1008	280	1032	401	488	121	42	6	6	10950
12.	46	46	124	184	307	624	303	146	266	272	280	112	286	142	115	138	6	2	2	3301
13.	282	282	705	648	1234	1797	1149	540	950	942	1032	286	1140	441	735	155	105	8	8	12475
14.	299	299	761	659	579	997	594	367	435	381	401	142	441	443	463	303	42	56	56	7718
15.	778	778	1382	1119	1016	1034	794	815	488	456	488	115	735	463	1431	350	310	34	34	12620
16.	255	255	650	486	273	375	293	222	162	117	121	38	155	303	350	320	36	82	82	4557
17.	127	127	186	154	138	87	76	128	42	40	42	6	105	42	310	36	156	2	2	1805
18.	29	29	98	74	22	34	30	20	15	6	6	2	8	56	34	82	2	37	37	621
19.	29	29	98	74	22	34	30	20	15	6	6	2	8	56	34	82	2	37	37	621

APPENDIX-IV-A

Direct Connectivity Matrix — 'C[1]' Matrix

	1	2	3	4	5	6	7	8	9	10	11	12	13	14	15	16	17	18	19	No.of direct connec-tions
1. Purulia	0	1	1	0	0	0	0	0	0	0	0	0	0	0	0	0	0	0	0	2
2. Asansol	1	0	1	0	0	0	0	0	0	0	0	0	0	0	0	0	0	0	0	2
3. Durgapur	1	1	0	1	0	0	0	1	0	0	0	0	0	0	1	0	0	0	0	5
4. Burdwan	0	0	1	0	1	0	0	0	0	0	0	0	0	0	1	0	0	0	0	3
5. Howrah	0	0	0	1	0	1	1	0	0	0	0	0	0	0	0	0	0	0	0	3
6. Calcutta	0	0	0	0	1	0	1	0	1	1	1	0	1	0	0	0	0	0	0	6
7. Kharagpur	0	0	0	0	1	1	0	1	0	0	0	0	0	0	0	0	0	0	0	3
8. Midnapore	0	0	1	0	0	0	1	0	0	0	0	0	0	0	0	0	0	0	0	2
9. Naihati	0	0	0	0	0	1	0	0	0	0	0	0	1	0	0	0	0	0	0	2
10. Basirhat	0	0	0	0	0	1	0	0	0	0	1	0	0	0	0	0	0	0	0	2
11. Habra	0	0	0	0	0	1	0	0	0	1	0	1	0	0	0	0	0	0	0	3
12. Bongaon	0	0	0	0	0	0	0	0	0	0	1	0	0	0	0	0	0	0	0	1
13. Santipur	0	0	0	0	0	1	0	0	1	0	0	0	0	1	0	0	0	0	0	3
14. Krishnanagar	0	0	0	0	0	0	0	0	0	0	0	0	1	0	1	0	0	0	0	2
15. Berhampore	0	0	1	1	0	0	0	0	0	0	0	0	0	1	0	1	0	0	0	4
16. Englishbazar	0	0	0	0	0	0	0	0	0	0	0	0	0	0	1	0	1	0	0	2
17. Siliguri	0	0	0	0	0	0	0	0	0	0	0	0	0	0	0	1	0	1	1	3
18. Jalpaiguri	0	0	0	0	0	0	0	0	0	0	0	0	0	0	0	0	1	0	0	1
19. Cooch Behar	0	0	0	0	0	0	0	0	0	0	0	0	0	0	0	0	1	0	0	1

APPENDIX-V

Route Distance Matrix (Distance in Kilometres)

	1	2	3	4	5	6	7	8	9	10	11	12	13	14	15	16	17	18	19
1.	0	241	390	235	113	244	729	50	374	193	226	656	331	441	215	740	306	550	325
2.	241	0	213	186	128	226	488	191	124	183	244	406	359	369	180	315	89	300	76
3.	390	213	0	92	210	79	701	273	337	30	97	619	202	212	73	397	97	513	116
4.	235	186	92	0	194	65	674	185	310	62	83	592	188	198	59	309	97	486	116
5.	113	128	210	194	0	231	616	63	252	145	113	534	218	228	102	187	193	428	212
6.	244	226	79	65	131	0	714	194	329	49	18	632	123	133	46	318	137	526	156
7.	729	488	701	674	616	714	0	679	364	690	732	294	837	847	587	803	577	188	558
8.	50	191	273	185	63	194	679	0	315	243	176	597	281	291	240	140	331	491	350
9.	374	124	337	310	252	329	364	315	0	113	349	282	452	462	110	448	213	250	194
10.	193	183	30	62	145	49	690	243	113	0	67	589	172	182	43	267	94	483	113
11.	226	244	97	83	113	18	732	176	347	67	0	650	105	115	64	300	155	544	174
12.	656	406	619	592	534	632	294	597	282	589	650	0	755	765	605	730	495	106	476
13.	331	359	202	188	218	123	837	281	452	172	105	755	0	10	169	257	260	649	279
14.	441	364	212	198	228	133	847	291	462	182	115	765	10	0	179	189	270	659	289
15.	215	180	73	59	102	46	587	240	110	43	64	605	164	179	0	289	91	480	110
16.	74	315	397	309	187	318	803	140	448	267	300	730	257	189	289	0	455	615	474
17.	306	89	97	97	193	137	577	331	213	94	155	495	260	270	91	455	0	487	19
18.	550	300	513	486	428	526	188	491	250	483	549	106	649	659	480	615	489	0	370
19.	325	76	116	116	212	156	558	350	194	113	174	476	279	289	110	474	19	370	0

APPENDIX-VI

Straight Line Distance Matrix (in kms.)

	1	2	3	4	5	6	7	8	9	10	11	12	13	14	15	16	17	18	19
1.	0	60	78	150	230	236	135	126	268	286	260	284	300	313	156	255	432	464	531
2.	60	0	24	96	176	182	159	150	214	230	206	230	203	190	115	214	391	423	491
3.	78	24	0	72	152	158	135	126	190	206	182	206	179	166	91	190	367	399	467
4.	150	96	72	0	80	86	207	198	118	134	110	134	164	151	76	175	352	384	452
5.	230	176	152	80	0	6	102	111	38	54	30	54	70	83	158	255	432	464	532
6.	236	182	158	86	6	0	102	111	32	48	24	48	64	77	152	251	428	460	528
7.	135	159	135	207	102	102	0	9	134	150	126	150	166	179	217	316	499	525	599
8.	126	150	126	198	111	111	9	0	143	159	135	159	175	188	226	325	502	534	602
9.	268	214	190	118	38	32	134	143	0	80	56	80	32	45	120	219	396	428	496
10.	284	230	206	134	54	48	150	159	80	0	24	48	112	125	200	299	476	506	576
11.	260	206	182	110	30	24	126	135	56	24	0	24	88	101	200	299	476	506	576
12.	284	230	206	134	54	48	150	159	80	48	24	0	112	125	200	299	476	506	576
13.	300	203	179	164	70	64	166	175	32	112	88	112	0	13	88	187	286	463	386
14.	313	190	166	151	83	77	179	188	45	125	101	125	13	0	75	174	351	383	451
15.	156	115	91	76	158	152	217	226	120	200	200	200	88	75	0	99	278	308	378
16.	255	214	190	175	255	251	316	325	219	299	299	299	187	174	99	0	177	209	277
17.	432	391	367	352	432	428	499	502	396	476	476	476	286	351	278	177	0	32	100
18.	464	423	399	384	464	460	525	534	428	506	506	506	463	383	308	209	32	0	132
19.	532	491	467	452	532	528	599	602	496	576	576	576	386	451	378	277	100	132	0

APPENDIX-VII

Growth of Registered Vehicles in the Districts of West Bengal (1967-1974)

Name of the District	Total number of registered vehicles								Growth Index							
	1967	1968	1969	1970	1971	1972	1973	1974	1967	1968	1969	1970	1971	1972	1973	1974
(a) *Goods Vehicles*:																
Burdwan	5949	6070	6625	6787	3597	4201	6553	4023	100	102	111	114	60	70	110	67
Bankura	1170	1245	1289	1036	1263	1339	1375	1411	100	106	110	88	107	114	117	120
Birbhum	613	630	666	674	694	712	734	763	100	102	108	109	113	116	119	124
Howrah	1655	1681	1931	2251	4077	4208	4376	4257	100	101	116	136	246	254	264	257
Hooghly	2608	3196	3230	3280	2554	2510	3029	3117	100	122	123	125	97	96	116	119
Midnapore	1366	1475	1588	1634	1666	1712	1292	1672	100	107	116	119	121	125	94	122
24-Parganas	4630	4711	4809	3800	5068	5108	5494	6754	100	101	103	82	109	110	118	145
Calcutta	13295	15649	15335	16521	21204	18269	19584	18639	100	117	115	124	159	137	147	140
Nadia	285	287	290	368	270	270	241	346	100	100	101	129	94	94	84	121
Murshidabad	742	766	813	879	927	985	370	390	100	103	109	118	124	132	49	52
Darjeeling	1084	1111	1146	1056	852	1256	1192	1044	100	102	105	97	78	115	109	96
Jalpaiguri	3106	3132	3210	3265	3318	3335	3512	3566	100	100	103	105	106	107	113	114
Malda	320	381	455	485	563	527	548	347	100	119	142	151	175	164	171	108
West Dinajpore	400	404	438	439	454	467	492	503	100	101	109	109	113	116	123	125
Cooch Behar	484	497	545	304	319	336	451	575	100	102	113	62	65	69	93	118
Purulia	463	502	561	605	643	695	814	1838	100	108	121	130	138	150	175	396
West Bengal	28768	41252	43034	43638	53059	45931	49967	50744	100	143	149	151	184	159	173	176

Contd.

APPENDIX VII (Contd.)

Name of the District	Total number of registered vehicles								Growth Index							
	1967	1968	1969	1970	1971	1972	1973	1974	1967	1968	1969	1970	1971	1972	1973	1974
(b) *Motor Cycles*:																
Burdwan	2203	1840	3822	4494	3900	4006	6652	6805	100	83	173	203	177	181	301	308
Birbhum	117	128	129	145	162	171	188	201	100	109	110	123	138	176	160	171
Bankura	174	215	271	311	358	338	354	414	100	123	155	178	205	194	203	237
Howrah	614	589	774	863	271	223	235	121	100	95	126	140	44	36	38	19
Hooghly	978	692	875	1015	1003	1031	1190	1259	100	70	89	103	102	105	121	128
Midnapore	698	598	948	1105	1126	1092	2341	963	100	85	135	158	161	156	335	137
24-Parganas	934	1035	1419	1548	1760	1792	1597	1597	100	110	151	165	188	191	170	170
Calcutta	9452	8889	10844	11129	13481	14469	18271	21279	100	94	114	117	142	153	193	225
Nadia	60	121	149	—	174	174	179	182	100	201	248	—	290	290	298	303
Murshidabad	167	181	267	334	408	423	283	316	100	108	159	200	244	253	169	189
Darjeeling	99	46	239	380	450	529	205	280	100	46	241	383	454	534	207	282
Jalpaiguri	655	461	367	527	814	838	581	618	100	70	132	80	124	127	88	94
Malda	77	93	107	128	135	150	165	229	100	120	138	166	172	194	214	297
West Dinajpore	43	40	48	60	62	68	73	76	100	93	111	139	144	158	169	176
Cooch Behar	252	271	365	237	282	343	424	533	100	92	144	94	111	136	168	211
Purulia	158	159	218	244	43	298	507	486	100	100	137	154	27	188	320	307
West Bengal	7436	15383	21332	22520	24086	25945	33246	35359	100	206	286	302	323	348	447	475

Contd.

APPENDIX VII (Contd.)

Name of the District	Total number of registered vehicles								Growth Index							
	1967	1968	1969	1970	1971	1972	1973	1974	1967	1968	1969	1970	1971	1972	1973	1974
(c) *Public Service Vehicles*:																
Burdwan	1351	2132	1436	1882	1250	1448	1966	1270	100	157	106	139	92	107	145	94
Bankura	315	349	347	360	387	375	379	414	100	110	110	114	122	119	120	131
Birbhum	230	200	223	247	258	259	263	277	100	86	96	107	112	112	114	120
Howrah	759	942	887	988	1071	1117	1275	949	100	124	116	130	141	147	167	125
Hooghly	928	630	540	553	591	417	427	480	100	67	58	59	63	44	46	51
Midnapore	925	1216	1058	1111	1152	1282	1074	1224	100	131	114	120	124	138	116	132
24-Parganas	1165	1447	1266	1512	1392	1665	1225	1489	100	124	108	129	119	142	105	127
Calcutta	9247	7751	7883	7888	8287	9069	11922	12252	100	84	85	85	89	98	128	132
Nadia	212	166	249	222	243	239	230	193	100	78	117	104	114	112	108	91
Murshidabad	278	300	312	326	339	351	190	200	100	107	112	117	121	126	68	71
Darjeeling	548	306	627	582	420	572	847	515	100	55	114	106	76	104	154	93
Jalpaiguri	359	718	555	482	441	472	690	463	100	200	154	134	122	131	192	128
Malda	199	209	231	242	294	343	374	275	100	105	116	121	147	172	187	138
West Dinajpore	199	189	196	192	205	220	253	293	100	94	98	96	103	110	127	147
Cooch Behar	298	366	384	301	326	350	425	509	100	122	128	101	109	117	142	170
Purulia	143	181	157	177	200	214	274	212	100	126	109	123	139	149	191	148
West Bengal	14445	17142	16337	17001	16939	18392	20106	21075	100	118	113	117	117	127	139	145

Contd.

APPENDIX VII (Contd.)

Name of the District	Total number of registered vehicles								Growth Index							
	1967	1968	1969	1970	1971	1972	1973	1974	1967	1968	1969	1970	1971	1972	1973	1974
(d) *Other Vehicles*:																
Burdwan	583	597	551	628	221	267	884	675	100	102	94	107	37	45	151	115
Bankura	36	39	47	53	59	28	28	44	100	108	130	147	163	.77	77	122
Birbhum	75	80	85	91	91	97	103	121	100	106	113	121	121	129	137	161
Howrah	300	318	333	327	278	294	357	476	100	106	111	109	92	98	119	158
Hooghly	158	14	37	30	48	51	130	156	100	8	23	18	30	32	82	98
Midnapore	85	112	123	139	142	171	172	107	100	131	144	163	167	201	202	125
24-Parganas	568	650	745	118	801	822	2340	2470	100	114	131	20	141	144	411	434
Calcutta	2127	1241	2517	1520	1860	1986	2621	2749	100	58	118	71	87	93	123	129
Nadia	102	102	31	49	80	84	88	114	100	100	30	48	78	82	86	111
Murshidabad	73	90	49	99	103	104	129	134	100	123	67	135	141	142	176	183
Darjeeling	368	382	433	307	333	345	781	5	100	103	117	83	90	93	212	1
Jalpaiguri	970	986	1003	593	619	635	641	635	100	101	103	61	63	65	66	65
Malda	57	61	63	72	21	25	77	20	100	107	110	126	36	43	135	35
West Dinajpore	29	35	34	65	81	89	90	92	100	113	117	224	279	306	310	317
Cooch Behar	43	43	77	6	6	23	23	5	100	100	179	13	13	53	53	11
Purulia	4	4	7	11	14	28	54	36	100	100	175	275	350	700	1350	900
West Bengal	5578	4739	6213	4108	4757	5049	8518	7837	100	84	111	73	85	90	152	140

Contd.

APPENDIX VII (Contd.)

Name of the District	Total number of registered vehicles								Growth Index							
	1967	1968	1969	1970	1971	1972	1973	1974	1967	1968	1969	1970	1971	1972	1973	1974
(e) *Motor Cars*:																
Burdwan	4751	4917	5321	5630	3761	4886	4082	3896	100	103	111	118	79	102	85	81
Bankura	303	327	355	388	401	362	380	427	100	107	117	128	132	119	125	140
Birbhum	246	256	263	272	274	273	287	292	100	104	106	110	111	113	116	118
Howrah	3497	3628	3981	4239	3673	3731	3741	2243	100	103	113	121	105	106	106	64
Hooghly	1944	1747	1933	2034	2176	1299	1354	1423	100	89	99	104	111	66	69	73
Midnapore	724	766	823	834	856	775	637	620	100	105	113	115	118	107	87	85
24-Parganas	5543	5839	6138	6402	6875	7197	7112	8534	100	105	110	115	124	129	128	153
Calcutta	45163	37966	42754	47526	51191	54728	60412	64847	100	84	94	105	113	121	133	143
Nadia	75	77	324	225	268	68	69	70	100	102	432	300	357	90	92	93
Murshidabad	437	392	486	536	1068	780	252	279	100	89	111	122	244	178	57	63
Darjeeling	2434	1443	2390	3363	3475	3562	3499	3584	100	59	98	138	142	146	143	147
Jalpaiguri	2275	2354	2336	1807	1637	1883	1957	1984	100	103	102	79	71	82	86	87
Malda	141	146	153	162	163	165	168	113	100	103	108	114	115	117	119	80
West Dinajpore	132	249	154	160	167	177	191	195	100	188	116	121	126	134	144	147
Cooch Behar	217	278	129	105	111	113	48	122	100	128	64	48	51	52	22	56
Purulia	346	279	223	235	459	287	364	737	100	80	64	67	132	82	105	213
West Bengal	68228	60664	67707	73918	75058	80302	84553	89366	100	88	99	108	110	117	123	130

Source: Home Transport Department, Government of West Bengal.

APPENDIX-VIII

Table Showing Total Length of Roads/Motors Vehicles on Road in the District of W.B. (1966-1977)

Year	Total length of roads	Total number of Motor Vehicles on road
1	2	3
District — Burdwan:		
1966	3585.00	10,683
1967	3727.02	11,340
1968	4013.00	12,968
1969	4066.11	13,313
1970	4070.26	14,506
1971	4071.41	13,544
1972	4133.00	18,310
1973	4138.56	19,300
1974	4142.39	19,595
District — Birbhum:		
1966	2039.00	530
1967	2042.00	466
1968	2236.00	515
1969	2250.00	670
1970	2268.00	695
1971	2275.00	715
1972	2280.00	745
1973	2280.00	1,097
1974	2280.00	938
District — Bankura:		
1966	2149.00	574
1967	2160.43	603
1968	2273.00	813
1969	2273.47	817
1970	2273.47	885
1971	2377.00	1,045
1972	2533.00	1,154
1973	2609.00	1,231
1974	2614.79	1,308
District — Hooghly:		
1966	2846.00	3,019
1967	2848.00	3,400

Contd.

APPENDIX VIII (Contd.)

1	2	3
1968	3061.00	4,229
1969	3061.00	3,897
1970	3064.08	3,881
1971	3068.00	4,923
1972	3226.00	5,638
1973	3266.00	6,130
1974	3140.93	6,438
District — Howrah:		
1966	2084.00	576
1967	2084.00	701
1968	2255.00	619
1969	2295.78	977
1970	2316.78	1,324
1971	2299.00	1,686
1972	2110.61	2,151
1973	2261.00	2,548
1974	2281.59	3,151
District — 24-Parganas:		
1966	9663.00	3,842
1967	9735.00	3,856
1968	10590.00	3,288
1969	10712.09	3,543
1970	10815.09	2,910
1971	10835.00	2,763
1972	10895.00	3,328
1973	10895.00	17,800
1974	10944.19	18,311
District — Murshidabad:		
1966	3515.00	976
1967	3545.00	1,158
1968	3673.00	1,281
1969	3676.92	1,268
1970	3679.92	1,592
1971	3684.00	1,498
1972	37'0.52	1,106
1973	5710.52	1,074
1974	3741.93	1,313
District — Midnapore:		
1966	4851.00	2,570
1967	5301.00	2,676

Contd.

APPENDIX VIII (Contd.)

1	2	3
1968	5388.00	2,838
1969	5631.69	2,995
1970	5680.69	4,219
1971	5880.00	2,246
1972	6173.00	2,609
1973	6275.00	2,677
1974	6375.14	2,480
District — Purulia:		
1966	1370.00	929
1967	1370.00	1,100
1968	1438.00	1,212
1969	1438.49	1,355
1970	1438.49	1,190
1971	1500.00	762
1972	1676.00	824
1973	1676.00	918
1974	1678.52	1,371
District — Malda:		
1966	1261.00	490
1967	1261.00	526
1968	1375.00	565
1969	1381.95	534
1970	1381.95	552
1971	1400.00	532
1972	1411.78	479
1973	1413.00	505
1974	1419.78	922
District — Darjeeling:		
1966	1413.00	7,739
1967	1416.00	7,974
1968	1416.00	8,267
1969	1423.00	8,534
1970	1423.00	8,628
1971	1423.00	8,981
1972	1465.98	9,325
1973	1466.00	5,434
1974	1467.85	6,794
District — Jalpaiguri:		
1966	1432.00	2,432
1967	1448.00	2,068

Contd.

APPENDIX VIII (Contd.)

1	2	3
1968	1633.00	1,891
1969	1633.00	1,685
1970	1636.00	2,777
1971	1636.00	2,785
1972	2007.80	2,869
1973	2007.80	7,101
1974	2007.80	7,283
District — West Dinajpore:		
1966	1688.00	357
1967	1688.00	357
1968	1886.00	366
1969	1943.30	387
1970	1943.30	429
1971	1921.00	452
1972	1788.00	506
1973	1788.00	580
1974	1723.66	586
District — Cooch Behar:		
1966	461.00	580
1967	462.00	696
1968	1359.00	808
1969	1360.00	925
1970	1360.00	953
1971	1360.00	1,044
1972	3617.00	1,165
1973	3617.00	1,371
1974	3624.85	1,749

APPENDIX-IX

Progress of Motor Vehicles on Road (1951–1976)

Year	Motor Cycles	Jeeps	Private Cars	Taxi	Bus	Goods Vehicles	Auto Rickshaws	Miscellaneous
1951	2,175	–	26,117	–	5,483	16,564	–	222
1956	5,775	768	48,183	2,785	3,629	19,970	–	5,363
1957	7,695	4,445	50,492	3,962	3,670	23,553	–	4,463
1958	8,526	4,521	53,000	4,500	4,000	25,000	–	4,701
1960	–	1,274	58,419	3,486	4,238	22,399	–	6,015
1961	10,593	1,191	60,185	3,394	4,721	23,766	–	5,716
1962	12,062	1,323	61,653	3,383	4,623	23,395	–	6,658
1963	12,935	1,228	62,168	3,735	4,910	24,135	–	9,234
1964	13,725	1,347	64,045	3,798	4,882	25,069	–	9,954
1965	14,323	1,450	67,398	4,184	4,637	26,914	–	11,368
1966	19,600	9,600	77,200	6,320	7,800	40,900	300	7,400
1967	20,910	1,700	76,650	5,050	8,150	31,750	280	13,300
1968	23,508	1,748	77,838	5,194	8,383	32,656	288	14,680
1969	26,106	1,796	79,026	5,338	8,400	33,560	296	16,060
1970	22,520	1,844	72,074	7,398	9,427	34,283	181	13,508
1971	31,302	1,892	82,390	5,770	8,700	35,368	322	18,820
1973	36,398	1,900	83,378	16,160	9,060	36,453	350	16,160
1976	–	7,797	81,393	10,231	8,521	37,105	3,191	–

Source: Basic Transport Statistics, 1961, 1965, 1966, 1967, 1968. Pocket Book on Transport in India, 1972-73, India, 1977-78.

APPENDIX-X

Growth of State Transport

The following Operational Statistics would indicate the growth of State Transport over 25 year (1951-1976)

Year	Kilometerage run (in lakhs)			Number of passengers (in lakhs)			Earnings (in lakhs)		
	C.S.T.C.	N.B.S.T.C.	D.S.T.C.	C.S.T.C.	N.B.S.T.C.	D.S.T.C.	C.S.T.C.	N.B.S.T.C.	D.S.T.C.
1951-52	89.60	8.16	–	548.00	–	–	48.37	–	–
1952-53	107.94	9.36	–	642.00	–	–	84.58	–	–
1953-54	141.36	12.38	–	851.00	–	–	85.22	–	–
1954-55	172.27	16.41	–	1170.00	–	–	109.39	–	–
1955-56	227.07	21.79	–	1645.57	–	–	159.74	–	–
1956-57	267.76	29.12	–	1997.00	–	–	190.45	–	–
1957-58	307.77	35.16	–	2351.25	–	–	258.89	–	–
1958-59	336.80	38.30	–	2839.00	–	–	307.65	–	–
1959-60	378.13	43.77	–	3437.00	–	–	369.40	–	–
1960-61	436.35	47.23	–	4235.80	–	–	445.40	–	–
1961-62	478.81	47.98	–	4691.42	54.02	–	441.15	42.10	–
1962-63	513.72	53.25	–	5035.42	60.06	–	491.41	45.91	–
1963-64	473.19	56.00	1.1	4930.95	68.54	18.45	462.12	51.50	5.16
1964-65	457.30	55.73	17.6	4895.00	72.68	50.75	510.00	56.42	9.8
1965-66	478.70	68.64	32.1	3955.89	92.63	135.05	560.50	72.19	20.00
1966-67	449.81	81.98	36.2	3963.79	131.84	119.91	555.94	97.60	29.00
1967-68	408.93	91.88	38.5	3901.73	157.95	115.12	542.32	112.91	30.16
1968-69	342.86	103.80	48.59	3726.66	170.04	111.62	542.03	126.01	31.31
1969-70	310.90	111.50	53.26	3509.90	181.54	114.96	493.19	141.75	38.33
1970-71	259.72	130.97	42.07	2899.00	200.44	95.80	399.38	159.70	28.91
1971-72	241.49	130.10	31.12	2553.46	202.08	67.00	370.12	171.52	20.39
1972-73	329.61	175.24	37.58	3996.00	223.91	71.45	525.17	208.30	27.16
1973-74	285.86	173.86	41.85	3188.00	255.50	90.08	455.40	231.23	36.54
1974-75	258.77	151.40	39.92	2821.62	248.20	84.96	461.00	222.62	44.55
1975-76	275.83	160.75	46.04	2719.48	260.03	110.90	574.89	259.21	64.55

Source: Calcutta State Transport Corporation, North Bengal State Transport Corporation, Durgapur State Transport Corporation.

APPENDIX-XI

Calutta State Transport Corporation

(A) Present Short Route Service:

Sl. No.	Route No.	Route Description	Length of the route (in kms.)	No of ordinary buses/limited buses
1		2	3	4
1.	2	Ballygunge Station-Paikpara via Esplanade	17.46	25/8
2.	2B	Ballygunge Station-Bagbazar via Esplanade	17.10	24
3.	3	Kiderpore-Shyambazar via Moulali	15.77	30
4.	3A	C.I.T. Road, Kankurgachi-Thakurpukur via B.B.D. Bag	21.56	22/14
5.	3B	Shyambazar-Shapore via Esplanade	17.20	4
6.	3C	Bangur Avenue-Esplanade via Shyambazar	11.10	4/8
7.	4	Kundghat-Baranagar via B.B.D. Bag/Bentinck Street	16.42	40
8.	5	Garia-Howrah Station via B.B.D. Bag	18.02	23/12
9.	6	Garia-Howrah Station via B.B.D. Bag	17.06	33/14
10.	7	Hazra Park-Sarsuna	10.78	12
11.	8	Ballygunge Station-Howrah Station via Eliot Road	15.53	13/8
12.	8B	Jadavpur-Howrah Station via Manicktala	17.22	31
13.	9	Jadavpur Station-Ultadanga Wooden Bridge via B.B.D. Bag/C.R. Avenue	17.60	23
14.	9A	Jadavpur-Santoshpur via Jadavpur Station	2.20	2
15.	9 Shuttle	Manicktala-Daspara	4.10	5
16.	10	Ballygunge Station-Howrah Station via Sundari Mohan Avenue	11.27	20/6

Contd.

APPENDIX XI (Contd.)

1		2	3	4
17.	11	Howrah Station-Rathtala via Sealdah	15.90	29
18.	11A	Dum Dum Junction-Howrah Station via Manicktala	10.80	28
19.	12D	Thakurpukur-Howrah Station via Mominpur/Kidderpur	18.50	14/8
20.	14	Bengal Chemical-Behala via Esplanade/C.R. Avenue/B.B.D. Bag	18.35	17/16
21.	15	Howrah Station-Ultadanga Wooden Bridge via Hatibagan	5.79	13
22.	16	Dhakuria-Shibpur Tram Depot via Sealdah	16.20	20/10
23.	33	Chetla-Paikpara via Sealdah	16.82	34
24.	34	Ariadaha-Esplanade via Shyambazar	14.97	19/14
25.	35	Joramandir-Sealdah	4.10	9
26.	35A	Joramandir-Howrah Station via Bowbazar/B.B.D. Bag	9.82	17/5
27.	35B	C.I.T. Building/Beliaghata-Sealdah	5.15	9
28.	36	Narikeldanga-Sealdah via Rajabazar	4.18	10
29.	38	Mathpukur-Sealdah via Bengal Pottery	4.67	10
30.		Esplanade-Nimtala	4.00	4 *
31.	L 14A	Esplanade-Salt Lake via Manicktala	11.50	6
32.	L-20	Esplanade-Barrackpore via Shyambazar/B.T. Road	29.00	25
33.	L-30B	Esplanade-Dum Dum Airport via Shyambazar	15.70	10
34.	L-7A	Sarsuna-B.B.D. Bag/Esplanade Via Kidderpore	14.50	6
35.	L-9	Gariahat (Golpark) — Dunlop Bridge	20.40	10
36.	S15	Dhakuria to Dum Dum Airport	25.0	10
37.	S16	Thakurpukur to Labony (Salt lake)	27.0	18
38.	S17	Chetla to Ariadaha	21.0	10
39.	S18	Salt Lake toHowrah Station	16.67	10
40.	S19	Jadavpur to Ultadanga	19.0	12
41.	S20	Garia to Jollygurge Tram Depot	7.08	4
42.	S21	Bagbazar to Garia	23.50	12
43.	S22	Sarsuna to Salt Lake	26.0	10

Contd.

APPENDIX XI (Contd.)

1	2	3	4
44. S23	Salt Lake to B.B.D. Bag	20.50	10
45. S24	Santoshpur to Babughat	18.50	5
46. S25	Tangra Housing Estate to Howrah Station	9.75	4
47. S26	Sakuntala Park to Ultadanga	23.0	6
48. S27	Sonarpur Rly.Stn. to Esplanade/ BBD Bag	24.7/ 25.7	5
49. S28	Sakuntala Park to Bagbazar	23.0	8
50. S29	Santoshpur to Jadavpur	15	3
51. S30	Budgebudge Stn. to Rabindra Sadan Ballygunge	21.75	3
52. L57	Howrah to Jagadishpur	13.0	6
53. L63	Howrah to Munshirhat	32.0	5
54. L75	Behala to Raipur	23.0	7
55. L91B	Shyambazar to Rajarhat	20.0	7
56. S1	Kasba to Howrah	15.50	5
57. S2	Kundghat to Howrah Stn.	13.19	8
58. S3	Esplanade to Nagar Bazar	11.57	4
59. S4	Parvashree to Howrah Stn.	15.52	6
60. S5	Esplande to Lake Town	8.97	7
61. S6	Howrah Stn. to Ballyguge Stn.	11.90	9
62. S7	Garia to Howrah Stn.	16.55	11
63. S8	Thakurpukur to Howrah Stn.	21.82	7
64. S9	Rathtala (Belghoria) to Jadavpur	23.18	12
65. S10	Dum Dum Airport to Esplanade	16.00	5
66. S11	Barrackpore to Esplanade	29.0	9
67. S12	CIT Bldg. to Howrah Stn.	11.90	6
68. S13	Santoshpur to Howrah Stn.	16.26	6
69. S14	Garia to Karunamayee	26.38	18
70. L16	Tangra To Shibpur B.E. College	13.15	5
71. L19	Esplanade to Garden Reach	12.0	5
72. L20A	Ultadanga tto Barasat	35.15	5
73. L20B	Esplanade to Barasat	27.00	4
74. L14C	Bagbazar to Salt Lake	11.60	5
75. L22	Esplanade to Oky Town	18.50	6
76. L31	Esplanade to Serampore Court	26.0	3
77. 33A	Paikpara to Park Circus	11.42	7
78. 35C	Salt Lake to Babughat	18.0	10
79. L14B	Esplanade to Sechbhavan	12.60	10
80. 14	Bengal Chemical to Rabindra Sadan	11.00	9

* No route No. has yet been allotted as the route has been opened in the latter part of May, 1973.

Source: D.K. Halder, *Urban Transport Problem*, (p. 194).

Contd.

APPENDIX XI (Contd.)

(B) Present Long Route Service:

Sl. No.	Route Description	Distance- (in kms.)	Fare for full distance (in Rs.)	Journey time	Date of inauguration
1	2	3	4	5 6	7
1.	Calcutta-Digha	252	12.50	6.00hrs.	14-4-68
2.	Calcutta-Keonjhar	372	20.14	9.00 "	15-4-71
3.	Calcutta-Berhampore	200	10.00	5.00 "	22-1-72
4.	Calcutta-Krishnanagar	116	4.65	3.00 "	15-8-72
5.	Calcutta-Suri	242	12.10	6.15 "	15-8-72
6.	Calcutta-Burdwan	121	4.85	3.50 "	15-8-72
7.	Calcutta-Midnapore	139	6.25	2.45 "	15-8-72
8.	(a) Calcutta-Haldia I	134	5.40	6.70 "	6-10-72
	(b) Calcutta-Haldia II	134	5.40	6.70 "	17-11-72
	(c) Calcutta-Haldia III	134	5.40	6.70 "	26-3-73
9.	Calcutta-Karimpur	192	7.65	4.35 "	15-8-73
10.	Calcutta-Tarakeswar	65	2.60	1.45 "	15-8-73
11.	Calcutta-Harinkhola	68	2.75	1.55 "	15-8-73
12.	Calcutta-Purulia	308	15.40	7.30 "	18-7-73
13.	Calcutta-Arambagh via Tarakeswar	94	4.70	2.35 "	1-6-75
14.	Calcutta-Karimpur	192	9.60	5.00 "	15-8-73
15.	Calcutta-Rampurhat via Burdwan	300	15.00	7.45 "	20-11-74
16.	Calcutta-Rampurhat via Berhampore	317	15.85	8.15 "	9-9-75
17.	Calcutta-Bankura via Burdwan	225	11.25	5.40 "	11-12-74
18.	Calcutta-Bankura via Arambagh and Bishnupur	192	9.60	3.50 "	15-10-75
19.	Calcutta-Katwa via Kalna and Nabadwip	159	7.95	4.45 "	11-10-75
20.	Calcutta-Bishnupur via Dankuni, Arambagh, Kamarpukur	148	7.40	3.55 "	25-12-75
21.	Calcutta-Namkhana	105	5.25	9.00 "	22-12-75 & 6-11-77
22.	Calcutta-Basirhat	67	3.35	2.10 "	4-2-75
23.	Calcutta-Jhargram	249	12.45	6.25 "	14-2-76
24.	Calcutta-Boira	115	5.75	3.00 "	24-5-76
25.	Calcutta-Dattafulia	117	5.85	3.15 "	1-4-77
26.	Calcutta-Santaldih	277	13.85	7.00 "	10-4-76
27.	Calcutta-Jiagunge	225	11.25	5.45 "	10-4-76

Contd.

APPENDIX XI (Contd.)

1	2	3	4	5 6	7
28.	Calcutta-Jayrambati via Dankuni, Harinkhola, Arambagh	104	5.20	2.45 "	23-9-76
29.	Calcutta-Bishnupur via Tarake-swar, Arambagh	159	7.95	4.20 "	19-5-76
30.	Calcutta-Chandrakona via Kolaghat, Ghatal	148	7.40	3.40 "	1-8-76
31.	Calcutta-Sikarpur via Krishnanagar, Karimpur	204	10.20	5.30 "	1-8-76
32.	Calcutta-Ranchi via Kharagpur, Ghatshila, Tatanagar	415	28.40	9.40 "	8-10-76
33.	Calcutta-Domkal via Krishnanagar, Karimpur, Jalangi	227	11.35	6.00 "	6-11-76
34.	Calcutta-Purulia via Durgapur and Matiara	308	15.40	7.30 "	18-7-73
35.	Calcutta-Bishnupur via Dankuni	148	7.40	5.55 "	20-11-77
36.	Calcutta-Basirhat	67	3.35	1.55 "	4-2-76
37.	Calcutta-Jhargram	249	12.45	6.25 "	14-2-76
38.	Calcutta-Sikarpur via Krishnanagar and Karimpur	204	10.20	5.30 "	1-8-76
39.	Calcutta-Domkal via Krishna-nagar, Karimpur, Jalangi	227	11.35	6.00 "	6-11-76
40.	Calcutta-Hasnabad	80	4.00	2.15 "	15-10-77
41.	Calcutta-Diamond Harbour	4	2.40	1.00 "	6-11-77
42.	Calutta-Garhbeta	163	8.15	4.15 "	18-12-77
43.	Calcutta-Purulia via Burdwan	337	16.85	8.25 "	15-8-77
44.	Calcutta-Kakdwip	91	—	1015-1300	8-4-81
45.	Calcutta-Kandi	232	—	1115-1730	31-10-78
46.	Calcutta-Amta	48	4.80	0600-0800	8-2-78
47.	Calcutta-Autpur	47	4.70	0715-0900	22-2-78
48.	Calcutta-Udayanarayanpur	48		0630-0841	31-3-78
49.	Calcutta-Hakimpur	95		0645-1015	16-12-78
50.	Calcutta-Nezut	94		1015-1300	16-12-78
51.	Calcutta-Chittaranjan	259		0915-1645	16-4-79
52.	Calcutta-Bagda	105		1045-1315	16-8-79
53.	Calcutta-Baduria	63	6.30	0800-1038	27-2-80
54.	Calcutta-Habra	50		0645-0815	14-4-80
55.	Calcutta-Katwa via Barasat & Krishnanagar	170		0725-1155	1-1-81
56.	Calcutta to Falta via Bakrahat Dongaria, Mullickpur	31		2200-0500	3-1-90
57.	Calcutta-Falta via Diamond Harbour, Dostipur			1045-1545	3-1-90

Contd.

APPENDIX XI (Contd.)

1	2	3	4	5	6	7
58.	Calcutta to Rajbalhat	50		0630-0830		20-4-81
59.	Calcutta to Palasipara	170				22-4-81
60.	Calcutta to Hariharpara	222		1415-2000		4-10-81
61	Calcutta to Dattafulia	117		0830-1145		3-3-82
62.	Calcutta to Noorpur	59		0615-0755		6-4-82
63.	Calcutta to Furfura Shariff	44		0710-0820		1-5-82
64.	Calcutta-Basanti	95		0630-1000		1-7-82
65.	Calcutta to Raidighi	74		0745-1107		15-11-83
66.	Calcutta to Taraklea	300		1200-1930		22-1-86
67.	Calcutta to Raghunath Ganj	255		1345-2000		8-5-86
68.	Calcutta to Hindaghat	72		0615-0815		2-6-86
69.	Calcutta to Raidighi via D.H. Road	92		1215-1445		25-8-86
70.	Calcutta to Kanmaribazar	62				4-4-88
71.	Calcutta to Jamtala via Baripur & Joynagar	74		0900-1200		14-4-88
72.	Calcutta to Jhillimilli	254		0615-1330		1-2-90
73.	Calcutta to Mukutmanipur	244		0630-1300		13-8-88
74.	Calcutta to Kalyani	65		0545-0745		1-6-88
75.	Calcutta to Basirhat	193		1245-1530		15-10-88
76.	Calcutta to Hazarduari	215		0600-1130		5-11-88
77.	Calcutta to Digha via Vivekananda Bridge	190		0900-1330		15-10-88
78.	Calcutta to Digha via Kharagpur (Night Service)	250		2130-0430		8-11-89
79.	Calcutta to Raipur (Bankura)	206		—		21-1-89
80.	Calcutta to Haridaspur	86		0745-1045		
81.	Calcutta to Khajuriaghat (Night Service)	308		0600-0750		9-2-89
82.	Calcutta to Diamond Harbour	48		0615-0805		15-5-89
83.	Calcutta to Bhangur	34		1800-1345		12-7-89
84.	Calcutta to Hazaribagh	400		0645-1645		25-7-89
85.	Calcutta to Rajgir (Nigh Service)	519		1800-0700		30-9-89
86.	Calcutta to Radhanagar	94		0830-1158		5-1-81
87.	Calcutta to Hetia	132		1530-1925		
88.	Calcutta to Basirhat to Digha (Night Service)	318		1730-1959		23-3-89
89.	Calcutta to Baduria	63		0545-0805		15-5-90
90.	Calcutta to Puri (Night Service)	571				14.6.90
91.	Calcutta to Raiganj (Night Service)	412		1930--530 (10 hrs)		25-6-90
92.	Calcutta to Kamkhana to Calcutta Digha (Night Service)	392 (105+287)		1445-1750 Namkhana 2100		25-6-90
93.	Calcutta-Kalyani-Digha	313 (65+248)		1745-2009 (9 hrs)		25-6-90

Source: Calcutta State Transport Corporation.

APPENDIX-XII

The Routes Operated by the Private Buses

Sl. No.	Route No.	Route Description	Kms. length of Route operated
1	2	3	4
1.	1	Paler Bazar-Bhawani Bhavan	6.50
2.	3B/3D	New Alipore-Milk Dairy Housing Estate	20.48
3.	3C	Esplanade-Bangur Avenue	16.05
4.	12	Esplanade-Raja Bagan	12.88
5.	12A	B.B.D. Bag to Raja Bagan	12.88
6.	12B	Esplanade to Akra Phatak	14.51
7.	12C	Barisha to Howrah Station	20.95
8.	13	Parnasree Colony to B.B.D. Bag	8.05
9.	17	Chetla to Howrah Station	14.00
10.	18	Sarsuna to Esplanade	16.00
11.	24/24A	Topsia to Bandhaghat	14.40
12.	30	Shyambazar to Madhyamgram	25.86
13.	30D	Shymbazar to Dum Dum Cantt.	25.86
14.	30E	Shyambazar to Krishnapur 2nd Canal	
15.	30A	Esplanade to Bangiya Unmad Ashram	8.05
16.	30B	Shyambazar to Dum Dum Airport	10.14
17.	30C	Esplanade to Hathiara	17.71
18.	32	Esplanade to Dakshineswar	14.49
19.	34B	Dunlop Bridge to Esplanade	12.88
20.	34C	Esplanade to Noapara	11.30
21.	37	Dhakuria Rly. Bridge to Esplanade	13.08
22.	39	Picnic Garden Road to High Court	10.86
23.	40	Karunamoyee Kali Bari to B.B.D. Bag	11.27
24.	41	Regent Estate to High Cout	15.74
25.	41/1	Rani Kuthi to High Court	17.45
26.	42	Bondel Gate too B.N.P. Office	14.08
27.	43	Bon Hooghly to Esplanade	8.05
28.	44	Baguihati to Howrah Station	14.04
29.	45	Padmasree Cinema to Dum Dum Airport	28.98
30.	46	Jessop Co. at Jessore Road to Esplanade	16.10
31.	47	Lake Town to Dhakuria Rly. Bridge via Gariahat Road	20.93
32.	47A	Lake Town to Dhakuria Rly. Bridge via Southern Avenue	20.95
33.	69	Noorpur too Mominpore	45.08
34.	72/72A	Basirhat to Nazat/Chaitalghat	27.36/21.73
35.	73	Naihati to Mogra	39.45
36.	74	Diamod Harbour to Hooghly Point	20.92
37.	75	Raipore to Esplanade	32.28
38.	76	Diamond Harbour to Esplanade	49.91

Contd.

APPENDIX XII (Contd.)

1	2	3	4
39.	76A	Mominpore to Charial	39.63
40.	77	Achipore to Esplanade	32.30
41.	77A	Birlapore to Esplanade	35.45
42.	78	Shyambazar to Barrackpore	19.31
43.	78B	Shyambazar to Ghola	16.09
44.	78C	Jessore Road Crossing to Esplanade	24.63
45.	78A	Bongaoon to Shyambazar via B.T. Road	86.44
46.	78E	Sodepore to Bongaon via Jessore Road	72.00
47.	78/1	Rahara to Esplanade	16.09
48.	79/79A	Shyambazar to Itindaghat	67.58
49.	79B	Barasat to Esplanade	17.07
50.	79C	Shyambazar to Berachampa	77.28
51.	80	Garia to Babli Bazar	46.66
52.	80A	Garia to Canning	42.18
53.	80B	Garia to Harinavi	10.47
54.	81	Barrackpore Court to Barasat Court	16.09
55.	82	Maslandpur to Basirhat	45.08
56.	83	Falta to Esplanade	23.79
57.	84	Songrampur to Sonarpur Hathkhola	33.79
58.	85	Barrackpore to Kanchrapara	43.47
59.	86	Berachampa to Haroa	9.66
60.	87	Barasat to Jagulia	26.56
61.	87A	Barasat to Naihati	20.12
62.	88	Barasat to Kanchrapara	40.29
63.	89	Diamond Harbour to Kakdwip	43.47
64.	89A	Diamond Harbour to Raidighi	45.08
65.	90	Shyambazar to Bivohi	52.03
66.	91	Shyambazar to Bhangar	34.06
67.	91A	Shyambazar to Haroa	37.03
68.	92	Bongaon to Boyra	33.79
69.	92A	Bongaon to Sindrani Ghat	36.04
70.	93	Shyambazar to Kharibari	27.36
71.	94	Kakdwip to Namkhana	14.84
72.	95	Barasat to Nagarukhra	39.45
73.	96	Bongaon to Gobardanga	29.07
74.	96D	Gobardanga to Bherigopalpur	48.27
75.	96C	Bongaon to Bherigopalpur	22.52
76.	97	Amtalla to Ghatakpur	48.27
77.	97A	Amtalla to Ghatakpur via Pyali	48.27
78.	99	Diamoond Harbour to Mograhat	44.29
79.	99A	Diamond Harbour to Dosherhat	40.32
80.		Namkhana to Frazergunge	19.32
81.		Kachuberia to Gangasagar	22.54

Source: D.K. Harder, *Urban Transport Problem*, pp. 104-105.

APPENDIX-XIII

Local Bus Services (District-wise)

Police Station	No. of bus routes through the P.S.	P.S. within the district connected by bus routes	Places outside the district connected by bus routes
1	2	3	4
(A) *Murshidabad*:			
Farakka	2	Berhampore, Shamsergamj Raghunathganj.	–
Samserganj	2	Jalangi, Farakka and Berhampore	–
Suti	1	Berhampore, Khargram	–
Raghunathganj	5	Berhampore, Farakka, Sagardighi	Birdhum district.
Sagardighi	5	Berhampore, Raninagar, Jalangi, Hariharpara, Nabagram, Raghunathganj.	–
Lalgola	1	Berhampore	–
Bhagawangola	N.A.	N.A.	N.A.
Raninagar	2	Jalangi, Berhampore, Sagardighi, Hariharpara	–
Jiaganj	1	Berhampore	–
Murshidabad	21	All P.S.	Birbhum district.
Nabagram	1	Berhampore, Sagardighi	–
Jalangi	3	Sagardighi, Berhampore, Raninagar	–
Nawada	2	Berhampore, Beldanga	–
Hariharpara	2	Jalangi, Berhempore, Raninagar, Sagardighi	–
Beldanga	4	Berhampore, Nawada	–
Berhampore	21	Raghunathganj, Jiaganj Lalgola, Beldanga	–

Source: Lead Bank Survey — Murshidabad, p., S20.

(B) *Bankura*:			
Bankura	63	With all other 18 P.S. in the district	Burdwan, Purulia, Midnapore, Hooghly, Calcutta, Birbhum.
Onda	5	Bankura, Borjora, Bishnupur, Taldanga, Indpur.	Purulia, Burdwan

Contd.

APPENDIX XIII (Contd.)

1	2	3	4
Saltora	11	Bankura, Borjora, Gangajalghati, Chhatna, Mejhia	Burdwan, Purulia
Chhatna	5	Bankura, Saltora, Mejhia Gangajalghati	Burdwan
Mejhia	8	Bankura, Borjora, Chhatna, Gangajalghati, Saltora	Burdwan.
Indpur	8	Bankura, Khatra, Onda	Purulia, Birbhum
Khatra	12	Bankura, Raipur, Ranibandh, Simlapal	–
Raipur	4	Bankura, Khatra, Taldangra, Simlapal	–
Ranibandh	1	Bankura, Khatra	–
Simlapal	9	Bankura, Khatra, Raipur, Taldangra	Birbhum
Bishnupur	24	Bankura, Onda, Indpur, Borjora, Taldangra, Patrasair, Kotulpur, Joypur, Sonamukhi, Indas	Purulia, Burdwan, Hooghly, Midnapore
Taldangra	8	Bankura, Raipur, Simlapal, Bishnupur, Onda	Birbhum
Borjora	12	Bankura, Onda, Bishnupur, Mejhia, Saltora, Sonamukhi, Patrasair, Indas	Burdwan, Birbhum
Gangajalghati	7	Bankura, Saltora, Mejhia, Chhatna	Burdwan
Sonamukhi	12	Bankura, Borjora, Patrasair Bishnupur, Indas	Burdwan
Patrasair	7	Bankura, Borjora, Sonamukhi, Bishnupur	Burdwan
Indas	2	Bankura, Borjora, Sonamukhi, Patrasair, Bishnupur.	–
Kotulpur	3	Bishnupur, Joypur	Hooghly
Joypur	9	Bankura, Bishnupur, Kotulpur	Hooghly

Source: Lead Bank Survey, Bankura.

(C) *Malda*:

Kaliachak	6	Englishbazar	–
Manikchak	3	Englishbazar, Ratna, Kharba, Harishchandrapur	–
Ratna	13	Englishbazar, Manikchak, Harishchandrapur, Kharba, Manikchak	–

Contd.

APPENDIX XIII (Contd.)

1	2	3	4
Kharba	8	Harischandrapur, Ratna, Manikchak, Englishbazar	–
Harishchandrapur	6	Kharba, Ratna, Manikchak, Englishbazar	–
Englishbazar	23	Kaliachak, Manikchak, Ratna, Kharba, Harish-chandrapur, Malda, Gazol, Bamangola, Habibpur	–
Old Malda	11	Englishbazar, Gazol, Bamangola, Habibpur.	–
Gazol	2	Englishbazar, Old Malda, Bamangola	–
Bamangola	–	Englishbazar, Malda, Gazol, Habibpur..	–
Habibpur	–	Englishbazar. Malda, Bamangola	

Source: Lead Bank Survey, Malda, p. S 26.

(D) *West Dinajpore*:

Hilli	1	Balurghat	–
Balurghat	15	Hillii, Kamarganj, Gangarampur, Banshihari Kushmundi, Kaliaganj Raiganj, Hemtabad, Itahar, Karandighi, Islampur, Chopra, Tapan.	Jalpaiguri, Siliguri, Kishanganj, (Bihar), Malda, Berhampore, Krishnagar, Calcutta.
Kumarganj	2	Balurghat	–
Tapan	3	Gangarmpur, Balurghat	–
Gangarampur	12	Balurghat, Banshihari, Kushmandi, Kaliaganj, Tapan, Itahar, Hemtabad, Raiganj, Karandighi, Islampur, Chopra	Jalpaiguri, Siliguri, Kishanganj (Bihar), Malda, Berhampore, Krishnanagar, Calcutta.
Banshihari	10	Balurghat, Gangarampur, Kushmundi, Kaliaganj, Raiganj, Hemtabad, Itahar, Karandighi, Islampur, Chopra.	Jalpaiguri, Siliguri, Kishanganj (Bihar), Malda.
Itahar	5	Raiganj, Kaliaganj, Kushm-undi, Hemtabad, Bansihari, Balurghat, Gangarampur, Raiganj	Malda
Hemtabad	6	Balurghat, Raiganj, Kalia-ganj, Kushmundi, Itahar, Banshihari	Jalpaiguri, Siliguri.

Contd.

APPENDIX XIII (Contd.)

1	2	3	4
Kushmundi	5	Balurghat, Gangarampur, Banshihari, Kaliaganj, Raiganj, Hemtabad, Itahar, Karandighi, Islampur, Chopra	Jalpaiguri, Siliguri, Kishanganj (Bihar)
Raiganj	11	Balurghat, Hemtabad, Kaliaganj, Kushmundi, Itahar, Banshihari, Karandighi, Islampur, Chopra	Jalpaiguri, Siliguri, Kishanganj (Bihar) Malda, Berhampore, Krishnanagar, Calcutta
Kaliaganj	5	Balurghat, Gangarampur, Banshihari, Kushmundi, Raiganj, Hemtabad, Itahar, Karandighi, Islampur, Chopra	Jalpaiguri, Siliguri, Kishnaganj (Bihar).
Islampur	3	Kaliaganj, Balurghat, Gangarampur, Banshihari, Kushmundi, Hemtabad, Raiganj, Karandighi, Chopra	Jalpaiguri, Siliguri, Kishanganj (Bihar) Malda.
Karandighi	3	Balurghat, Gangarampur, Bansihari, Kushmundi, Kaliaganj, Hemtabad, Raiganj, Islampur, Chopra.	Jalpaiguri, Siliguri, Kishanganj, (Bihar) Malda.
Chopra	3	Balurghat, Gangarampur, Banshihari, Kushmundi, Kaliaganj, Hemtabad, Raiganj, Karandighi, Islampur	Jalpaiguri, Siliguri, Kishanganj (Bihar), Malda.

Source: Lead Bank Survey, West Dinajpur, p. S 28.

(E) *Purulia*:			
Arsha	2	Purulia, Manbazar	–
Bagmundi	9	Burdwan, Balarampur, Barabazar, Purulia, Jhalda	–
Balarampore	9	Bagmundi, Burdwan, Barabazar, Purulia, Manbazar	Tatanagar, Sindri.
Barabazar	7	Purulia, Burdwan, Bagmundi, Balarampur, Manbazar, Hura, Puncha.	Khatra (Bankura) Sindhi (Bihar).

Contd.

APPENDIX XIII (Contd.)

1	2	3	4
Burdwan	6	Purulia, Barabazar, Bagmundi, Balarampur, Manbazar.	Khatra (Bankura), Tatanagar (Bihar).
Hura	9	Purulia, Puncha, Barabazar, Manbazar, Raghunathpur, Kashipur.	Bankura.
Jaipur	3	Purulia, Jhalda	Dhanbad, (Bihar) Ranchi
Jhalda	4	Purulia, Jaipur, Bagmundi	Ranchi (Bihar).
Kashipur	8	Purulia, Raghunathpur, Hura, Puncha.	–
Manbazar	7	Purulia, Balarampur, Barabazar, Burdwan, Hura, Puncha, Arsha	–
Neturia	–	–	–
Para	7	Purulia, Puncha Raghunathpur	–
Puncha	6	Purulia, Barabazar, Para, Manbazar, Raghunathapur	Bankura
Purulia	52	All police stations within the district.	Ranchi, Dhanbad, Tatanagar(Bihar) Khatra, Bankura, Saltora, Indpur } Bankura; Burnpur, Durgapur } Burdwan. Calcutta and Sindri.
Raghunathpur	17	Purulia, Santuri, Kashipur, Hura, Para	Bankura, Saltora.
Santuri	3	Purulia, Raghunathpur	Bankura, Saltora.

Source: Lead Bank Survey, Purulia, p. S 18.

APPENDIX-XIV

This Table Shows the Selected Nodes with 10,000 and above Population

Sl. No.	Nodes/Centres	Population		
		1951	1961	1971
1	2	3	4	5
1.	Burdwan	75,376	108,224	143,318
2.	Katwa	23,682	20,621	28,832
3.	Kalna	17,324	22,603	28,594
4.	Asansol	76,277	103,405	155,968
5.	Kulti	–	–	–
6.	Raniganj	25,939	30,113	40,104
7.	Ondal	–	18,645	21,810
8.	Durgapur	–	41,696	206,638
9.	Memari	–	–	11,046
10.	Chittaranjan	–	28,957	40,736
11.	Suri	18,135	22,841	30,110
12.	Dubrajpur	12,205	13,917	15,797
13.	Bolpur	14,802	23,355	29,636
14.	Rampurhat	15,144	19,897	23,770
15.	Bankura	49,369	62,833	79,129
16.	Bishnupur	23,981	30,958	38,135
17.	Midnapore	45,476	59,532	71,326
18.	Kharagpur	129,636	147,253	161,257
19.	Ghatal	21,148	26,971	27,570
20.	Chandrakona	17,502	20,807	27,250
21.	Tamluk	13,599	17,986	22,478
22.	Jhargram	–	13,965	19,237
23.	Contai	12,738	22,094	27,355
24.	Howrah	433,630	512,598	737,877 *
25.	Bally	63,138	101,159	38,892
26.	Domjur	–	Bally + Lilua	10,892
27.	Uluberia	12,575	18,509	20,095
28.	Bowrea	12,,977	13,599	–
29.	Chinsurah	56,805	83,104	105,241
30.	Singura	–	–	10,757
31.	Magra	30,622	45,463	61,748
32.	Tarakeswar	–	–	11,959
33.	Serampore	126,672	174,368	219,639
34.	Uttarpara	51,536	90,472	124,881
35.	Chandranagar	49,909	67,105	75,238
36.	Bhadreswar	36,292	35,489	45,586
37.	Arambagh	11,460	16,551	25,592
38.	Tollygunge	149,817	–	14,118

Contd.

APPENDIX XIV (Contd.)

1	2	3	4	5
39.	Sonarpur	16,310	24,812	34,383
40.	Metiabruz	109,160	130,770	154,913
41.	Baruipur	–	13,608	20,501
42.	Joynagar	13,355	14,177	15,218
43.	Barrackpore	16,189	16,912	96,889
44.	Dum Dum	87,549	174,177	312,332
45.	Naihati	55,313	58,457	82,080
46.	Barasat	16,027	29,281	42,642
47.	Bongaon	23,364	41,082	50,538
48.	Canning	–	12,575	18,706
49.	Hasnabad	13,138	17,560	20,931
50.	Diamond Harbour	–	–	13,072
51.	Baduria	16,385	23,573	27,647
52.	Basirhat	34,823	53,943	63,816
53.	Habra	18,777	26,466	51,435
54.	Calcutta	2,548,677	2,927,289	3,148,746
55.	Krishnanagar	50,042	70,044	85,923
56.	Nabadwip	56,298	72,861	94,204
57.	Santipur	42,413	51,190	61,166
58.	Ranaghat	31,957	55,100	71,749
59.	Chakdah	27,391	35,089	46,345
60.	Berhampore	55,613	62,317	72,605
61.	Kandi	15,220	19,780	26,225
62.	Samserganj	15,935	17,220	22,068
63.	Raghunathaganj	18,255	24,201	29,872
64.	Lalgola	–	10,657	13,419
65.	Jiaganj	19,148	23,675	26,535
66.	Murshidabad	10,756	16,990	17,110
67.	Balurghat	18,121	26,999	67,088
68.	Islampore	–	–	15,715
69.	Raiganj	15,473	32,290	43,191
70.	Kaliaganj	–	–	21,191
71.	Englishbazar	30,663	45,900	61,335
72.	Gangarampur	–	–	14,809
73.	Jalpaiguri	41,259	48,738	55,159
74.	Dhupguri	–	10,637	16,808
75.	Alipurduar	24,886	28,927	36,667
76.	Mainaguri	–	20,014	23,514
77.	Darjeeling	33,605	40,651	42,873
78.	Kurseong	11,719	13,410	16,425
79.	Siliguri	32,480	65,471	97,484
80.	Kalimpong	16,677	25,105	–
81.	Cooch Behar	33,242	41,922	53,684
82.	Purulia	41,461	48,134	57,708
83.	Kashipur	10.577	13,215	18,838
84.	Raghunathpur	–	10,556	12,721

* Howrah City (including Golabari, Howrah, Bantra, Sibpur, Jagacha, P.S. and Bally municipalitty and two mouzas of Sankrail P.S. i.e., J.L. No. of 39 and 40).

Source: Population from West Bengal Census 1951, 1961 and 1971.

APPENDIX-XV

Comparison of Space Potential Analysis (1956)

Sl. No.	Town	Space potential/person per sq. kms.		
		Straight line distance *	Road distance	Difference
1	2	3	4	5
1.	Burdwan	78304.32	77509	795.32
2.	Katwa	26639.60	25836.35	803.27
3.	Kalna	20285.20	19480.95	804.25
4.	Asansol	79204.81	78409.63	795.18
5.	Kulti	64337.24	63539.76	797.48
6.	Raniganj	28895.32	28092.39	802.93
7.	Ondal	28895.32	–	802.93
8.	Durgapur	–	–	–
9.	Memari	–	–	–
10.	Chittaranjan	–	–	–
11.	Suri	21095.74	20291.61	804.13
12.	Dubrajpur	15169.10	14364.06	805.04
13.	Bolpur	17764.63	16959.99	804.64
14.	Rampurhat	18106.44	17301.85	804.59
15.	Bankura	52312.05	51512.73	798.32
16.	Bishnupur	26938.43	26135.20	803.23
17.	Midnapore	48421.28	47621.33	799.93
18.	Kharagpur	132533.59	131746.62	786.97
19.	Ghatal	24107.04	23303.37	803.67
20.	Chandrakona	20463.10	19658.87	804.23
21.	Tamluk	16362.31	15757.49	804.82
22.	Jhargram	–	–	–
23.	Contai	15701.80	14896.84	804.96
24.	Howrah	436355.42	435615.20	740.22
25.	Bally	66073.25	65276.05	797.20
26.	Domjur	–	–	–
27.	Uluberia	15538.89	14733.91	804.98
28.	Bowrea	15940.66	15135.74	804.92
29.	Chinsurah	59743.84	58945.66	798.18
30.	Mogra	33575.67	32773.46	802.21
31.	Serampore	129571.27	128783.84	787.43
32.	Uttarpara	54477.83	53678.83	799.00
33.	Chandernagar	52851.75	52052.51	799.24
34.	Arambagh	70767.59	69971.11	796.48
35.	Tollygunge	152703.16	151919.29	783.87

Contd.

APPENDIX XV (Contd.)

1	2	3	4	5
36.	Sonarpur	14424.52	13619.37	805.15
37.	Metiabruz	112069.19	11279.06	790.13
38.	Joynagar	16318.45	15513.59	804.86
39.	Barrackpore	19150.84	18346.42	804.42
40.	Dum Dum	90470.43	89676.98	793.45
41.	Naihati	58252.69	57454.28	798.41
42.	Barasat	18988.94	18184.48	804.46
43.	Bongaon	26321.78	25518.46	803.32
44.	Hasnabad	16101.57	15296.68	804.89
45.	Baduria	19346.73	18542.34	804.39
46.	Basirhat	37774.29	36972.73	801.56
47.	Calcutta	2550204.54	2549789.66	414.88
48.	Krishnanangar	52984.67	52185.45	799.22
49.	Nabadwip	59237.13	58438.87	798.26
50.	Santipur	45359.99	44559.60	800.39
51.	Ranagahat	34909.91	34107.91	802.00
52.	Chakdah	30346.50	29543.80	802.70
53.	Berhampore	58552.52	57754.15	798.37
54.	Kandi	18182.39	17377.82	804.57
55.	Samserganj	18896.99	18092.52	804.47
56.	Raghunathganj	21215.67	20411.56	804.11
57.	Jiaganj	22108.17	21304.20	803.97
58.	Murshidabad	13720.92	12915.66	805.26
59.	Balurghat	21081.75	20277.62	804.13
60.	Raiganj	18435.25	17630.71	804.54
61.	Englishbazar	33616.65	32814.45	802.20
62.	Jalpaiguri	44206.65	43406.07	800.58
63.	Alipurduar	27842.92	27039.83	803.09
64.	Darjeeling	36556.98	35755.23	801.75
65.	Kurseong	14683.38	13878.26	805.12
66.	Siliguri	35432.62	34630.70	801.92
67.	Kalimpong	19638.57	18834.22	804.35
68.	Cooch Behar	36194.19	35392.38	801.81
69.	Purulia	44408.53	43607.99	800.54
70.	Kashipur	13542.02	12736.73	805.29

* Distance is computed from P.W.D. Road Map.

APPENDIX-XV (Contd.)

Comparison of Space Potential Analysis (1966)

Sl. No.	Town	Space potential/person per sq.kms.		
		Straight line distance	Road distance	Difference
1	2	3	4	5
1.	Burdwan	111169.59	110487.35	682.24
2.	Katwa	23607.63	22915.89	691.74
3.	Kalna	25588.70	24897.17	691.53
4.	Asansol	106352.84	105670.09	682.75
5.	Kulti	37260.23	36542.28	717.95
6.	Raniganj	33095.18	32376.76	718.42
7.	Durgapur	44672.75	43955.64	717.11
8.	Suri	25826.59	25107.35	719.24
9.	Dubrajpur	16906.77	16186.52	720.25
10.	Bolpur	26340.35	25637.90	702.45
11.	Rampurhat	22883.97	22192.15	691.82
12.	Bankura	65799.85	65112.69	687.16
13.	Bishnupur	33939.78	33249.16	690.62
14.	Midnapore	62500.40	61812.88	687.52
15.	Kharagpur	150180.30	149502.30	678.00
16.	Ghatal	29954.65	29263.60	691.05
17.	Chandrakona	23793.54	23101.82	691.72
18.	Tamluk	20973.86	20281.83	692.03
19.	Jhargram	16954.75	16262.28	692.47
20.	Contai	25079.94	24388.35	691.59
21.	Howrah	515354.15	514715.79	638.36
22.	Bally	104107.90	103424.89	683.01
23.	Uluberia	21496.62	20804.65	691.97
24.	Bowrea	16588.92	15896.41	692.51
25.	Chinsurah	86061.36	85376.39	684.97
26.	Magra	48437.99	47748.94	689.05
27.	Serampore	94474.41	92390.36	684.05
28.	Chittaranjan	31939.72	31248.88	690.84
29.	Uttarpara	93425.90	92741.74	684.16
30.	Chandarnagar	70069.85	69383.15	686.70
31.	Bhadreswar	38468.66	37778.53	690.13
32.	Arambagh	19539.53	18847.35	692.18
33.	Tollygunge	65901.80	65214.65	687.15
34.	Sonarpur	27796.66	27105.38	691.28
35.	Methiabruz	28115.51	27424.26	691.25

Contd.

APPENDIX XV (Contd.)

1	2	3	4	5
36.	Joynagar	17166.65	16474.20	692.45
37.	Barrackpore	19900.36	19208.22	692.14
38.	Dum Dum	177091.69	176416.61	675.08
39.	Naihati	61425.90	60738.27	687.63
40.	Barasat	32263.57	31572.71	690.86
41.	Bongaon	44059.04	43369.52	689.52
42.	Canning	15565.40	14872.78	692.62
43.	Hasnabad	20548.06	19855.99	692.07
44.	Baduria	26558.24	25866.82	691.42
45.	Basirhat	56914.02	56225.89	688.13
46.	Calcutta	2928913.92	2928537.57	376.35
47.	Krisnanagar	73443.29	72716.95	726.34
48.	Nabadwip	75823.15	75137.08	686.07
49.	Habra	29449.89	28758.78	691.11
50.	Santipur	54162.31	53473.88	688.43
51.	Ranaghat	58070.47	57382.47	688.00
52.	Chakdah	38068.85	37378.68	690.17
53.	Berhampore	65284.09	64596.88	687.21
54.	Kandi	22767.02	22075.19	691.83
55.	Samserganj	20208.22	19516.11	692.11
56.	Raghunathganj	27185.95	26494.60	691.35
57.	Lalgola	13648.29	12955.47	692.82
58.	Murshidabad	19978.33	19286.19	692.14
59.	Balurghat	29982.64	29291.59	691.05
60.	Raiganj	35271.16	34580.68	790.48
61.	Englishbazar	48874.78	48185.79	688.99
62.	Jalpaiguri	51711.45	51022.76	688.69
63.	Dhupuri	13628.30	12935.49	702.82
64.	Alipurduar	31909.74	31218.90	690.84
65.	Mainaguri	23000.91	22309.10	691.81
66.	Darjeeling	43626.24	42938.67	689.57
67.	Kurseong	16400.01	15707.48	692.53
68.	Siliguri	68436.62	67749.74	686.88
69.	Kalimpong	28087.53	27398.27	691.26
70.	Cooch Behar	44898.65	44209.22	688.43
71.	Purulia	51107.74	50418.98	688.76
72.	Kashipur	16205.10	15512.55	692.55
73.	Raghunathganj	13547.34	12854.51	692.83

APPENDIX-XV (Contd.)

Comparison of Space Potential Analysis (1974)

Sl. No.	Town	Space potential/person per sq.kms.		
		Straight line distance	Road distance	Difference
1.	Burdwan	146710.17	145998.12	712.05
2.	Katwa	32273.81	31551.34	722.47
3.	Kalna	32035.92	31313.42	722.50
4.	Asansol	159354.69	158643.78	710.91
5.	Kulti	47724.11	47003.04	721.07
6.	Raniganj	43540.92	42819.48	721.44
7.	Ondal	25254.86	24531.74	723.12
8.	Durgapur	210002.72	209296.42	707.30
9.	Suri	33551.26	32828.90	722.36
10.	Memari	14495.52	13771.43	724.09
11.	Dubrajpur	19244.46	18520.06	723.66
12.	Bolpur	33077.46	32355.06	722.40
13.	Rampurhat	27214.01	26491.07	722.94
14.	Bankura	82549.00	81831.11	717.89
15.	Bishnupur	41572.78	40851.15	721.63
16.	Midnapore	74749.39	74030.78	718.61
17.	Kharagpur	164641.39	163930.97	710.42
18.	Ghatal	31012.36	30289.77	722.59
19.	Chandrakona	30692.50	29969.88	722.62
20.	Tamluk	25922.57	25199.51	723.06
21.	Jhargram	22682.97	21959.62	723.35
22.	Contai	30797.45	30074.84	722.61
23.	Howrah	741011.37	740353.43	657.94
24.	Bally	42329.45	41607.89	721.56
25.	Domjur	14341.59	13617.48	724.11
26.	Uluberia	23540.60	22817.33	723.27
27.	Bowrea	14059.71	13335.58	724.13
28.	Chinsurah	108649.68	107934.16	715.52
29.	Singur	14024.65	13482.53	542.12
30.	Magra	65175.54	64456.06	719.48
31.	Tarakeswar	15408.13	14684.12	724.01
32.	Serampore	105433.08	104717.26	715.82
33.	Chittaranjan	44172.65	43451.26	721.39
34.	Uttarpara	128281.16	127567.43	713.73
35.	Chandarnagar	78659.69	77941.44	718.25
36.	Bhadreswar	49020.55	48299.60	720.95
37.	Arambagh	29035.22	28312.45	722.77

Contd.

APPENDIX XV (Contd.)

1	2	3	4	5
38.	Tollygunge	192250.81	191667.71	583.10
39.	Sonarpur	37832.40	37110.43	721.97
40.	Metiabruz	62449.72	61709.78	739.94
41.	Baruipur	23946.42	23223.19	723.23
42.	Joynagar	18665.71	17942.00	723.71
43.	Barrackpore	100301.30	19585.02	716.28
44.	Dum Dum	315650.89	314954.21	696.68
45.	Naihati	85498.72	84781.10	717.62
46.	Barhasat	46077.82	45356.61	721.21
47.	Bongaon	53970.40	53181.51	788.89
48.	Canning	22065.64	21360.42	705.22
49.	Hasnabad	24289.68	23584.65	705.03
50.	Diamond Harbour	16434.09	15728.35	705.74
51.	Baduria	31002.77	30298.35	704.42
52.	Basirhat	67156.08	66454.96	701.12
53.	Habra	54780.45	54078.20	702.25
54.	Calcutta	3150748.40	3150390.51	315.89
55.	Krishnanagar	89253.50	88554.39	699.11
56.	Nabadwip	97530.91	96832.55	698.36
57.	Santipur	64507.23	63805.87	701.36
58.	Ranaghat	74815.78	74115.34	700.44
59.	Chakdah	49692.66	48589.95	702.71
60.	Berhampore	75941.27	75240.95	700.32
61.	Kandi	29581.38	28876.84	704.54
62.	Samserganj	25426.18	24721.26	704.92
63.	Raghunathganj	33226.80	32522.59	704.21
64.	Lalgola	16780.93	16075.23	705.70
65.	Jiaganj	28991.25	29186.73	704.52
66.	Murshidabad	20470.33	19764.96	705.37
67.	Islampur	19075.94	18370.44	705.50
68.	Balurghat	70426.66	69725.84	705.50
69.	Raiganj	46540.03	45837.03	703.00
70.	Kaliaganj	24527.57	23822.57	705.00
71.	Englishbazar	64676.16	63974.81	705.00
72.	Gangarampur	18170.33	17464.75	705.58
73.	Jalpaiguri	58502.84	57800.93	705.58
74.	Dhupguri	20168.47	19436.07	705.40
75.	Alipurduar	40018.85	39315.26	705.59
76.	Mainaguri	26871.56	26166.77	704.79
77.	Darjeeling	46222.16	45519.14	703.02
78.	Kurseong	19785.63	19080.20	705.43
79.	Siliguri	100809.48	100111.42	698.06

BIBLIOGRAPHY

Abler, Ronald, Adams, John S. and Grald Peter : *The Spatial Organisation, Geographer's View of the World*, 1971, New Jersey, p. 501-505.

Banerjee, A. : Road Development in West Bengal : A Review, Indian Road Congress, *Statesman*, 19th April, 1977, p.10.

Berry, Brian J.L. : Recent Studies Concerning the Role of Transportation in the Space Economy, *Annals of the Association of America Geographers*, Vol. 49, 1-4, 1959, p. 342.

Bhattacharya, Dhires : Focus on West Bengal, 1972, Calcutta, p. 115-125.

Blunden, John, Haggett, Peter, Hamnett, Christopher and Sarre, Philip : *Fundamentals of Human Geography*, 1978, London.

Bose, Nirmalendu : Transport in Bengal, *Geographical Review of India*, Vol. XIII, No. 4, 1951, p. 43-48.

Bose S.C. : Geography of West Bengal, 1968, New Delhi, p. 119-124.

Central Bank of India : *Lead Bank Survey Report, Cooch-Behar District*, 1972.

Ibid., Darjeeling District, 1971.

Ibid., Jalpaiguri District, 1972.

Chatterjee, A.B., Gupta, Avijit and Mukhopadhyay P.K. : *West Bengal, Presidency College*, 1970, Calcutta, p. 140-146.

Chatterjee, S.P. : Bengal in Maps, 1949, Calcutta p. 8-12.

Chattopadhyay, Arup Ratan : *Development of Transport in 24-Parganas*, 1964, M.A. unpublished Thesis, Calcutta.

Chopra, P.N.: Economic Structure and Activities, Ministry of Education and Social Welfare, *The Gazetteer of India*, Vol. III, 1975, p. 727-741.

Cole, J.P. and King, C.A. : *Quantitative Geography, Techniques and Theories in Geography*, 1968, London, p. 559-560.

Cox, Kevin R. : *Man, Location and Behaviour: An Introduction to Human Geography*, 1972, Calcutta.

Datta Gupta, Arghya Kusum : *Focus on West Bengal, Problems and Prospects*, Calcutta.

Davies, Ross L. : A Note on Centrality and Population Size, *Professional Geographer*, Vol. XXI, No. 2, March, 1969, p. 108.

Disney, G.W. : *Manual for Roads Work in Bengal*, 1906, Calcutta.

Dutta, Ruddar and Sundharam, K.P.M. : *Indian Economy*, 1979, New Delhi, p. 652-63.

Gananathan, V.S. : Roads as Means of Surface Transport in India, *National Geographer*, Vol. VIII, 1973, p. 15-24

Gananathan, V.S. and Patil, Charulata : Transportation in Kerala, *Deecan Geographer*, Vol. X, No. 2, p. 23.

Ganguli, D.S. : *Regional Economy of West Bengal : A Study in Urbanization, Growth Potential and Optimization of Industrial Location*, 1979, Orient Longman, p. 99-175.

Garrison, W.L. : Connectivity of the Interstate Highway System, *Papers and Proceedings of the Regional Association* 6 (1960), 121-37.

Gauther, Howard L. : Geography, Transportation and Regional Development, *Economic Geography* 46 (October 1970) p. 612-19.

Ghosh, Sankar : *Changing West Bengal*, State Planning Board, West Bengal, 1975, p. 7-23.

Ghosh, Sankar : *West Bengal Today*, State Planning Board, West Bengal, 1976, p. 123-24.

Government of India : Committee on Transport Policy and Co-ordination – Preliminary Report, Planning Commission, 1961, New Delhi.

Ibid., Final Report, 1961, p. 104.

Government of India, First Five Year Plan, Planning Commission.

Ibid., Second Five Year Plan, Planning Commission.

Ibid., Third Five Year Plan, Planning Commission.

Ibid., Fourth Five Year Plan, Planning Commission.

Government of India : Reports on the Administration of Bengal, 1901, Calcutta, p. 129.

Ibid., 1903.

Ibid., 1905.

Government of India : Report of the Indian Road Development Committee, Vol. I, Central Publication Branch, 1928, p. 81.

Government of India : Regional Transport Surveys, Summary, Joint Technical Group for Transport Planning, Planning Commission, 1968.

Government of West Bengal : Regional Planning for West Bengal – A Statement of Needs, Problems and Strategy, C.M.P.O., Development and Planning (Town and Country Planning) Department, 1985, Calcutta.

Government of West Bengal : Basic Development Plan, Calcutta Metropolitan District, 1966-86, Calcutta Metropolitan Planning Organisation, Development and Planning (Town and Country Planning) Department, 1966, Calcutta.

Government of West Bengal : Howrah Area Development Plan – 1966-1986, Calcutta Metropolitan Planning Organisation, Development and Planning (Town and Country Planning) Department, 1967, Calcutta.

Government of West Bengal : Interim Development Plan for Siliguri (Siliguri Planning Organisation) Development and Planning (Town and Country Planning) Department, 1965, Calcutta, p. 3-15.

Government of West Bengal : Interim Development Plan for Asansol-Durgapur (Asansol Planning Organisation) Development and Planning (Town and Country Planning) Department, 1966, p. 13-57.

Government of West Bengal : Regional Planning for West Bengal, Calcutta Metropolitan Planning Organisation, 1965, p. 43-9.

Government of West Bengal : Road Transport Survey of West Bengal (Town and Country Planning) Department, 1966, Calcutta.

Government of West Bengal : Final Report, Metropolitan Planning Commission, 1963, Calcutta, p. 61-8.

Government of West Bengal : West Bengal's Approach to Fifth Five Year Plan (1974-'79), State Planning Board, 1972, Calcutta, p. 105-7.

Government of West Bengal : *Economic Review*, (1976-'77), 1977, West Bengal, p. 63-9.

Government of West Bengal : Twenty Year Road Development Plan (1981-2001) for West Bengal, Public Works (Roads) Directorate 1984, Calcutta p. 1-4.

Haggett, Peter : *Geography – A Modern Synthesis*, 1972, p. 335-9.

Haggett, Peter, Cliff, Andrew and Frey, Alan : *Locational Analysis in Human Geography*, p. 315.

Halder, D.K. : *Urban Transport Problem*, 1977, Calcutta, p. 106-25.

Hay, Alan : *Transport for the Space Economy : A Geographical Study*, 1973, London, p. 34-8.

Hoyle, B.S. : *Transport and Development*, 1973, London, p. 45-9.

Hurst, Michael E. Eliot : *Transportation Geography – Comments and Readings*, 1974, U.S.A.

Hurst, Michael E. and Fraser, Simon : Transportation and the Societal Framework, *Economic Geography*, Vol. 49, No. 1-4, 1973, p. 163.

Ibid., p. 92-100.

Hullur, S.I. and Sinha, B.N. : Accessibility of Roads in Mysore State, *The National Geographical Journal of India*, Vol. XVII, Part 2-3, 1971, p. 77.

Johnston, R.J. : *Multi-variate Statistical Analysis in Geography*, 1978, New York, p. 138-53.

Kansky, K.J. : Structure of Transportation Network – Relationships between Network Geometry and Regional Characteristics, Research Paper No. 84., 1963, Chicago, p. 5-31.

Kayastha, S.L. and Singh, D.N. : Some Aspects of Transportation in Dhanbad, *National Geographical Journal of India*, Vol. 8, Part 1-4, 1972, p. 64.

King, A.J. : *Comprehensive Report on Road Development Projects in Bengal*, Vol. I, II and III, Part I, 1937, Calcutta.

Krishnamurthy, S.R. : The Lead Bank Survey Report, Burdwan, United Commercial Bank, Economics Department, 1971, Calcutta, p. 21.

Lahiri, Kalidas : *Road Problems of West Bengal*, 1950.

Leinback, Thomas, R. : Transportation and the Development of Malaya, *Annals of the Association of American Geographer*, Vol. 65, 1975, p. 279-80.

Mathur, Om Prakash : The Problem of Inter-Regional Disparities (The Indian Background), *Indian Journal of Regional Science*, Vol. V, No. 1, 1973, p. 98-9.

Mishra, R.P. : *Million Cities of India*, 1978, p. 46.

Mitchell, K.K. and Kirkness, L.H. : Report on the Present State of Road and Railway Competition and the Possibilities of their future co-ordination, Development and Cognate Matters, 1933, Government of India.

Munshi, Sunil Kumar : *Geography of Transportation in Eastern India under the British Raj*, 1980, Calcutta, p. 27-51.

National Council of Applied Economic Research : *Techno-Economic Survey of West Bengal*, 1962, New Delhi, p. 170-74.

Pathak, C.R., Aziz, A. and Chattopadhyay, R.N. : Identification of Planning Areas in the Three State Region, Bihar, Orissa and West Bengal with respect of their levels of Development and Planning Regions, *India Journal of Regional Science*, Vol. II, No. 1, 1970.

Ramachandran, H. : Connectivity – Some Extended Aspects of Graph Theory Techniques, *Indian Journal of Regional Science*, Vol. VI, No. 2, 1974, p. 113-14.

Ray, B. : *District Census Handbook*, Cooch Behar, West Bengal, 1961, Calcutta, p. 119-21.

Sadhukhan, Sunil Kumar : Sectoral and Regional Linkage Analysis in West Bengal, *Indian Journal of Regional Science*, Vol. VII, No. 2, 1975, p. 136.

Samaddar, S.K. : Development and Planning, *India Highways Annual* No. 2, Vol. 5, Indian Road Congress, 38th Annual Session, 1977, New Delhi.

Sarkar, B.B. : Problems of Rural Development in Backward Districts of Bankura and Purulia in West Bengal, *Indian Journal of Regional Science*, Vol. V, No. 1, 1973, p. 49.

Sharma, T.C. and Coutinho, O. : *Economic and Commercial Geography of India*, 1977, New Delhi, p. 345-47.

Singh, Dinanath : Studies in Transportation Geography, *National Geographical Journal of India*, Vol. 14-15, 1969, p. 138.

Singh, D.N. : Transportation and Regional Development with special reference to India, A Geographical Perspective, *Geographical Outlook*, Vol. VIII, 1972, p. 47.

Singh, Jagdish : Transport Geography of South Bihar, Varanasi, 1964, p. 98-112.

Singh, Ram Briksh : *Transport Geography of Uttar Pradesh*, Varanasi, 1966, p. 59-73.

Sinha, Bimal Chandra : West Bengal – Land and People, City College Commerce Department, 1956, Calcutta, p. 86-9.

State Planning Board : *West Bengal (1974-'76)*, 1976, p. 426.

Taafe, Edward. J and Guathier, Howard. L. : *Geography of Transportation*, 1973, New Jersey, p. 62-3.

Taafe, E.J., Morvill, R.L. and Gould P.R. : Transport Expansion in Underdeveloped Countries, *Geographical Review*, 1963, p. 503-29.

Tata, Robert, J. : A Space Potential Derived Measure of Transportation Efficiency, Symposium on Quantitative Methods in Geography, *21st International Geographical Congress*, 1966, p. 50-65.

Thurstone, L.L. : Multiple Factor Analysis – A Development and Expansion of Vectors of Mind, 1947, Chicago, p. 1.

Tindswell, Vincent : *Pattern and Process in Human Geography*, 1976, New Jersey, p. 259.

United Bank of India : Report of the Fact Finding Survey on Murshidabad District, 1971, West Bengal, Department of Economic Studies, Calcutta, p. 5-20.

Ibid., Bankura, p. 17.

Ibid., Malda, p. 9-20.

Ibid., West Dinajpore, p. 21.

Ibid., Purulia, p. 16.

United Commercial Bank : Lead Bank Survey Report, Birbhum, 1971, Department of Economics, p. 19.

Ibid., Howrah, p. 25.

West Bengal Bureau of Applied Economics and Statistics : Some Basic Statistics on Economy of West Bengal, 1967, Calcutta.

West Bengal Bureau of Applied Economics and Statistics : Backwardness of the Districts of West Bengal; A Comparative Study, 1971, Calcutta.

Yeats, Maurice : *An Introduction to Quantitative Analysis in Human Geography*, U.S.A. p. 200-9, 227-30.

INDEX